Internationalizing US Student Affairs Practice

Grounded in research and theory, *Internationalizing US Student Affairs Practice* presents an inclusive framework for enhancing the intercultural competencies of practitioners, students, and faculty in institutions of higher education. This cutting-edge book explores how student affairs practitioners are well positioned to integrate internationalization strategies across student affairs divisions and functions. Each chapter intentionally incorporates theories and literature from higher education and student affairs disciplines infused with international and multicultural education. "Promising Practices"—case studies written and submitted by practitioners around the world—appear throughout the book to demonstrate practical applications in non-US settings. The strategies in this book help student affairs practitioners enhance the intercultural development of support programs and services, all without leaving the home campus.

Tamara Yakaboski is Full Professor of Higher Education and Student Affairs Leadership at the University of Northern Colorado, USA.

Brett Perozzi is Vice President for Student Affairs at Weber State University, USA.

Internationalizing US Student Affairs Practice

An Intercultural and Inclusive Framework

Tamara Yakaboski and Brett Perozzi

NEW YORK AND LONDON

First published 2018
by Routledge
711 Third Avenue, New York, NY 10017

and by Routledge
2 Park Square, Milton Park, Abingdon, Oxon, OX14 4RN

Routledge is an imprint of the Taylor & Francis Group, an informa business

© 2018 Taylor & Francis

The right of Tamara Yakaboski and Brett Perozzi to be identified
as authors of this work has been asserted by them in accordance with
sections 77 and 78 of the Copyright, Designs and Patents Act 1988.

All rights reserved. No part of this book may be reprinted or
reproduced or utilised in any form or by any electronic, mechanical, or
other means, now known or hereafter invented, including photocopying
and recording, or in any information storage or retrieval system,
without permission in writing from the publishers.

Trademark notice: Product or corporate names may be trademarks or
registered trademarks, and are used only for identification and
explanation without intent to infringe.

Library of Congress Cataloging-in-Publication Data
A catalog record for this title has been requested

ISBN: 978-0-415-79192-2 (hbk)
ISBN: 978-0-415-79193-9 (pbk)
ISBN: 978-1-315-21214-2 (ebk)

Typeset in Perpetua
by Florence Production Ltd, Stoodleigh, Devon, UK

Contents

List of Figures and Tables		vi
Acknowledgments		vii
Preface		ix
1	Introduction: Internationalization for US Student Affairs	1
2	Connection of Internationalization to Multiculturalism, Diversity, Social Justice and Inclusion	31
3	Intercultural and Related Competencies for Student Affairs	55
4	Organizational Alignment of Student Affairs for Internationalization	81
5	Student Engagement and the Cocurriculum	107
6	An Internationalized Context for Professional Development	133
7	Recommendations and Implications for Practice	159
	Biographies of the Authors and Promising Practices Contributors	177
	Index	185

Figures and Tables

FIGURES

4.1 Global Citizens in a Learning Society. Internationalization at THUAS 2015–2020   84–85

TABLES

0.1 Global Promising Practices   xiv–xv

1.1 Strategies for Internationalization "At Home"   8–9

3.1 Knowledge and Skills Needed to Have Intercultural Competency   59

3.2 Personal Attributes of Interculturally Competent Professionals   61

4.1 Documents Inclusive of International Goals/Activities   87

4.2 Prioritization of Internationalization   87

4.3 International Services Supervised by the Student Affairs Division   95

4.4 Student Affairs Division/Staff Engagement in International Activities   96

6.1 Experiences Needed to be Considered Interculturally Competent   152

Acknowledgments

We are forever grateful to our student affairs and services and international education colleagues worldwide who have inspired this publication, influenced its content and helped shape our world views. Members of ACPA, IASAS, and NASPA have been influential in supporting the internationalization of student affairs and services, and we are indebted to these many thoughtful scholars and practitioners.

Tamara would like to thank the following individuals for their support during the idea development, proposal, researching and writing, and/or final editing phases of this book: Leah Reinert, Karla Perez-Velez, Margaret Sebastian, Elaine Steneck, and Emalie Whan. Additionally, Tamara acknowledges her graduate students in the Higher Education and Student Affairs Leadership program and international education colleagues at the University of Northern Colorado who have contributed to her personal and professional development over the years.

Brett would like to thank colleagues at Weber State University for their support, as well as many global student affairs and services colleagues for providing experiences and learning over time that have led to the ability to publish this book. Brett would also like to thank his partner, Teri Bladen, for her ongoing understanding and support.

Preface

INTERNATIONALIZING US STUDENT AFFAIRS PRACTICE

Historically in US higher education, student affairs has been considered a "home away from home" for students, from college unions to residence halls to recreation centers to cultural centers. Student affairs offers many opportunities for students to find a place of belonging and connection that support a culture of learning. Increasingly, the ability to support a wider diversity of students requires intercultural understanding and global frameworks. To do this, *Internationalizing US Student Affairs Practice* reframes the conversation from mobility-focused programs to campus-based efforts through various levels of the institution. One of this book's unique features is that it incorporates a framework, Internationalization at Home (IaH), which is more common outside of the United States, to refocus on "at home" strategies. This publication targets US-based student affairs practitioners, administrators, and faculty and offers a foundational argument to support inclusive internationalization of student affairs divisions and the intercultural development of professionals and students.

We have intentionally sought out emerging and promising practices from around the world to balance the attention on US-based practice. Through 14 selected promising practices from global practitioners, readers can explore and adapt new approaches to their practice. This will allow readers to engage in learning from other regions' and countries' higher education systems and practices, all of which enhances the intercultural global competencies of practitioners, students, and faculty. Combined with these global examples, chapters review relevant theories and research related to internationalizing student programs and services, competency and professional development for student affairs, and organizational structures and policies.

PREFACE

WHAT'S IN A NAME? TERMINOLOGY

Internationalization is far from a new term or trend, but it has increasingly become a buzzword across all institutional types and within various departments in higher education institutions (HEIs). However, it may be useful to review some commonly associated terms.

- **Cocurricular** describes programs and services that occur outside of the academic curriculum. The cocurriculum reinforces transferable skills and abilities learned in the classroom to out of class situations, where students are interacting with peers, faculty, and staff. Some scholars make a distinction between cocurricular and extra-curricular; however, in this book, we use cocurricular to talk about US student affairs practices.
- **Globalism** is the term used in the ACPA and NASPA (2015) professional competencies to discuss another layer of knowledge, where practitioners are aware of issues at local, national, regional, and global levels once they advance beyond the basic level. As will be discussed later, we use interculturalism over globalism in this book.
- **Globalization** is commonly seen as a force and references economic flows of goods and services, including higher education ideas, technologies, and personnel, across national borders (Altbach, 2007; Knight, 2007). Compared to internationalization, globalization suggests supra-regional phenomenon or global patterns that affect higher education (de Wit, 2010).
- **Internationalization** is a process that involves strategies and activities around global or intercultural learning, functions or programs, and policies (Altbach, 2007; Knight, 2007). In review of the past 50 years of internationalization-related terminology, internationalization maintains a focus on a process of change (Knight, 2012, 2013).
- **Internationalization at Home (IaH)** is the "purposeful integration of international and intercultural dimensions into the formal and informal curriculum for all students within the domestic learning environments" (Beelen & Jones, 2015, p. 6).
- **International education**, while common in higher education, is reserved primarily for activities involving education abroad, academic programs, or delivery of modern languages (Olson, Evans, & Shoenber, 2007) and has developed as its own discipline parallel to student affairs.
- Throughout the book, we use the term **"domestic students"** to refer to local students and **"international students"** to refer to non-local students. The term international or domestic may be inclusive of refugee, immigrant, or undocumented students depending on context.

x

International students may hold US citizenship if, for example, they were born in the US but grew up in their home country. The use of these terms is for ease of reading rather than creating monolithic binaries.

- **Intercultural** learning is the "process of learning among diverse international and multicultural others" (Killick, 2017, p. 30). While intercultural often refers to cultural diversity within and between (Knight, 2012), intercultural competency is about appropriate attitudes, behavior, and communication in specific situations as shown in Deardorff's (2006) Intercultural Competence Model. **Intercultural competence**, while more often used in international education, offers student affairs additional guidance in intercultural competencies. For a thorough review of the history and evolution of intercultural competence, see Deardorff and Jones (2012).
- Within the US, **multiculturalism** and multicultural education have focused mainly on domestic diversity, at times omitting global perspectives. Similar to internationalization, multiculturalism is a process of personal, institutional, and societal transformation (Killick, 2017; Olson et al., 2007).
- We use the term **practitioner** over professional in many cases, except in reference to professional development and competencies, to be inclusive of staff often in non-US countries who perform the work of student affairs but may work outside of a traditional student affairs unit, may not have graduate degrees in student affairs, or view themselves as professionalized.
- A **promising practice**, rather than best practice, implies that an excellent practice in one situation may be adapted in part or creatively for a different setting or outcome without implying a one-size-fits-all approach. This book shares innovative, culturally appropriate, and impactful programs and services to aid in learning from each other as a global community of practitioners.
- The most common definition of **social justice** used in student affairs defines it as a process and goal where resources are equitably distributed and all societal members are safe and secure both physically and psychologically (ACPA & NASPA, 2015; Bell, 1997). Up until recently, social justice has had a narrow US-based focus with less global connections and implications (Killick, 2017), yet student affairs practitioners around the world report using social justice perspectives with contextual variations (Bardill Moscaritolo & Roberts, 2016).
- While we recognize that the preferred term when speaking globally is student affairs and services, because this publication is specifically targeted to US-based practitioners, the term **student affairs** is used throughout the book.

PREFACE

ABOUT THIS BOOK

Foundational Elements to *Internationalizing US Student Affairs Practice*

The three critical foundational elements woven throughout *Internationalizing US Student Affairs Practice* include interdisciplinary, international literature; original survey data from US SSAOs (Senior Student Affairs Officers); and, global Promising Practice cases.

Each chapter intentionally incorporates theories and literature from higher education and student affairs disciplines infused with international education and multicultural education disciplines both in the US and outside of the US when available. We believe that incorporating global, multidisciplinary literature with US-based student affairs scholarship aids readers in developing a broader understanding of paradigms and expands global knowledge that complement the global Promising Practices included throughout the book.

Since internationalization of US student affairs is a newer trend, there is a paucity of existing data; therefore, we, as the researchers, a graduate preparation program faculty member and a senior student affairs officer, collaborated to create an exploratory survey. The purpose of the survey was to explore student affairs' role in this change process, if at all, and if so, how SSAOs incorporate internationalization throughout their division related to programs, services, staff, and the extent of relationships with other divisions around international and global concepts. We employed a primarily qualitative methodology using an electronic survey as the data collection tool. We designed the survey to cover a wide range of topics under the umbrella of SSAOs' perceptions about their institution's internationalization, including the role of student affairs in the broader institutional plan to internationalize, how their division implements internationalization, and the global competency development of student affairs staff. The survey consisted of several response formats, including open-ended questions, forced choice, and priority responses. Most of the 34 total questions were open-ended, with 11 questions being demographic-related. The open-ended questions yielded 35 single-spaced pages of responses that we then coded thematically. From 101 survey respondents, data spanned 53 public and 33 private HEIs across 31 US states (numbers may not add up as some responses did not answer demographic questions at the end). The SSAOs were chief officers, as well as assistant, associate, and vice/deputy vice presidents/chancellors ("AVPs"). We contextualize our US SSAO research within the broader themes of literature from higher education, student affairs, and international education. Thereby our survey of US SSAOs' perceptions of internationalization informs some discussions throughout the book as we share data and quotes.

To demonstrate practical applications, each chapter contains Promising Practices submitted and written by practitioners around the world to further expand

xii

the student affairs global framework, as shown in Table 0.1. An understanding of how non-US institutions and organizations provide services and support for students can be incredibly instructive for practitioners, particularly because the basic paradigms and conceptualizations force a different way of thinking. Realistic and approachable illustrations of points through examples are inserted wherever possible. Similarities and differences are shared across student affairs work globally. These should be understood and explored without value judgements and within cultural context. The Promising Practices are examples of culturally appropriate programs and initiatives from a number of non-US countries.

Goals

- Help define what internationalization and intercultural development means for student affairs in the US to support more inclusive practices.
- Use an IaH framework to promote inclusive internationalization that stimulates intercultural development for all without prioritizing outbound international travel.
- Showcase Promising Practices that are international and intercultural in nature, to expand knowledge of US practitioners and graduate preparation curriculum.
- Provide strategies for integrating internationalization into US student affairs divisions, departments, graduate preparation curriculum, and professional development.

Wrrant and Rationale

Throughout this book, we address the capacity for US practitioners to move internationalization beyond academic curriculum and into the cocurriculum by more fully engaging and mobilizing student affairs. We posit the need for US student affairs practitioners to become internationally and interculturally competent to better prepare themselves and students as inclusive, global citizens. As student affairs practitioners see themselves responsible for creating "inclusive, respectful, and equitable space," this extends to being intercultural facilitators who work with students and colleagues from various backgrounds (Ward, 2016, p. 8). Embracing a global perspective is an educational responsibility, thereby requiring student affairs to expand the scope beyond understanding and supporting local diversity to a broader, global understanding of diversity (Ping, 1999).

HEIs cannot rely on outbound mobility as the primary way to expose students to global and intercultural competencies. Likewise, the recent trend and expansion of short-term education abroad opportunities for student affairs practitioners and graduate students may help expand worldviews, but this alone cannot be the main strategy to internationalize US student affairs and practitioners' work. Without attention to what faculty and practitioners can do on their own local campuses,

Table 0.1 Global Promising Practices

Promising Practice Program Title	Higher Education Institution(s)	Country	Program Focus	PP Author(s)	Page Location
Internationalization at Home at Rhodes	Rhodes University	Eastern Cape, Grahamstown, South Africa	Community Engagement; Orientation; Student Engagement	Orla Quinlan	13–16
Community-Based Experiential Learning	University of British Columbia	Vancouver, British Columbia, Canada	Community Engagement; Leadership; Diversity, Social Justice & Inclusion	Peter Wanyenya	19–22
Listen, Live and Learn at a South African University	Stellenbosch University	Stellenbosch, South Africa	Living Learning Community; Residential Life; Diversity, Social Justice & Inclusion	Birgit Schreiber	38–40
Cultural Encounters at CUHK	The Chinese University of Hong Kong	Hong Kong, People's Republic of China	Student Engagement	Raymond Leung	44–47
Intercultural Communication and Learning Program	Cheong Kun Lun College, University of Macau & Zhide College of Fudan University	Macau, People's Republic of China; Shanghai, People's Republic of China	Partnership & Collaboration; Community Engagement	Peter Yu & Sisi Sun	66–68
Global Citizenship & Equity Learning Experiences	Centennial College	Toronto, Canada	Service Learning; Global Citizenship; Diversity, Social Justice & Inclusion	Yasmin Razack & Neil Buddel	71–75
The "Opening-Up" of Student Affairs Initiative	Fudan University	Shanghai, People's Republic of China	Research; Partnerships & Collaboration; Professional Development	Rounsaville	92–95

NTU's Global Lounges	Nottingham Trent University	Nottingham, United Kingdom	Student Engagement	Cheryl Jin Xu & Dun Mao	98–101
Student Leadership Development Program	Duke Kunshan University	Kunshan, Jiangsu Province, People's Republic of China	Student Leadership; Diversity, Social Justice & Inclusion	Howard S. Wang & Jia Zheng	109–112
Leadership and Student Activism Studies	Pontificia Universidad Católica de Chile	Santiago & Villarrica, Chile	Leadership; Activism; Diversity, Social Justice & Inclusion	María Soledad Cruz, Priscila Gallardo, Ivonne Moraga, & William Young	115–119
Student Employment Program	American University of Kuwait	Salmiya, Kuwait	Student Engagement; Student Employment	Tadd Kruse & Bader Al-Sayed Ahmed	123–126
Embedding Cultural Competence in Student affairs: An Australian Perspective	University of Sydney, Sydney NSW, Australia	Sydney, Australia	Professional Development; Leadership; Diversity, Social Justice & Inclusion	Juanita Sherwood & Jordi Austin	136–139
QU Student Life and Services—Professional Development Certificate Program	Qatar University	Doha, Qatar	Professional Development	Courtney Stryker	143–146
Systemic University Change Toward Internationalization: Courses for Administrative Staff	Universitat Rovira i Virgili	Tarragona, Spain	Professional Development	Marina Casals Sala	148–151

PREFACE

it may be difficult to achieve the significant goals and learning outcomes of internationalization. IaH relates both to formal and informal curriculum to develop international and intercultural knowledge, skills, and attitudes for all, regardless of whether they are international or domestic students or regardless of participation in education abroad experiences. IaH also requires a focus on support staff so they are prepared to work appropriately with students.

Much research and countless publications address internationalizing curriculum and education abroad, but far less focus is on what is considered the cocurriculum or the primary domain of student affairs. Society and the workplace expect students to graduate with some level of intercultural competency to be successful global citizens in an increasingly connected economy. Yet, how can those who work in student affairs increase students' global or intercultural competencies if they are not integrating internationalization tenets and strategies themselves? Associations like NAFSA: Association of International Educators work to prepare a global workforce by developing intercultural competencies of international educators, but student affairs does not mirror this yet. Even though most student affairs practitioners understand that global competency is a worthy goal, they may not see the day-to-day application or relevancy to their work.

Audience and Use

The audiences of this publication are broad and varied. The number of student affairs practitioners has continued to grow over the last few decades as demonstrated in the growth of graduate preparation programs. For example, the ACPA graduate directory lists 130 programs while NASPAs list includes 315 records. Whatever the number, this is a major jump from a decade ago when there were about 90 programs located primarily in the US. The book targets US graduate preparation programs, graduate students, and faculty as well as all levels of practitioners within US student affairs, such as chief and senior student affairs officers, directors, program heads, and other practitioners interested in internationalization and providing staff and students with a global perspective. International educators and administrators who are housed outside of student affairs divisions may benefit from developing ways to connect more intentionally to their student affairs colleagues and departments on campus. US-trained practitioners working outside the US, and non-US practitioners may also be interested in the book's content as it relates to preparing oneself and others (particularly students) for a global environment. However, cultural context drives all decisions outside the Western paradigm of student affairs, and readers will want to reflect on these practices within the context of their own cultural mores, norms, and assumptions.

US student affairs associations see global competencies as an important and growing area for development, and they encourage members to be aware of, and embrace, these competencies. This positions the membership of associations

xvi

was perfect audiences for this publication. The membership of NASPA—Student Affairs Administrators in Higher Education, ACPA—College Student Educators International, the Association of College and University Housing Officers-International (ACUHO-I), the Association of College Unions International (ACUI), and the International Association of Student Affairs and Services (IASAS) may all be interested in the contents of this publication. NAFSA members may also benefit from developing a better understanding of how to best connect international and domestic students within a broader student affairs umbrella and engage with student affairs colleagues in this globally rich environment.

Organization and Layout

In the first three chapters, we present a foundation to the internationalization of student affairs and, more specifically, what an IaH framework offers practice by incorporating intercultural competencies into existing diversity, multicultural, and social justice and inclusion (SJI) work. To build upon this foundation, we discuss internationalization of student affairs at the divisional, cocurricular, and professional levels in Chapters 4–6. To reflect the foundational elements of this book, each chapter incorporates the following:

1. Discussion of applicable theoretical and/or related scholarship from higher education and student affairs, international education, and multicultural education disciplines.
2. Inclusion of non-US perspectives from literature and applied scholarship.
3. Original survey data from our study of US SSAOs' perspectives and implementation of internationalization.
4. Promising practices from practitioners at institutions or programs outside of the US.

In the final chapter, we offer implications for practice around strategies to foster discussions and organizational change.

REFERENCES

American College Personnel Association—College Student Educators International (ACPA) and The National Association of Student Personnel Administrators—Student Affairs Administrators in Higher Education (NASPA). (2015). Professional competency areas for student affairs practitioners. Washington, D.C.: Authors.

Altbach, P. G. (2007). Globalization and the university: Realities in an unequal world. In J. J. F. Forest and P. G. Altbach (Eds.), *International handbook of higher education* (pp. 121–139). Dordrecht, The Netherlands: Springer.

PREFACE

Bardill Moscaritolo, L., & Roberts, D. (2016). Global competencies for student affairs. In K. Osfield, B. Perozzi, L. Bardill Moscaritolo, & R. Shea (Eds.), *Supporting students globally in higher education* (pp. 109–126). Washington, D.C.: NASPA.

Beelen, J., & Jones, E. (2015). Redefining internationalization at home. In A. Curaj, L. Matei, R. Pricopie, J. Salmi, & P. Scott (Eds.), *The European higher education area: Between critical reflections and future policies* (pp. 67–80). New York: Springer.

Bell, L. E. (1997). Theoretical foundations for social justice education. In M. Adams, L. Bell, & P. Griffin (Eds.), *Teaching for diversity and social justice: A sourcebook* (pp. 3–15). New York: Routledge.

Deardoff, D. K. (2006). Identification and assessment of intercultural competence as a student outcome of internationalization. *Journal of Studies in International Education*, *10*(3), 241–266.

Deardorff, D. K., & Jones, E. (2012). Intercultural competence: An emerging focus in international higher education. In D. K. Deardorff, H. de Wit, J. D. Heyl, & T. Adams (Eds.), *SAGE handbook of international higher education* (pp. 283–303). Thousand Oaks, CA: Sage.

de Wit, H. (2010). *Internationalisation of higher education in Europe and its assessment, trends and issues*. The Netherlands: Nederlands-Vlaamse Accreditatieorganisatie (NVAO).

Killick, D. (2017). *Internationalization and diversity in higher education: Implications for teaching, learning and assessment*. London: Palgrave.

Knight, J. (2007). Internationalization: Concepts, complexities and challenges. In J. J. F. Forest and P. G. Altbach (Eds.), *International handbook of higher education* (pp. 207–227). Dordrecht, The Netherlands: Springer.

Knight, J. (2012). Concepts, rationales, and interpretive frameworks in the internationalization of higher education. In D. K. Deardorff, H. de Wit, J. D. Heyl, & T. Adams (Eds.), *SAGE handbook of international higher education* (pp. 27–42). Thousand Oaks, CA: Sage.

Knight, J. (2013). The changing landscape of higher education internationalisation—for better or worse? *Perspectives: Policy and Practice in Higher Education*, *17*(3), 84–90.

Olson, C., Evans, R., & Shoenberg, R. E. (2007). *At home in the world: Bridging the gap between internationalization and multicultural education*. Washington, D.C.: ACE.

Ping, C. J. (1999). An expanded international role for student affairs. *New Directions for Student Services*, *86*, 13–21.

Ward, H. H. (2016). *Internationalizing the co-curriculum: Part three: Internationalization and student affairs*. Washington, D.C.: ACE. Retrieved from www.acenet.edu/newsroom/Documents/Intlz-In-Action-Intlz-Co-Curriculum-Part-3.pdf

Chapter 1

Introduction

Internationalization for US Student Affairs

Proponents of internationalizing higher education espouse that it has many benefits for students, such as increasing employability (Ripmeester, 2016), developing global citizenship (Knight, 2007), and offering global student learning outcomes through an internationalized curriculum (Jones, 2016; Leask, 2016). At the institutional level, internationalization may increase campus prestige or reputation, promote strategic international partnerships, advance academic knowledge markets, and increase revenue sources (Rumbley, Altbach, & Reisberg, 2012). Student affairs is a leader in the higher education sector for helping students gain experiences and develop concomitant skills and abilities to develop as global citizens. While student affairs practitioners have increased their international involvement and activities over the last decade (Dalton & Sullivan, 2008; Osfield & Terrell, 2009), this is a more recent development when compared to peers in academic affairs who deal with student and scholar mobility and recruitment, transnational or joint degrees, programs in English, and collaborative research (Knight, 2013; Roberts & Komives, 2016). Yet, internationalization of higher education in the US lags behind other countries (Green, 2015) and student affairs remains under-involved in ventures that will have significant impact in a rapidly changing world.

The attention given to student affairs in internationalization literature comes predominately labeled as "extra-curricular" or "cocurricular" and focuses mostly on clubs and services for international students and diversity programming (Knight, 2007, 2012; Ward, 2016) or on how to improve services or programming for international students and domestic students (Dalton & Sullivan, 2008; Latham & Dalton, 1999; Walker, Hart, Jackson, Roberts, & Ludeman, 2014). Practitioners who have a solid understanding of the global stage and its influence on higher education can contribute meaningfully to internationalization processes and dialogues taking place on their campuses, prepare themselves to operate in this challenging milieu, and prepare students to be global citizens who can incorporate interculturally inclusive practices. An understanding of the ubiquity of internationalization in higher education and the role that student affairs plays requires knowing that bringing international students to US campuses and sending US students abroad are only two components of the larger work to internationalize. Increasingly, the changing societal and institutional contexts require student affairs practitioners to integrate internationalization strategies and pay more attention to the experiences and development of all diverse students.

Today, internationalization requires more critical work from faculty and student affairs practitioners to support intercultural development and global competencies. Significant new or growing trends are likely to affect internationalization efforts of higher education institutions (HEIs) and the work of student affairs globally for years to come. Polarization in societies around the world, as evidenced by the "Brexit" vote in the United Kingdom, the election of Donald Trump in the US, many countries' response to the refugee crisis, and tribal politics in many African countries' elections, to name a few, will influence internationalization in both the short and long term. Violence and hate related to neo-Nazism, anti-Semitism, and anti-Muslim sentiments reverberate around the world. The narrow emphasis on mobility within US internationalization, combined with these trends, limit HEIs' ability to offer a positive response to anti-immigration and anti-internationalization acts (de Wit, 2017). Calls for racial justice such as with the Black Lives Matter movement, which has spread around the world, reflect global demands for racial equity and the end of oppression and discrimination against minoritized and Indigenous peoples. The polarization of these trends elicits student unrest and campus protests, not to mention damage to values of inclusivity and sense of belonging. Cultural and affinity centers on US campuses have borne the "brunt of the responsibility for cultural education and programming" (Patton & Hannon, 2008, p. 139); however, these trends show that all stakeholders have responsibility for creating inclusive communities. Student affairs practitioners have to practice within global and intercultural frameworks so that diversity and social justice and inclusion (SJI) efforts, policies, and programs are inclusive of various identities including nationalities, citizenship status, religious practice, languages, and more. *Internationalizing US Student Affairs Practice* builds a case for why it is necessary to address internationalization at multiple levels within US student affairs, and how to promote continued intercultural development of students, student affairs practitioners, graduate students in higher education and student affairs (HESA) graduate preparation programs, and the faculty who support these programs and services, all without having to leave the home campus.

THE INTERCONNECTION OF GLOBALIZATION, INTERNATIONALIZATION, AND INTERCULTURALISM

While similar in nature and occasionally used interchangeably, globalization and internationalization are closely related but distinct concepts. Globalization broadly involves economic, social, and political forces that create an interdependence and connection between nation states. Specifically, in relation to higher education, globalization is "the reality shaped by an increasingly integrated world economy, new information and communications technology, the emergence of an international knowledge network, the role of the English language, and other forces beyond the control of academic institutions" (Altbach, Reisberg, & Rumbley, 2009, p. 7). With that, internationalization flows from globalization in how government, business, and HEIs respond to the forces of an ever-expanding society. As many scholars (e.g., de Wit, 2010; Hudzik, 2015; Knight, 2007) note, the term internationalization has varied meaning, occasionally is used interchangeably, albeit incorrectly, with related terms of globalization and interculturalism, and is applied in a variety of ways around the world. However, most scholars agree that internationalization is a process.

A holistic perspective expands the worldviews and education of all students, helps them develop global or intercultural competencies, and infuses student affairs programs and services with global perspectives and practices, all of which are desirable components of internationalization for student affairs. The most common definition for internationalization, used in US and European higher education literature, explains internationalization at national, sector or regional, and institutional levels as "the process of integrating an international, intercultural or global dimension in the purpose, functions or delivery of post-secondary education" (Knight, 2007, p. 214). Where internationalization was once seen as the "toolkit" companion to globalization, it is now seen as core or imperative to higher education institutions (Hudzik & Stohl, 2012; Knight, 2007, 2012; Rumbley et al., 2012). Internationalization has two components: Internationalization at Home (IaH) and Internationalization Abroad (de Wit, 2010), also called cross-border education or education abroad, which refers specifically to mobility of people, programs, services, and policies (Knight, 2012).

To combat a world of political instability, interculturalism is a "response both to the increased mixing of peoples in that world and the skills needed to interact with people from varying cultural backgrounds and social locations" (Cornwell & Stoddard, 1999, p. 17). The concept of interculturalism connects to internationalization by relating to the learning and individual development of attitudes, behaviors, knowledge, and communication skills (Deardorff, 2006). "Internationalization is also about relating to diversity of cultures that exist within countries, communities, institutions, and classrooms so *intercultural* is used to address aspects of cultural diversity" (Knight, 2012, p. 30, italics in original). With this definition as a guide, throughout this book, we connect internationalization and interculturalism to US contexts of multiculturalism, diversity, and SJI work.

Given the advanced development of student affairs as a profession in the US, practitioners have great potential to contribute to campus internationalization and students' intercultural development in many ways (Dalton & Sullivan, 2008;

Osfield & Terrell, 2009). Recently, the American Council on Education (ACE) published a report on student affairs involvement in serving the increase of international students and facilitating all students' intercultural competencies because "student affairs is on the front lines of internationalization" (Ward, 2016, p. 5). However, there has been little guidance outside of graduate preparation programs' education abroad trips and international or comparative courses, and professional associations' pre-conference workshops and conference sessions (e.g., Kruger & Dungy, 1999; Perozzi & Havlic, 2011; Schultz, Lee, Cantwell, McClellan, & Woodard, 2007; Yakaboski & Birnbaum, 2017). By understanding why and how to internationalize, practitioners can enhance the intercultural development competencies and practices for high quality programs and services that meet the needs of institutional and student affairs divisional goals and place student learning at the heart of the process. The term internationalization gained dominance during the 1980s to promote international studies and educational mobility; now it largely refers to the international dimension of higher education as implemented through the various frameworks of Comprehensive Internationalization, Internationalization of the Curriculum, and Internationalization at Home.

COMMON INTERNATIONALIZATION FRAMEWORKS

Comprehensive Internationalization

Comprehensive Internationalization (CI) is the most dominant framework used in the US as an "institutional imperative, not just a desirable option" (Hudzik & Stohl, 2012, p. 66). The usage of the term "comprehensive internationalization" increased in the early 2000s with a series of American Council on Education (ACE) publications and the creation of NAFSA: Association of International Educators' Paul Simon Award for Comprehensive Internationalization (Hudzik, 2015). Before that, beginning in the 1960s as a response to growing anxiety over the increasing reality of globalization, US higher education mainly internationalized the curriculum with geographical areas of study and language programs (Hudzik & Stohl, 2012). ACE (2017) defines CI as "a strategic, coordinated process that seeks to align and integrate international policies, programs, and initiatives, and positions colleges and universities as more globally oriented and internationally connected" (para 1). Furthermore, CI is not just campus focused but influences "the institution's external frames of reference, partnerships and relationships" (Hudzik & Stohl, 2012, p. 66). While CI includes internationalizing the curriculum, cocurriculum, and learning outcomes as one of its six interconnected target areas, its structure implies a top-down process that may remove agency from faculty and programs, as well as student affairs divisions. Interestingly, it places student mobility, outgoing and incoming, as separate from the curriculum. For a more comprehensive review of CI, see Hudzik's (2015) *Comprehensive Internationalization: Institutional Pathways to Success*.

The CI framework is meant to be systematic and inclusive, yet it is not accessible to all areas of higher education or all institutions, as recently revealed by the UNESCO-based worldwide association of HEIs, International Association of Universities (IAU) *4th Global Survey of Internationalization of Higher Education* (Egron-Polak & Hudson, 2014; Hudzik, 2015). The IAU survey showed that US institutions have not prioritized internationalization like that of their global counterparts. Specifically, outgoing student mobility is the most important internationalization activity across Europe, Latin America, the Caribbean, and North America. In the US, the top activity is increasing the recruitment of fee-paying international students. In Africa, Asia and Pacific islands, and the Middle East, increasing international research is the most important activity (Egron-Polak, & Hudson, 2014). Only 14% of the survey respondents (1,336 institutions across 131 countries) view internationalizing the campus curriculum as important, which sets up the need for this book's emphasis on internationalizing the cocurriculum and broader student affairs work. Overall, IAU's survey leads to two questions. What is the role of educators in preparing students for life and work in a global economy when preference is still being given to heavy reliance on mobility and online opportunities to internationalize student learning (Egron-Polak, & Hudson, 2014)? And we would add: what is the role of student affairs practitioners as educators in the cocurriculum in supporting internationalization?

This overview does not assume to do justice to all work on CI, but given the limitations that exist in the implementation of such a comprehensive framework, the focus here is on cocurriculum through an alternative but complementary framework. ACE's work on CI in the early 2000s failed to fully acknowledge the role of the cocurriculum within the internationalization movement. The cocurriculum did not receive specific attention until 2016 when an ACE's *Internationalization in Action* series report highlighted student affairs (Ward, 2016). Therefore, throughout this book, we argue for the application of an alternative framework that can assist US student affairs' shift to the holistic intercultural development of all individuals without prioritizing mobility.

Internationalization of the Curriculum

Similarly to defining other terms, internationalization of the curriculum (IoC) takes on a variety of meanings and applications that depend upon individual, disciplinary, institutional, local, regional, and national contexts (Leask, 2015). Most research and training on IoC has come out of Australia through Betty Leask's work with the local government and HEIs and is more prevalent there and in the United Kingdom than in the US. The definition of IoC is "The incorporation of international, intercultural, and/or global dimensions into the content of the curriculum as well as the learning outcomes, assessment tasks, teaching methods, and support services of a program of study" (Leask, 2015, p. 9). The curriculum refers to formal, informal, and hidden elements with student affairs aspects existing largely in the informal and hidden curriculums or what often is termed the cocurriculum or extra-curriculum. The most likely formal curriculum that relates to student affairs is in leadership programs, first-year experiences, and related coursework.

IoC follows many of the same steps as general curriculum design or redesign with the inclusion of a critical stage that allows for creativity and reimagining academic disciplines (Leask, 2015). This stage is necessary to not only question the dominant paradigm and ways of knowing but to also incorporate alternative knowledge traditions, which connects well to student affairs practitioners as transformative, social justice educators (Rhoads & Black, 1995). Research has shown that student affairs graduate preparation programs reproduce White privilege (Bondi, 2012), so it is critical to reimagine curriculum through new and alternative global paradigms that are interculturally inclusive.

Internationalization at Home (IaH)

Internationalization at Home (IaH) essentially developed out of a need to move beyond mobility to emphasize "teaching and learning in a culturally diverse setting" (Wachter, 2003, p. 6). The overarching concept of IaH was developed by Bengt Nilsson after he became the vice president for international affairs at a newly founded university in Malmö, Sweden, in the late 1990s. Nilsson chose the concept of IaH over other forms of internationalizing because he recognized that most students at his new institution would never study abroad. This new Swedish university catered to a regional student population, minimizing attention to recruiting international students but utilizing the local diversity of students who came from immigrant roots (Wächter, 2003). Now, throughout Europe, between 56% and 64% of universities report including IaH in their internationalization policies due to a grassroots effort over the past couple of decades (Beelen & Jones, 2015). The IaH movement has grown to include Australia, the UK, and more recently, select institutions throughout South Africa and Latin America.

The current concept of IaH, coined by the European Association of International Educators (EAIE) (Crowther, Joris, Otten, Nilsson, Teekens, & Wächter, 2000), addresses how internationalization efforts ignore students, staff, and faculty who might never participate in outbound mobility opportunities, such as education abroad or exchanges. IaH in Europe, specifically, focuses on the formal curriculum because student affairs is delivered from a different paradigm than in the US and is less developed as a profession overall. Since its conception in 1999, IaH offers a counter option or paradigm shift to the dominant thinking that equates internationalization primarily with outbound and inbound mobility. Four characteristics define IaH:

1. Efforts are aimed at all students and part of the required curriculum.
2. Efforts focus on developing international and intercultural competencies in all students.
3. IaH assumes that the majority of students will not travel for study-related purposes.
4. Efforts may include short-term outgoing mobility when part of the compulsory curriculum.

There is a strong message embedded in the fact that in Europe, where international travel is far easier and less costly than it is for students in the US, the IaH concept was developed to refocus efforts on the local curriculum, as they recognized that most students will not travel abroad for academic purposes. Similarly, in the US, only 10% of college graduates participate in credit-bearing education abroad experiences (Institute of International Education, 2016). Institutional stakeholders cannot rely on mobility as the method for 90% of students to gain exposure to intercultural learning opportunities. In the US, what little examination exists on the informal curriculum or the cocurriculum concentrates on the role that international offices play in developing social activities for international students and how it could expand to develop more intentional interactions between international and domestic students (Beelen, 2013). While international offices often connect to the larger internationalization of campus, they have to focus their time and resources on immigration and related support services for incoming and outgoing students and scholars. As such, international offices may be separated from the cocurriculum if they are not intentionally structured to coordinate with student affairs. Thus, an IaH focus advocates for collaboration across divisional boundaries to benefit intercultural development for all students, staff, and faculty alike.

A sampling of common IaH strategies listed below, in Table 1.1, shows how IaH can incorporate activities across all areas of the institution from academic curriculum, faculty and institutional research, and assessment to more common cocurricular and student affairs programs. IaH can also include external organizations that achieve learning outcomes most closely associated with education abroad by leveraging local communities, inner-city neighborhoods, and/or rural areas. Many activities already occur within student affairs and span these areas meaning there is already a foundation for internationalization.

Multiple forms of internationalization have evolved over time, but we argue that the IaH concept has great application potential for the US context of student affairs because divisions may fall outside of internationalization strategies of HEIs. Across many universities, internationalization activities and efforts are centralized in international education offices rather than being dispersed across the institution. Likewise, diversity and inclusion efforts are centralized in cultural and affinity centers and are not always incorporated within internationalization

Table 1.1 Strategies for Internationalization "At Home"

Areas	Strategy Ideas
Curriculum and Programs	Infuse international, cultural, global, or comparative dimensions into existing courses, including first-year programs
	Encourage additional language study outside of native language
	Focus on area or regional studies
	Develop joint or double degrees
Teaching/Learning Process	Involve international students, returned education abroad students, and cultural diversity of classroom in teaching/learning process
	Use technology and social media to support cross-border learning through joint courses or assignments and research projects
	Incorporate international scholars and teachers and local international or intercultural experts
	Integrate international, intercultural case studies, role plays, problem solving scenarios, project-based learning, teams, learning communities, and resource materials
	Incorporate promising practice examples from around the world into graduate preparation curriculum
	Develop cultural local community-based service learning
	Integrate global learning outcomes and assessment
Research and Scholarly Activity	Create joint research projects
	Host international conferences and seminars
	Publish articles and papers to promote internationalization and intercultural work
	International research agreements
	Research exchange programs
	International research partners in academic and other sectors
	Integrate visiting researchers and scholars into academic and student activities on campus
Cocurricular Activities	Create:
	– International/global leadership development programs
	– Student activism leadership programs
	– Global citizenship programs
	– Interdisciplinary seminars and workshops
	– International or returning scholar speaker seminar
	– Language partners or conversational groups for English or additional language learning
	– Friendship, or ambassador programs

	– International student speaker programs
	– Peer support groups and programs
	Encourage intercultural development through student clubs, organizations, and associations training
	Collaborate on international and intercultural campus events
	Liaison with community-based cultural and ethnic groups
	Partner with cultural, multicultural, and affinity centers on campus
Local Community Involvement	Involve students in local cultural and ethnic organizations through internships, volunteering, placements, and applied research
	Involve representatives from local cultural and ethnic groups in teaching/learning activities, research initiatives, and cocurricular events and projects

Adapted from Knight 2012, p. 35

and international education. This segregation was demonstrated in the responses from 101 US SSAOs in our survey conducted in conjunction with this book, as described in the Preface. One overarching point was that US SSAOs associated internationalization with mobility-related programs, such as the recruitment of international students and sending students through education abroad programs, and if they did not supervise these areas then they were not involved with internationalization. This understanding was evident at private and public universities alike, regardless of geographical location, size of the institution, or Carnegie classification. However, US SSAOs recognized internationalization as an opportunity for competency development for student success through meaningful programs and initiatives that support a diverse environment. IaH offers a globally based foundation to explore the internationalization of student affairs and intercultural development.

A FOCUS ON INTERCULTURAL STUDENT LEARNING FOR ALL

A primary IaH goal is to improve inclusivity and intercultural development by being mutually beneficial. Domestic and international students require intentional experiences to develop cultural sensitivities and skills to learn how to work with others from different backgrounds (Yefanova & Johnstone, 2015). Student learning related to internationalization comes in the form of programs that expand global knowledge and increase understanding of diverse peoples and cultures. Connecting internationalization with multicultural and diversity work can create a more inclusive environment through cocurriculum, student services, and curriculum. Research from the UK on inclusive internationalization shows that "diversity initiatives that are based on the 'integration and learning' perspective—rather than access and legitimacy or discrimination and fairness perspectives—are most likely to motivate in a sustained manner to ensure long term change" (Caruana & Ploner, 2010, p. 11).

Spelling out several critical student competencies and desired learning outcomes, an SSAO in our study said of their research university in Florida,

> We envision a [institution name] where students, faculty, and staff embrace an inclusive learning community with respect, responsibility, and acceptance for all cultures. Graduates will make meaningful contributions to a global society through character, competence, and integrity. They will make ethical decisions and be committed to a life of service and leadership.

A goal of student learning connects with the desire to graduate global citizens and interculturally competent individuals. Within European institutions, researchers note that even when institutions consider themselves internationalized, they may not have strategies or data to demonstrate that their graduates have increased intercultural competencies (Gregersen-Hermans, 2016). Often perpetuated is the belief that if HEIs offer diversity in terms of structural diversity or numerical representation of various identities and national origins, then this exposure will lead to intercultural development. However, representational diversity does not equal transformational experiences. While most HEIs provide mandatory intercultural training for international students through activities such as international student orientation, they may not provide similar training for domestic students. Student affairs can concentrate on intentional, integrated programs and services that incorporate international students' and domestic students' needs and cultures while focusing on intercultural learning for all students.

International Students

The statement that "True social justice had come to be understood as the development of a community that allowed for those who had traditionally been marginalized the ability to prosper without having to forfeit their cultural heritage" (Landreman & MacDonald-Dennis, 2013, p. 7) can be inclusive of international students, all students' intercultural learning, and linguistically diverse students. International students offer unique and mutual benefits to US HEIs, such as filling needed teaching assistantship positions when there is not a pipeline of US students to fill them, and providing economic contributions to institutions and local/national economies (Glass, Wongtrirat, & Buss, 2015; Peterson, Briggs, Dreasher, Horner, & Nelson, 1999). As more US HEIs expand or actively recruit international students, practitioners will want to revisit existing programs and services for inclusivity related to the variations of culture, nationality, religion, and additional identities that students hold as well as incorporate ethical considerations around the recruitment of international students (Andrade & Evans, 2009).

As one UK study shares, "international students effectively cannot escape from inter-cultural experience, whether positive or negative, but many of their home peers are just not aware of the presence of international students or tend to avoid interaction" (Caruana & Ploner, 2010, p. 13). Some international and immigrant students experience high levels of discrimination, neo-racism, neo-nationalism, and/or microaggressions within HEIs that prevent their ability to develop a sense of belonging and negatively affect learning (Kim & Díaz, 2013; Kim & Kim, 2010; Lee & Rice, 2007). Neo-racism and neo-nationalism add cultural, linguistic, and national origin biases to discrimination and is a direct response to the rise of non-European immigrants in the US over the last decades. International students may experience a hostile or chilly campus climate like many students of color and minoritized students given expectations to "assimilate into the White racial fabric of PWIs [predominately White institutions] and accept the existing institutional culture—a culture plagued by racism, oppression, and discrimination" (Patton & Hannon, 2008, p. 142). However, international students have the added challenge of cultural and country transitional issues and perhaps not being aware of why their differences are targets or how to report and cope with these experiences.

All students may face similar adjustment issues, academic challenges, family and social commitments, and financial considerations. International students also navigate in a new culture, possibly a very different educational system and structure, operate in English, which may not be their native language, and watch changing immigration laws (Terzian & Osborne, 2011). The belief that international and immigrant students have to adapt and assimilate is a form of stereotyping that relies on deficit modeling to perpetuate the idea that international students lack social and cultural capital and have to change to be successful (Leask, 2015; Rose-Redwood & Rose-Redwood, 2013). This deficit framework ignores that international students have intercultural capital, which is:

> [A] compliment [to] "original" cultural perspectives without imposing a need to abandon them in favor of assimilation to "new" ones. And by doing so, it may lead people to appreciate cultural diversity and develop an understanding for previously unfamiliar and perhaps "strange" situations and contexts.
>
> (Pöllmann, 2013, p. 2)

The often-unchecked bias of the dominant or US academic culture privileges some US students and expects international students, as well as minoritized students, to behave, engage, and perform in ways that stereotypes and discriminates against them (Killick, 2017). For example, assuming all students should vocally discuss in large group events or classroom discussions is a bias against students from cultures that may not debate with authority figures (Yakaboski, Perez-Velez, & Almutairi, 2017). Or faculty may favor or preference students from Asian countries due to a model minority stereotype. Educating international students on US race relations and cultural contexts may be left to international offices who, if they have any programs on this, often take a tolerance approach and focus primarily on undergraduate students (Althen, 2009). Therefore, within a US context, it is important to educate all students about US race relations and immigration history through a social justice framework. Practitioners and faculty can make efforts to reduce stereotyping that blames international students for behaviors or ways of engagement. With intentional connections between internationalization, multicultural or cultural centers, and other inclusion work, the needs and experiences of non-majority students can be more adequately addressed.

International and Domestic Student Interaction

In our US SSAO survey, some administrators agreed that internationalization of student affairs would reflect more direct interaction between international and domestic students. An SSAO at a Washington public research university said: "We are formulizing better ways to work with and interact with international students, and we are not doing our jobs as student development professionals if we do not determine better ways to do so." In line with this higher level of engagement, internationalization was a high priority for both this institution and student affairs division. Prioritizing internationalization for student affairs allowed the SSAO to think intentionally about how to create engagement and interaction. Another example from an SSAO at a private master's university in Connecticut viewed that offering "current issues discussions focusing on global issues, global/cultural awareness development in students" was a way to "foster relationships between domestic and international students," which can engage dissimilar peers in meaningful interactions that lead to significant learning and growth.

Part of being intentional about interactions is ensuring students are aware of why they are grouped interculturally or cross-nationally and that intercultural communication is an expectation where students are provided with the skills to do so effectively (Yefanova & Johnstone, 2015; Yefanova, Woodruff, Kappler, & Johnstone, 2014). As an illustration, JAMK University of Applied Sciences in Jyväskylä, Finland, graduate students and faculty developed an intercultural game, called New Horizons, to encourage cross-cultural understanding and learning between homogenous Finnish students and the growing refugee community (JAMK, 2016). The idea for the project emerged in a cross-cultural management course and the game teaches refugees about Finland and exposes Finnish participants to all the other cultures represented by their growing immigrant populations. The campus-based group, JAMK United for Refugees, facilitates the game at JAMK events, in classes, and venues around the city of Jyväskylä.

12

INTERNATIONALIZATION FOR US STUDENT AFFAIRS

Much literature and examples from around the world demonstrate the importance of intentionally designing group or partner work for programs and learning opportunities. At the University of Leeds in the UK, the International Student Office and Accommodation Services turned a small residence hall into the Ellerslie Global Residence to house about 100 UK and international students interested in intercultural learning and interaction. Each year begins with a week of programming to develop community and bonding as well as start cultural exploration (Manns, 2014). In another example, as shown in the Promising Practice Internationalisation at Home at Rhodes University in South Africa, staff work to internationalize student services by operating an "integrated residential system where international and South African students not only live together, but engage in residential housing and are given leadership training to intentionally create academically conducive, inclusive environments" (Quinlan, 2015, p. 19). This example connects domestic and international students in various structured and meaningful ways, while providing a focus on international student learning and their adjustment to academic life in a new environment. Rhodes University demonstrates the importance of strategies that cut across academic and student services from the beginning of students' journey with orientation and throughout programming that gets students connected to diversity within the community and campus. The strategies show how staff respond within the cultural context of the university and what their students need to develop within that framework.

PROMISING PRACTICE: Internationalisation at Home at Rhodes

Institution: Rhodes University

Location: Eastern Cape, Grahamstown, South Africa

Author: Orla Quinlan, Director, International Office

Background and Context:
Rhodes University is an English language institution of 8,002 students, situated in one of the poorest provinces in South Africa. Of the 2,464 graduates in 2017, 59% were women, and 21% were international students, mainly originating from other countries in Africa, but also from exchange programmes with Australia, Canada, China, Europe, and the USA. Under the apartheid system, it was a "white" institution in a predominantly Xhosa-speaking region. Now 71% of the student body are black students. Additionally, there are 63 languages spoken on campus. A minority of French and Portuguese mother tongue African students and some local South African students struggle with English as the medium of instruction. Increasingly, departments provide tutorials in Xhosa. The student body in public higher education encompasses fee-paying students, those who are eligible for government financial aid (NSFAS), and students who are ineligible for NSFAS

13

funding and unable to afford university fees. These students were the dominant group involved in the Fees Must Fall movement, which disrupted universities beginning in 2015.

On arrival, every student is provided with an **orientation** programme that introduces all aspects of academic life, and encompasses an introduction to social and cultural aspects of university life and the reality of living with other people who come from various cultural and social backgrounds. The orientation responds to the changing context of South Africa and alerts students to academic programmes, study skills, and facilities, as well as the pertinent social issues and challenges of race, gender, and behavioural concerns such as substance abuse. Additional topics include the politics and culture of South Africa, the possibilities of protests, how these are conducted, and what they can expect. Students are advised about cultural sensitivities and, while the general environment might initially appear familiar and similar to home, there are differences. Students are given examples of where others have inadvertently made mistakes, and are advised to treat their visas with respect and not to engage in any activity that might jeopardise them. For example, getting arrested and getting a police record can have a lifelong impact on securing visas for returning to South Africa and traveling beyond.

Community Engagement (CE) is a key pillar of the university and ranges from involvement at government policy level and ground-breaking research, to practical, strategic volunteer interventions at a community level. Volunteerism forms an important part of the student experience and learning at Rhodes. The CE Office runs a 19-week project planning process to support students who seek to build meaningful relationships with community organisations, while working toward a shared co-created project from start to finish. The Student Volunteer Programme provides special provisions for incoming exchange students to volunteer for a semester with mandatory training provided for participants. Volunteer options include: Arts and Alternative Education, High School Tutoring, Literacy and Homework, and Mentoring. Each residence hall is paired with an Early Childhood Development site. Volunteering provides nearly 1,000 Rhodes students with opportunities to learn outside the classroom environment, acquiring essential critical thinking, leadership, project management and interpersonal skills, and is a team experience, promoting civic consciousness and critical engagement.

Further Description: Internationalisation at Home

The most highly visible and concentrated set of activities in the Internationalisation at Home programme take place in May. The programme opens with an International parade that includes university and community partners, featuring children who have been involved in community engagement programmes and organizations.

There is also an **academic seminar**, lecture, or panel discussion with an international theme; usually in partnership with the Law faculty; the Politics and International Relations Department or the Pan African Youth Dialogue student group. Topics have included the treatment of immigrants and refugees in South Africa; Africa and the International Criminal Court; and the contemporary status of Western Sahara. Students are made aware of the importance of internationalisation and remaining open to under

INTERNATIONALIZATION FOR US STUDENT AFFAIRS

standing people from other parts of the world. Awareness-raising campaigns have also been part of the activities, including anti-xenophobia campaigns.

An intercultural competency component has included running workshops to get middle-management staff and students to reflect on the attributes of intercultural competence. We encourage people to **learn other languages** and introduced a pilot 30-minute Language Carousel event, during International week, to inspire interest and participation, where each student has five minutes to teach five basic phrases from their language, before switching to another partner and language; the activity was so popular that it will be expanded going forward.

The **Student Representative Council** also gets involved by offering snacks from different parts of the world, organising a themed wall mural each year or providing a photo booth with flags for students to identify with. The week ends with an African Ball, celebrating Africa Day and the continent's multiculturalism; students come in the formal wear of their choosing, the food and music comes from different countries on the African continent. Later in the year, the **postgraduate students** collaborate with the International office to organise events such as the "Nigeria Dialogues," an academic event organised entirely in a Nigerian style and discussing topics pertinent to Nigeria.

Goals and Outcomes of the Rhodes Internationalisation at Home programme:

- Ensure that all students can engage in social and education spaces that expose them to dimensions of life from places outside of South Africa. These dimensions include knowledge, culture, customs, and current affairs.
- Encourage international students to work with the societies representing their home country and invite South Africa students specifically to find out about the international students' countries.
- Create specific interventions to develop intercultural competencies in a context, where different social groups are interacting for the first time in their lives, as most South African students cannot afford to go on a study abroad experience.
- Provide the opportunity to discuss multiple heritages by internationalising Heritage Day, to ensure that meaningful learning conversations happen. There is always more learning than if people just invite each other to sample food, such as the "show me your roots" programme.

Assessment:

We have seen that the South African students decided spontaneously to have internationally themed days themselves, during international week, and that internationally oriented activities make the diversity on the campus more visible to the South African students. The programs have been well received and established, and most of those who participated in the programmes are interested in continuing.

Lessons Learned:

The principles that inform the specific nature of the Internationalisation at Home programme include:

15

INTERNATIONALIZATION FOR US STUDENT AFFAIRS

1. Work with the specific context you have on campus.
2. Optimise any aspects that are international, by increasing their visibility and level of activity.
3. Create social spaces for intercultural engagements that are new and different to those that take place in the established social spaces.
4. Bring in new and different perspectives to current debates.
5. Cultivate a core group of active students, who truly believe that people from different backgrounds can live and work together and become friends and who model intercultural competence, to help with the organisation of the programme.

While this extremely diverse and dynamic, continuously transforming post-Apartheid environment shows much promise, risks are posed by a deteriorating political context, narrow nationalism, racism and occasional flashes of xenophobia and there is no room for complacency. Much work is needed, on an ongoing basis, if the vision of an open society welcoming of all people is ever to be fully realised.

Media Links:

Orientation Programme 2017: www.ru.ac.za/media/rhodesuniversity/content/deanofstudents/documents/Orientation%20Booklet%202017%20for%20website%20final.pdf

Community Engagement: www.ru.ac.za/communityengagement/

Student Volunteer Handbook 2018: www.ru.ac.za/media/rhodesuniversity/content/communityengagement/images/SVP%20Handbook%202018%20for%20WEB.pdf

International Office website: www.ru.ac.za/international/

International Office Facebook: www.facebook.com/RUInternationalOffice/

THE NEED TO INTERNATIONALIZE STUDENT AFFAIRS GRADUATE PREPARATION CURRICULUM

In the US, the preparation of student affairs practitioners through graduate programs has been an ongoing research area and topic because master's level new practitioners coming directly out of higher education and student affairs (HESA) graduate programs comprise 15–20% of the US student affairs workforce (Renn & Jessup-Anger, 2008). Much of the socialization to the profession begins during this time of graduate school (Tull, Hirt, & Saunders, 2009); therefore, it is important for curriculum to reflect the values of the profession and to have internationalization and intercultural development included within those values. In the limited, albeit growing body of scholarship on international student affairs and services, much of the literature does not address how graduate preparation programs can internationalize the curriculum. The employability of student affairs graduates requires that they know how to best work with diverse students, staff, and faculty within a global world. There are increasing opportunities for HESA

16

graduates to work in cross-border environments, be they at international campuses of US universities, national institutions in other countries, or their home campus. Faculty have a responsibility to ensure all graduate students have access and opportunity to gain intercultural competencies and develop their knowledge about research in international education and ethical methods for comparative and international work.

In a 2007 survey of 63 US student affairs graduate preparation programs' efforts to internationalize, researchers found that "student affairs has not kept adequate pace" in internationalization (Schultz et al., 2007, p. 627). It is important for graduate programs to play a more vital role in internationalization through helping students develop cross-cultural acumen. Their survey shows that internationalized activities in HESA programs are less often staples of the program or faculty, and more so student-driven activities, which come with ebbs and flows and fails to institutionalize internationalization. Since that research, anecdotally, graduate preparation programs have increased short term, a few days to a couple weeks, education abroad trips as evidenced by advertisements over listservs.

Outside of that one study, the conversation about the need and how to internationalize US curriculum is in its infancy. A panel session at the Annual Convention for ACPA held in Montreal, Canada on "infusing international perspectives in professional preparation programs" showcased three examples from presenters' experiences, which were in a course assignment, a stand-alone course on global higher education, and short-term graduate education abroad trip (Niehaus, Seifert, & Wawrzynski, 2016). At the 2017 Annual International Symposium at NASPA in San Antonio, Texas, Yakaboski, Ramos, and Hornak facilitated a session titled "Infusing globalism: A dialogue on internationalizing curriculum." The three facilitators discussed the narrow focus of using education abroad to internationalize, how curriculum needs to vary depending on world region, the limited guidance from US-based professional standards and competencies, and finally, the danger to student learning and inclusion efforts of not internationalizing. From the discussion, attendees and presenters developed these suggestions for curriculum revision:

- Creating globalism or its equivalency as its own competency.
- Involving international students in cocurricular planning and programming.
- Teaching ethnocentrism through social justice curriculum.
- Using local resources to connect to intercultural learning opportunities; developing better partnerships between student affairs and faculty.
- Ensuring professional associations are not furthering US ethnocentric dialogues or neocolonizing behaviors through partnerships and abroad trips.

If graduate preparation programs are to adequately prepare students and practitioners, then faculty can look to revising existing US-centric graduate curriculum. As faculty assess their program's assumptions about ways of knowing and what knowledge the curriculum provides, they can evaluate if North American and US values and ideology dominate. An historically US-centric practitioner curriculum may fail to meet the needs of domestic and international students in programs without intentional curriculum development and revision.

THE LOCAL GLOBAL CONNECTION FOR COMMUNITY ENGAGEMENT

An IaH framework encourages connection to the local community for opportunities to collaborate in intercultural learning while supporting the global needs of the community. In our study, an SSAO at a private research university in New York shared that internationalization means the "Equal measure and consideration for local and global awareness, education, engagement, contradictions, and community building." At this institution, the SSAO reported they are "intentionally imbedding language, goals and principles that clearly identifies objectives to engage international students." Ultimately, there are ways to gain additional skills and knowledge by focusing on local areas that are intercultural to the students at hand, be they domestic or international students.

Local engagement supports intercultural development and internationalization because these programs often include diverse teams, international organizations, or nonprofits (Ward, 2015b). The local community is a great connection for internationalization strategies and student affairs programs to intentionally collaborate with immigrant or refugee populations, linguistically diverse communities, or culturally diverse organizations for service learning, volunteer experience, or other community-engaged partnerships. Community service and service learning programs foster important skills for students as well as providing communities needed support and aid (Ward, 2015a). Service learning and alternative spring break programs are cocurricular programs that can be internationally located or, what IaH would argue, locally based options with cultural and ethnic communities. Local, off-campus, volunteer opportunities provide all students with an expanded view and experience of US cultures and individuals (Ward, 2015a).

A focus on globally framed, local opportunities addresses the concern over increases in education abroad trips, found to exoticize destinations and cultures while remaining limited to students with more financial and social capital (Killick, 2015). As much of the internationalization efforts in US graduate preparation programs have come in the form of short-term education abroad trips, looking more at the local global connection can provide opportunities for all students. For student affairs practitioners, there are ways to capitalize on global learning or professional development without having resources for international travel.

18

For example, the Modern Languages Department at Oakton Community College in Illinois developed a program, Internationalizing Ourselves, where a lunch-hour program for staff and faculty met weekly and worked on language development (Korbel, 2002). One goal of the program was to increase awareness of cultural and linguistic diversity. Program assessment found that it was humbling to be inarticulate in another language, thus, hopefully creating greater patience, empathy, and sensitivity when working with students and staff who are non-native English speakers, as well as learning another language.

One program at Johnson County Community College in Kansas, USA is a cocurricular course called Intercultural Semester where students enroll to "go global while staying local" (Korbel, 2002, p. 130). The course incorporates knowledge, skills, and experiential learning related to intercultural communication, language, and culture through pairing with a partner, and an internship or service learning requirement in the community. A bonus of the program is that upon successful completion, students receive a scholarship that can be used toward an education abroad opportunity. Relatedly, the University of Cape Town in South Africa offers local volunteering through their Student Health and Welfare Centres Organisation that intentionally incorporates international and domestic students together to work in poorer local communities and townships in the Western Cape (Beelen, 2007).

As shown in the Promising Practice Community-Based Experiential Learning (CBEL) from the University of British Columbia (UBC) below, programs that incorporate international students into service learning experiences within the local community can assist intercultural interactions. In UBCs CBEL program, community members from the Metro Vancouver Regional District become co-educators to work with the international student leaders on selected issues affecting local communities. Local organizations on the theme of health promotion and environmental sustainability have included farmer's markets, the Vancouver Aquarium, the David Suzuki Foundation, and the Little Mountain Neighborhood House (Drexhage, 2015).

PROMISING PRACTICE:
Community-Based Experiential Learning
(component of an international, undergraduate awards program)

Institution: The University of British Columbia

Location: Vancouver, British Columbia, Canada

Author: Peter Wanyenya, International Student Advisor, Special Populations & Programs, International Student Development, International Student Initiative and Ph.D. Student, UBC Social Justice Institute

INTERNATIONALIZATION FOR US STUDENT AFFAIRS

Background and Context:

In 2001, the University of British Columbia (UBC) launched the International Scholars Program (ISP) as a means to provide a high quality, global education to deserving international, undergraduate students by offering them the opportunity to study at UBC as fully funded award students. Selected students have proven financial need, demonstrated evidence of potential for academic success, and experiences with community engagement. At the time, for UBC this initiative served the general altruistic spirit of public, post-secondary institutions, which aims to provide access to education, based on merit and financial need, to those most deserving. Within the Canadian context, such arrangements are not new. Canadian post-secondary institutions, through collaborations with organizations such as the World University Service of Canada, have been collaborating to provide such access to education to the most deserving young people from around the world through resettlement services and education to refugees as early as the 1980s.

Since the 1980s, the global phenomenon of internationalization has intensified with the Canadian government actively engaging in coast-to-coast internationalization efforts at all levels of education and in institutions of all sizes. Through the support of the 2011 national policy, International Education Strategy, the goal is to make Canada a preferred destination for more international students.

With this governmental support, many institutions have implemented internationalization strategies including UBC, which has been touted as North America's "most international university" by *Times Higher Education* University Rankings. UBC has 62,923 undergraduate and graduate students between the Vancouver and Okanagan campuses with 14,434 international students from 162 countries across both campuses with the majority at the Vancouver campus.

UBCs Internationalization Strategic Plan (2011) aims to:

- Foster global inclusivity among all its constituents.
- Transform how we develop knowledge, how we teach, and how we learn at the intersections of local, national, and international imperatives.
- Develop in students, faculty and staff the critical and intercultural skills and values that empower them to be global citizens and leaders.

Part of implementing UBCs Internationalization Strategic Plan (ISP) includes increasing opportunities for international engagement through "at home" programs.

However, there can be tensions with "at home" strategies if the mindsets that work behind the model view international students as lacking certain skills and abilities which need to be addressed toward those initiatives (Knight, 2004, 2007). It is imperative that we move from viewing international students as "deficits" to viewing educational systems as "an ecological place of and for connections, relationships, reciprocity, and mutuality" (Sackney, 2007, p. 2). In line with these cautions, UBCs "at home" international education programming seeks to expand the possibilities of interconnection and mutual learning for students, academic institutions, and the broader community.

Therefore, as ISP has continued to attract top international students, we have integrated the strategic benefits of offering comprehensive supports that enhance students'

20

entire UBC academic experience, from their academic advisors, to their student health and wellness advisors (Lee & Metcalfe, 2017). Through community-based learning and leadership, our programs help develop students into confident, resilient graduates, who are global leaders that make meaningful contributions across different societies. In 2014, we had an opportunity to examine how our ISP award students were engaging beyond academics, and what could be done to deepen their connections to the priorities and activities of communities within the Metro Vancouver Regional District, with the desire of furthering their learning, and levels of community engagement. As part of the broader ISP, in 2014 we launched our Community-Based Experiential Learning (CBEL) award program pilot, which since then has annually engaged about 60 diverse, international, undergraduate award students with more than 10 community organizations. Through engaging with local initiatives, students are challenged in their assumptions about volunteering, charity, and the priorities of communities within the Vancouver district.

After meeting selected community partner organizations and learning of their work, students are assigned to interdisciplinary teams, or engage in self-directed community-based projects. Students commit a minimum of 40 hours over the regularly scheduled academic term, which begins in September and lasts until April, including engagement in monthly development workshop with program staff. Community partners are in turn invited to serve as co-educators for students to learn about the complexity of local communities, and their priorities, in relation to student's international experiences. During the time students are engaged in CBEL, program staff provide timely skill-building workshops, one-on-one and team-based advising that includes reflection and project planning, and liaise with, or support student engagement with community partners on project scoping and delivery.

Goals and Outcomes:

The CBEL program allows for first- and second-year scholars to draw from their own past experiences of community engagement in cross-cultural contexts, develop their interdisciplinary skills, and apply them in a new region of the world, where they now live and study, while learning the complexities of social and ecological inequities in realities outside of the University. Global citizenship becomes less of an ideal, or rhetoric, but embodied learning experiences for our award students who continue to learn grounded in realities of their new home. As such, the program aims to enhance international students' local, personal, and professional networks as work experience and career pursuit are significant concerns of theirs while they are at UBC and in their home country, or elsewhere.

Therefore, specific goals for the CBEL program are to:

- Increase international student awareness of the value of and their ability to gain future experiential learning opportunities to enhance employability.
- Increase international student awareness of local community issues and their complexity as the more students feel connected to others even through issue-based challenges, the better they learn.

21

INTERNATIONALIZATION FOR US STUDENT AFFAIRS

- Forge relationships between diverse international students and members of local communities to reduce the possibility of xenophobic bias while working towards solutions to solve community issues.
- Enhance international student appreciation for community-engaged learning and its contributions to social change in the promotion of civic engagement and global citizenship.

Assessment:

Annually, we have conducted assessments and evaluations on how CBEL has allowed our award students to strengthen their understanding of what it means to be working "from here." This is done through multiple methods including, using photos, taken with permission, in communities to create photo journals, pre- and post-surveys, and focus groups to get the rich qualitative feedback about the seemingly "small" things that when taken together as a cohort become systemic issues that may require structural change. All students are also offered the opportunity to meet one-on-one with program staff on any concerns they may have, or ideas that they would like to develop. Moreover, it is vital that students understand what it means to live in an ethno-linguistically diverse community such as Vancouver, BC. It is equally important that they begin to learn, understand, and embody the protocols, personal and collective responsibilities in living on the traditional, ancestral and unceded territory of the *xʷməθkʷəy̓əm* (Musqueam), *səlilwətaʔɬ* (Tsleil-Waututh) and *Skwxwú7mesh* (Squamish) Peoples, as we maintain and continue efforts at reconciliation with Indigenous Peoples in Canada.

Lessons Learned:

1. Given the multifaceted nature of supporting multiple CBEL experiences, we found as award program staff that institutionally manage and coordinate these efforts, that a program planning and development approach in the structure and delivery of CBEL is best to meet the needs of our diverse CBEL stakeholders.
2. We developed a conceptual model called the experiential education process that maps out and connects the learner to broader learning objectives of complexity of community and interdisciplinary skills. This served as an important and accessible tool to illustrate and articulate to students and community partners the broader learning outcomes that we hoped to achieve with CBEL.
3. We enhanced our learning around partner engagement with international students and were affirmed in that fostering long-term community partner relationships is of great benefit to our students' learning both in the immediate and long term. As well, it helps to ensure our work with students in community is done in the most responsible and ethical manner.

Media Links:

International Scholars Program: http://internationalscholars.ubc.ca/

22

STUDENT AFFAIRS FRAMEWORKS AND PRACTICES BEYOND THE US

While student affairs is a well-established profession in the US, it takes on different forms in other countries but the work with and for students' development and welfare is still being done (Ludeman, Osfield, Iglesias Hidalgo, Oste, & Wang, 2009). One goal of incorporating non-US Promising Practices in this book is to showcase innovative, culturally appropriate, and impactful programs and services to aid learning within a global community of practitioners. Regardless of location, the influence of common elements of globalization and internationalization provide a connective tissue among a global community of student affairs and services practitioners. As student affairs advances, those doing the work can embrace learning about practices and perspectives beyond the US and Western-centric model of current practice to discover commonalities and celebrate differences.

The following illustrates the complex perspective about how to internationalize student affairs, highlighting that practitioners will want to learn about practices and frameworks outside of the US. An SSAO at a small private college in Ohio shared in our survey some critical needs for internationalization of the field:

- Acquiring competencies relevant to understanding and supporting international student needs.
- Providing opportunities for students to gain knowledge and appreciation for other world perspectives.
- Effectively challenging institutional assumptions that only pertain to US students, understanding, and embracing practices employed in other countries/regions to serve students.

To achieve the first two points about supporting international students and helping all students gain intercultural competencies, practitioners and student affairs broadly needs to continue gaining knowledge about practices beyond the US.

To the SSAOs' last point, one way to expand knowledge about non-Western frameworks and practices is to learn what practitioners, often faculty, in other world regions are doing to serve and support within various cultural and historical contexts. For example, in Chinese higher education, faculty members often are charged with the senior leadership of student affairs, staff members have broad responsibilities, and select students are relied upon for high levels of work and responsibilities (Xia, 2014). In the UK, practitioners believe that "the skills and expertise of the staff within student support services contribute directly to the total student learning experience" (Rowley, 1996, p. 166). Kenyan student services practitioners and faculty face similar challenges to others around the world, such as increasing costs, political influences on students and campus climate, and need for training in leadership (Yakaboski & Birnbaum, 2013). In Finland, the students' union organizations fulfill much of the responsibilities for providing students with similar services such as housing, dining, health care, and general student advocacy to the institutional administrators and government officials. These are just a few examples of the growing work in English and here are some additional publications that explore the internationalization of student affairs globally: Osfield and Associates (2008), Osfield, Perozzi, Bardill Moscaritolo, and Shea (2016), Ludeman and Associates (2009), and UNESCO (2002).

CONCLUSION

The phenomenon of globalization has become better understood over time, and the movement and ideology has led to widespread internationalization of the higher education sector, thus influencing the field of student affairs, practitioners, and their work with students and services. A common conception is that international-ization means having and working with international students. Assisting inter-national students is one of the most common student services around the world; almost every HEI now recruits or attracts international students. Yet, equating internationalization with international students ignores the need to focus on domestic students' intercultural competence and create environments where they can experience and practice this competency. Rather, helping international and domestic students learn key skills for productive intercultural interaction and engagement is a core challenge and responsibility for student affairs practitioners that cannot be assigned as only the work of international education or multicultural and cultural centers. As such, to advance IaH and broader internationalization in student outcomes practitioners and programs can focus on (1) local community engagement over international mobility, (2) intentional interactions between international and domestic students, and (3) intercultural competency develop-ment for all students.

For practitioners to effectively advance inclusive internationalization, they must increasingly understand the global student affairs and services context, and realize that other paradigms and conceptualizations of this work are valid and cul-turally and contextually bound. Approaches steeped in Western ideology and research are not always applicable in a global context, and keeping international-ization as a guiding philosophy will help practitioners facilitate broader inclusion in their work environments. IaH is one useful framework to ensure practice focuses on serving all students inclusively. To achieve this, our book offers: (1) knowledge incorporation of non-US models of student affairs and services through global Promising Practices and international, interdisciplinary literature, (2) development of intercultural professional competency as a companion to multicultural develop-ment and SJI work, and (3) acquisition of professional development to enhance international and intercultural skills and knowledge.

24

REFERENCES

Altbach, P., Reisberg, L., & Rumbley, L. (2009). *Trends in global higher education: Tracking an academic revolution*. A Report Prepared for the UNESCO 2009 World Conference on Higher Education. Paris, France: UNESCO.

Althen, G. (2009). Educating international students about "race." *International Educator, 18*(3), 88–93.

American Council on Education. (2017). Leading internationalization: CIGE model for comprehensive internationalization. Retrieved from www.acenet.edu/news-room/Pages/CIGE-Model-for-Comprehensive-Internationalization.aspx

Andrade, M. S., & Evans, N. W. (Eds.). (2009). *International students: Strengthening a critical resource*. Lanham, MD: Rowman & Littlefield Education.

Beelen, J. (2007). *Implementing internationalisation at home*. EAIE Professional Development Series for International Educators, 2. Amsterdam, The Netherlands: EAIE.

Beelen, J. (2013). Internationalisation at home, history and conceptual notions. In J. Beelen, A. Boddington, B. Bruns, M. Glogar, & C. Machado (Eds.), *Guide of good practices Tempus Corinthiam* (pp. 123–131), Vol. 3. Brussels, Belgium: Tempus Corinthiam.

Bondi, S. (2012). Students and institutions protecting Whiteness as property: A critical race theory analysis of student affairs preparation. *Journal of Student Affairs Research and Practice, 49*(4), 397–414.

Caruana, V., & Ploner, J. (2010). *Internationalisation and equality and diversity in higher education: Merging identities*. Leeds, UK: Leeds Metropolitan University.

Cornwell, G. H., & Stoddard, E. W. (1999). *Globalizing knowledge: Connecting international & intercultural studies*. Washington, D.C.: AAC&U.

Crowther, P., Joris, M., Otten, M., Nilsson, B., Teekens, H., & Wächter, B. (2000). *Internationalization at home: A position paper*. Amsterdam, The Netherlands: EAIE.

Dalton, J. C., & Sullivan, M. H. (2008). Expanding global horizons. In K. J. Osfield & Associates (Eds.), *Internationalization of student affairs and services: An emerging global perspective* (pp. 7–12). Washington, D.C.: NASPA.

de Wit, H. (2010) *Internationalisation of higher education in Europe and its assessment, trends and issues*. The Netherlands: Nederlands-Vlaamse Accreditatieorganisatie. NVAO.

de Wit, H. (2017, February 25). Internationalisation of HE may be accelerating. *University World News*. Retrieved from www.universityworldnews.com/article.php?story=20170225091655310

Deardorff, D. (2006). Identification and assessment of intercultural competence as a student outcome of internationalization. *Journal of Studies in International Education, 10*(3), 241–266.

Drexhage, G. (2015). UBC's international undergrads partner with local community groups. UBC News. Retrieved from http://news.ubc.ca/2015/04/28/beyond-the-classroom-ubcs-international-undergrads-partner-with-local-community-groups/

Glass, C. R., Wongtrirat, R., & Buus, S. (2015). *International student engagement: Strategies for creating inclusive, connected, and purposeful campus environments*. Sterling, VA: Stylus.

Green, M. F. (2015, May 29). US lags behind on internationalization. *University World News.* Retrieved from www.universityworldnews.com/article.php?story=2015052711 0733116

Gregersen-Hermans, J. (2016). From rationale to reality in intercultural competence development: Working towards the university's organizational capability to deliver. In E. Jones, R. Coelen, J. Beelen, & H. de Wit (Eds.), *Global and local internationalization* (pp. 91–96). Rotterdam, The Netherlands: Sense Publishers.

Hudzik, J. K., & Stohl, M. (2012). Comprehensive and strategic internationalization of U.S. higher education. In D. K. Deardorff, H. de Wit, J. D. Heyl, & T. Adams (Eds.), *SAGE handbook of international higher education* (pp. 61–80). Thousand Oaks, CA: Sage.

Institute of International Education. (2016). Open Doors data. Retrieved from www.iie.org/opendoors

JAMK University of Applied Sciences *(Jyväskylän ammattikorkeakoulu).* (2016). New Horizons and JAMK United for Refugees Project Profile. Retrieved from www.jamk.fi/globalassets/palvelut—services/koulutus-ja-kehittaminen/kansainvalistyminen/new-horizons/jufr-new-horizons-profile-01.10.16.pdf

Jones, E. (2016). Mobility, graduate employability and local internationalisation. In E. Jones, R. Coelen, J. Beelen, & H. de Wit (Eds.), *Global and local internationalization* (pp. 107–116). Rotterdam, The Netherlands: Sense Publishers.

Killick, D. (2015). *Developing the global student: Higher education in an era of globalization.* New York: Routledge.

Killick, D. (2017). *Internationalization and diversity in higher education: Implications for teaching, learning and assessment.* London: Palgrave Teaching & Learning.

Kim, E., & Díaz, J. (2013). *Immigrant students and higher education* (ASHE Higher Education Report No. 38(6)). San Francisco, CA: Jossey-Bass.

Kim, S., & Kim, R. H. (2010). *Microaggressions experienced by international students attending U.S. institutions of higher education.* In D. W. Sue (Ed.), *Migroaggressions and marginality: Manifestation, dynamics, and impact* (pp. 171–191). Hoboken, NJ: Wiley.

Knight, J. (2012). Concepts, rationales, and interpretive frameworks in the internationalization of higher education. In D. K. Deardorff, H. de Wit, J. D. Heyl, & T. Adams (Eds.), *SAGE handbook of international higher education* (pp. 27–42). Thousand Oaks, CA: Sage.

Knight, J. (2013). The changing landscape of higher education internationalisation—for better or worse? *Perspectives: Policy and Practice in Higher Education, 17*(3), 84–90.

Korbel, L. A. (2002). Small projects that promote an international campus culture. In R. M. Romano (Ed.), *Internationalizing the community college* (pp. 125–134). Washington, D.C.: Rowman & Littlefield Publishers.

Kruger, K. W., & Dungy, G. J. (1999). Opportunities for international travel and professional exchange for student affairs professionals. *New Directions for Student Services, 86,* 23–31.

Latham, S., & Dalton, J. C. (1999). International skills and experiences for a global future. *New Directions for Student Services, 86,* 89–92.

Landreman, L. M., & MacDonald-Dennis, C. (2013). The evolution of social justice education and facilitation. In L. M. Landreman (Ed.), *The art of effective facilitation: Reflections from social justice educators* (pp. 3–22). Sterling, VA: Stylus.

Leask, B. (2015). *Internationalizing the curriculum.* New York: Routledge.

Leask, B. (2016). Internationalizing curriculum and learning for all students. In E. Jones, R. Coelen, J. Beelen, & H. de Wit (Eds.), *Global and local internationalization* (pp. 49–54). Rotterdam, The Netherlands: Sense Publishers.

Lee, J. J. & Rice, C. (2007). Welcome to America? International student perceptions of discrimination. *Higher Education, 53*(3), 381–409.

Lee, Y. I., & Metcalfe, A. (2017). Academic advisors and their diverse advisees: Towards more ethical global universities. *Journal of International Students, 7*(4), 944–962.

Ludeman, R., Osfield, K., Iglesias Hidalgo, E., Oste, D., & Wang, H. (2009). *Student affairs and services in higher education: Global foundations, issues and best practices.* Paris, France: UNESCO.

Manns, K. (2014). Ellerslie global residence. In H. Spencer-Oatey, D. Dauber, & S. Williams (Eds.), *Promoting integration on campus: Principles, practice and issues for further exploration* (p. 29). Coventry, UK: UKCISA.

Niehaus, E., Seifert, T., & Wawrzynski, M. (2016). Infusing international perspectives in professional preparation programs. Panel presentation at annual ACPA Convention, Montreal, Canada.

Osfield, K. J. & Associates. (2008). *Internationalization of student affairs and services: An emerging global perspective.* Washington, D.C.: NASPA.

Osfield, K. J., Perozzi, B., Bardill Moscaritolo, L., & Shea, R. (2016). *Supporting students globally in higher education: Trends and perspectives for student affairs and services.* Washington, D.C.: NASPA.

Osfield, K. J., & Terrell, P. S. (2009) Internationalization in higher education and student affairs. In G. S. McClellan, & J. Stringer (Eds.), *The handbook of student affairs administration in higher education* (pp. 120–143). San Francisco, CA: Jossey-Bass.

Patton, L. D., & Hannon, M. D. (2008). Collaboration for cultural programming: Engaging culture centers, multicultural affairs, and student activities offices as partners. In S. Harper (Ed.), *Creating inclusive campus environments: For cross-cultural learning and student engagement* (pp. 139–154). Washington, D.C.: NASPA.

Perozzi, B., & Havlic, M. K. (2011). *Professional development in student affairs and services around the world.* NASPA Knowledge Communities: Celebrating ten years of educating for lives of purpose. Washington, D.C.: NASPA.

Peterson, D. M., Briggs, P., Dreasher, L., Horner, D. D., & Nelson, T. (1999). Contributions of international students and programs to campus diversity. *New Directions for Student Services, 86*, 67–77.

Pöllmann, A. (2013). Intercultural capital: Toward the conceptualization, operationalization, and empirical investigation of a rising marker of sociocultural distinction. *SAGE Open, 3*(2), 1–7.

Quinlan, O. (2015). South Africa: Small steps in the right direction. *EAIE Forum: Internationalisation at Home*, 17–19.

Renn, K. A., & Jessup-Anger, E. R. (2008). Preparing new professionals: Lessons for graduate preparation programs from the National Study of New Professionals in Student Affairs. *Journal of College Student Development*, *49*(4), 319–335.

Ripmeester, N. (2016). Internationalisation and employability: Making the connection between degree and the world of work. In E. Jones, R. Coelen, J. Beelen, & H. de Wit (Eds.), *Global and local internationalization* (pp. 121–127). Rotterdam, The Netherlands: Sense Publishers.

Rhoads, R. A., & Black, M. A. (1995). Student affairs practitioners as transformative educators: Advancing a critical cultural perspective. In E. J. Whitt (Ed.), *ASHE Reader on College Student Affairs Administration* (pp. 407–415). Boston, MA: Pearson.

Roberts, D. & Komives, S. (2016). *Enhancing student learning and development in cross-border higher education: new directions for higher education*. San Francisco, CA: Jossey-Bass.

Rose-Redwood, C., & Rose-Redwood, R. (2013). Self-segregation or global mixing? Social interactions and the international student experience. *Journal of College Student Development*, *54*(4), 413–429.

Rowley, R. (1996). Student support services. In D. Warner & D. Palfreyman (Eds.), *Higher education management: The key elements* (pp. 166–180). Buckingham, UK: Open UP.

Rumbley, L. E., Altbach, P. G., & Reisberg, L. (2012). Internationalization within the higher education context. In D. Deardorff, H. de Wit, J. Heyl, & T. Adams, (Eds.), *The SAGE handbook of international higher education* (pp. 3–26). Thousand Oaks, CA: Sage.

Sackney, L. (2007). Systemic reform for sustainability. *Government of Saskatchewan*. Retrieved from www.publications.gov.sk.ca/

Schulz, S., Lee, J. J., Cantwell, B., McClellan, G., & Woodard, D. (2007). Moving toward a global community: An analysis of the internationalization of student affairs graduate preparation programs. *NASPA Journal*, *44*(3), 610–632.

Terzian, S. G., & Osborne, L. A. (2011). International college students. In M. J. Cuyjet, M. F. Howard-Hamilton, & D. L. Cooper (Ed.), *Multiculturalism on campus: Theory, models, and practices for understanding diversity and creating inclusion*, 1st ed. (pp. 237–263). Baltimore, MD: Johns Hopkins UP.

Tull, A., Hirt, J. B., & Saunders, S. A. (2009). *Becoming socialized in student affairs administration: A guide for new professionals and their supervisors*. Sterling, VA: Stylus.

United Nations Educational, Scientific, and Cultural Organization (UNESCO). (2002). *The role of student affairs and services in higher education: A practical manual for developing, implementing and assessing student affairs programmes and services*. Paris, France: Author.

Wächter, B. (2003). An introduction: Internationalisation at home in context. *Journal of Studies in International Education*, *7*(1), 5–11.

Walker, K. L., Hart, J. L., Jackson, T., Roberts, G., & Ludeman, R. B. (2014). Global citizenship and tertiary education: Looking to the future. *ACPA Developments*, *12*(3), Retrieved from www.myacpa.org/publications/developments/volume-12-issue-3

Ward, H. H. (2015a). *Internationalizing the co-curriculum: Part one: Integrating international students*. Washington, D.C.: ACE. Retrieved from www.acenet.edu/news-room/Documents/Intlz-In-Action-Intlz-Co-Curriculum-Part-1.pdf

Ward, H. H. (2015b). *Internationalizing the co-curriculum: Part two: Global and intercultural education in the co-curriculum*. Washington, D.C.: ACE. Retrieved from www.acenet.edu/news-room/Documents/Intlz-In-Action-Intlz-Co-Curriculum-Part-2.pdf

Ward, H. H. (2016). *Internationalizing the co-curriculum: Part three: Internationalization and student affairs*. Washington, D.C.: ACE. Retrieved from www.acenet.edu/news-room/Documents/Intlz-In-Action-Intlz-Co-Curriculum-Part-3.pdf

Xia, M. (2014). *A comparative study: Student affairs in Chinese and American higher education* (Unpublished master's thesis). University of Denver, Denver, CO.

Yakaboski, T., & Birnbaum, M. G. (2013). The challenges of student affairs at Kenyan public universities. *Journal of Student Affairs in Africa*, *1*(1&2), 33–48.

Yakaboski, T., & Birnbaum, M. G. (2017). Case study: (Re)Blending Mayan and Mexican interculturalism with social justice in a U.S. graduate preparation program. In D. K. Deardorff & L. A. Arasaratnam-Smith (Eds.), *Intercultural competence in international higher education* (pp. 289–293). New York: Routledge.

Yakaboski, T., Perez-Velez, K., & Almutairi, Y. (2017). Breaking the silence: Saudi graduate student experiences on a U.S. campus. *Journal of Diversity in Higher Education*. Advance online publication. http://dx.doi.org/10.1037/dhc0000059

Yakaboski, T., Ramos, E., & Hornak, A. (2017). Infusing globalism: A dialogue on internationalizing curriculum. NASPA International Symposium, San Antonio, TX.

Yefanova, D., & Johnstone, C. (2015). Maximising the educational impact of international students. *EAIE Forum: Internationsation at Home*, 9–11.

Yefanova, D., Woodruff, G., Kappler, B., & Johnstone, C. (2014). *The study of the educational impact of international students in campus internationalization at the University of Minnesota: Phase 1*. Retrieved from https://global.umn.edu/icc/documents/15_EducationalImpact-IntlStudents.pdf

Chapter 2

Connection of Internationalization to Multiculturalism, Diversity, Social Justice and Inclusion

The increasing plurality of societies and diversification of nations and higher education require that students, practitioners, and faculty possess intercultural skills to communicate and manage cultural differences while recognizing one's own biases and stereotypes to be able to combat those of others (Olson, Evans, & Shoenberg, 2007; Thom, 2010). A prevailing assumption that higher education institutions (HEIs) are places of liberal culture where people from all backgrounds, identities, and cultures are supported and included is a false one (Killick, 2017). Quite the opposite, there are calls for scholars, faculty, and practitioners to use their work to advance racial equality in US higher education (Lederman, 2017). For instance, ACPA—College Student Educators International (2017) created the Strategic Imperative on Racial Justice and Decolonization to address how "all forms of oppression are linked," and that "racism and colonization all are real, present, enduring, intersectional, and systemic forms of oppression" that "have informed the experience of all of us in higher education" (p. 2). There has been much good work done in advancing diversity and multiculturalism in HEIs through multi-cultural, cultural, and affinity centers, who have been serving as expert facilitators of cross-cultural learning (Stewart, 2011). However, the more recent shift to social justice and inclusion (SJI) acknowledges the need for all practitioners across all functional areas to focus on individual, institutional, and social change to address issues of equity, privilege, power, and institutionalized oppression. Connecting internationalization to issues within the local community is a key element to ensuring global learning related to Internationalization at Home (IaH).

Social and economic background continues to largely determine who partici-pates in higher education with abounding concerns of access and inequity including who gains entrance to global mobility programs (OECD, 2012; Usher & Medow, 2010). This combines with the trend that more and more HEIs are increasing or adding international student recruitment as part of their internationalization or diversity strategies and enrollment management plans. Often the assumption is that recruiting international students is equivalent to internationalization, and

31

yet international student increases may not come with adequate addition of support staff positions, a cultural change, or addition of services. Recruitment plans may ignore that international students require assistance due to their large transitions often without local family support and that they experience discrimination on campuses and even in the surrounding communities. Yet, the European Student Union in its *Kaunas Declaration* (2013) spoke out against using international students as a revenue stream and stated that those students should receive ample services and support comparable to domestic students.

While not a part of any definition currently used in the US, other professional associations connect internationalization to SJI and social responsibility, in part to ensure students are not treated primarily as revenue streams. The Canadian Bureau for International Education's *Internationalization Statement of Principles* (2014) states:

> internationalization aims to educate students as global citizens, including attributes of openness to and understanding of other worldviews, empathy for people with different backgrounds and experience to oneself, the capacity to value diversity, and respect for indigenous peoples and knowledge.
>
> (p. 1)

Combining this perspective with social justice in a global context can support students, staff, and faculty developing inclusive, intercultural competencies and their development as local and global citizens (Olson et al., 2007; Patel & Lynch, 2013). While there is undoubtedly much need to focus on domestic diversity within US higher education, it is a missed opportunity to leave out global and international frameworks and international students from these same conversations, policies, and programs. Just as inclusive diversity work matters and positively impacts students (Harper, 2008; Stewart, 2011), promoting broad intercultural competency development would positively change the culture and climate for all students. For instance, at the 2017 Association for the Study of Higher Education (ASHE) conference, Shaun Harper's presidential address keynote spoke about the continued prevalence of White Supremacy in perpetuating how White faculty and staff continue to hold power in determining what is taught, and what the norms of behavior and academic expectations are (Lederman, 2017). These are good considerations for student affairs to reexamine knowledge and practices within the profession to prevent an assimilation framework from being applied to diverse international students, for instance.

"Internationalization is also about relating to diversity of cultures that exist within countries, communities, institutions, and classrooms so *intercultural* is used to address aspects of cultural diversity" (Knight, 2012, p. 30, italics in original). In part, internationalization addresses the need to develop intercultural skills, knowledge, and attitudes of students, faculty, and staff alike to reach the vision of

32

DIVERSITY AND INCLUSION CONNECTION

embracing a pluralistic, multicultural society. Internationalization can build upon this work to support systemic changes that transform structural components that privilege dominant groups and, instead, create global learning opportunities for all (Caruana & Ploner, 2010). HEIs' internationalization strategies can include reflection on the "why," or the purpose of internationalizing (de Wit, 2016), and, as such, prevent a disconnect from the rest of the institutions' strategies, including diversity initiatives. When strategies are separate, internationalization conversations may omit or silence racism, inequities, or power hierarchies. If internationalization is isolated, then it can create an artificial separation between global and multicultural local contexts that exist in many US cities and towns where HEIs are located. Without links to SJI work, internationalization risks being viewed as a buzzword, similar to diversity and multiculturalism on some campuses, where the focus is more on understanding and tolerance rather than systemic change and access for all (Goodman, 2011). Also, separations make it easy to omit social justice and social responsibility from internationalization strategies. This chapter offers a foundational argument for the shift from structural or numerical representation of internationalization to one that combines efforts with diversity, multicultural, and SJI work to advance a more inclusive application of internationalization.

STRUCTURAL DIVERSITY DOES NOT EQUAL INTERNATIONALIZATION

Structural diversity or numerical representation through increased recruitment of diverse students, staff, and faculty, does not directly or automatically equate to increased engagement, curricular diversity, or cross and intercultural interactions (Chun & Evans, 2016). The sheer number of international students may raise the internationalization profile of HEIs, yet structural diversity itself has little substantive impact, and could negatively influence campus culture. HEI campuses are the "ideal setting within which cultural barriers can be overcome through intercultural dialogue and social interaction . . . however, spatial and social proximity do not always coincide" (Rose-Redwood & Rose-Redwood, 2013, p. 414). Nevertheless, structural diversity is the most common diversity and internationalization strategy for many HEIs in the US.

A focus on recruitment and representation of international students reflects a structural diversity plan or intent. In our US SSAO study, institutions with small international student populations assumed that the lack of structural diversity or larger numerical representation was an issue for developing an internationalized student affairs division. The belief was that internationalization required a significant sized international student population to allow for interaction and representation. An example comes from an SSAO in New York who stated, "I believe that our division doesn't regard itself as internationalized. We have a very small international student population and few staff from other countries." Of course, it may be easier

33

DIVERSITY AND INCLUSION CONNECTION

to develop interactive programs with more diverse students, however teaching domestic students intercultural skills can occur by other means.

Structural diversity alone has little effect on students' intercultural learning because it relies on the contact hypothesis, which posits that brief interactions "can reinforce stereotypes and prejudices if critical incidents are not evaluated on cognitive, affective, and behavioural levels" (Caruana & Ploner, 2010, p. 12). Research consistently shows that students and educators deny equity to international students in US classrooms (Valdez, 2016). Therefore, having international students on campus does not increase the intercultural competency for any students (Otten, 2003) and may serve to reinforce stereotypes or cause international students to experience harm (Lee & Rice, 2007; Hanassab, 2006). It is important for international and immigrant students to develop a sense of belonging to improve resiliency and retention, as well as experience (Glass, Wongtrirat, & Buss, 2015; Kim & Díaz, 2013). Structural diversity-related thinking alone is limiting because it removes internationalization as a responsibility of practitioners to provide all students with global understanding and intercultural development regardless of student representation.

LINKS TO MULTICULTURALISM AND DIVERSITY

Multicultural education in the US grew out of the civil rights and women's movements of the 1960s and 1970s that brought with it the establishment of campus cultural centers (Patton, 2010; Stewart, 2011). On the other hand, US internationalization is primarily a top-down initiative through Comprehensive Internationalization (ACE) and a response to the Cold War and need for US citizens who could serve as ambassadors around the world (Cornwell & Stoddard, 1999). Within multicultural education there is a need to rewrite and retell history and stories to include minoritized individuals. This is true for internationalization as well, given the dominant narratives that privilege some over others. For example, to what degree do US graduate preparation program curriculum or student affairs professional development address issues around colonization, neo-colonization, neo-racism, or neo-nationalism? Do they include students from diaspora movements, from the borderlands, who are refugees, who are undocumented, who are international students, or who occupy multiple spaces, inbetweenness, or third spaces, such as Puerto Ricans or those in the US who have homes in more than one place/country, as examples? Internationalization and intercultural development can begin to address this absence of knowledge and the effect on student affairs practice, and work to end the harm to these populations, which limit student affairs' ability to advance SJI.

On US campuses, multicultural education broadly addresses "groups marginalized by race, ethnicity, gender, sexual orientation, religion, and/or other cultural characteristics" (Cuyjet, Howard-Hamilton, & Cooper, 2011, p. 12). With this:

34

DIVERSITY AND INCLUSION CONNECTION

> the argument is often made that successful pursuit of multicultural education requires an exclusive focus on matters of domestic diversity, that embracing global education in this conversation is an unnecessary distraction that takes away from what is and should be an increasing and deserving focus on ethnic diversity in the United States.
>
> (Charles, Longerbeam, & Miller, 2013, p. 47)

The significant body of literature on multiculturalism in higher education largely attends to domestic US diversity and is not always inclusive of international students and cultures (Cornwell & Stoddard, 1999; Olson et al., 2007), or receives brief mention. Although the literature includes international students as one of the many cultural populations on campuses, global frameworks may often be left out of diversity and inclusion conversations and international students may be discussed in monolithic terms.

From a multicultural framework, there is no one American or US culture, there is instead US citizenship or nationality, and "[d]ifferences of nationality are but one in a multidimensional matrix of differences that define most intercultural encounters" (Cornwell & Stoddard, 1999, p. 17). A false monolithic interpretation views culture as a fixed entity with a common collective identity, physical attributes, and characteristics devoid of power differentials or external political, structural, or economic contexts (Chun & Evans, 2016). For example, to understand the African American experience and history requires knowledge about the African diaspora, which then requires information about West African culture (Cornwell & Stoddard, 1999). To focus solely on a US-only perspective does not represent history and interconnections. Likewise, to see only the US as incredibly multicultural is also a false reality as other countries have been influenced by colonization, diasporas, migration, missionary work, and other movements that make what is seemingly homogeneous also multicultural. For example, Australia shares a long history of migration flows that have led to a multicultural society that has influenced their higher education system as well (Caruana & Ploner, 2010). These monolithic or privileged interpretations speak a bit to the American elitism that views the US as more advanced or progressive, whereas this perspective may not be held by members of other nations with more social welfare systems that privilege welfare and community over capitalism and individualism (Cornwell & Stoddard, 1999).

Internationalization and interculturalism can complement multiculturalism because:

> International and intercultural must be framed as complementary aspects of the broader notions of equity, diversity, and inclusion within our institutions, something not yet accepted in all universities. Relevant intercultural learning outcomes will need to be incorporated into curricula for all students, not simply

35

> opportunities for international mobility, and innovative assessment tasks developed which measure whether the outcomes have been achieved.
>
> (Jones, 2016, p. 114)

While many student affairs practitioners support and advocate for multiculturalism and inclusion (Jenkins & Walton, 2008), it is not clear how and if current cultural, social justice work in higher education considers interculturalism for all students or the diversity of and within international student populations. In practice, multiculturalism addresses domestic diversity and internationalization focuses on cultures outside of the US; they share common goals and overlaps in knowledge, such as "how students can see systems, make meanings, and understand connections between cultures and identity concepts" (Olson et al., 2007, p. 12). There are several shared learning outcomes between multicultural education and internationalization, many of which have commonality with SJI learning objectives, such as reduce one's own prejudice, develop empathy, and create perspective consciousness. In fact, American Council on Education (ACE) has advanced a collaborative initiative called, At Home in the World, which promotes global connections and local diversity commitments to support students' cultural and global learning because of these shared learning outcomes. Additionally, Chun and Evans (2016) cite six commonalities in the definitions of intercultural, multicultural, and cultural or diversity competence:

> (a) recognition of cultural dominance and historical forms of exclusion that take shape through the channels of power and privilege; (b) recognition and respect for cultural differences; (c) a dynamic understanding of the contested and fluid nature of culture; (d) the connection of culture with identity and positionality; (e) the self-determination and self-affirmation involved in identity formation; (f) the skillsets needed to engage and communicate with those who are different from oneself.
>
> (p. 45)

Some scholars have argued for the combination of multicultural, intercultural, diversity, and internationalization work to develop students' deeper critical analysis skills and ability to apply concepts beyond the US (e.g., Charles et al., 2013; Cortés, 1998; Killick, 2017; Olson et al., 2007).

In the UK, there is growing synergy with diversity and multicultural education in that internationalization helps students develop intercultural skills and competencies (Killick, 2017). Also in the UK, like the US, there is a local multicultural context where "an expansive conceptualization of multiculturalism can support internationalisation and needs to be considered a key element of strategy. Creative inter-cultural pedagogy should be exploited to offer a global outlook for the majority of students who are not internationally mobile" (Jones, 2011, p. 29).

In some contexts, equity and inclusion work can be parallel to and even compete with internationalization efforts unless institutions intentionally combine efforts (Atherton, 2015). Leeds Metropolitan University in the UK designed its curriculum to use internationalization to assist all students' ability to see the broader global perspective even if they work and remain local (Jones, 2011). Unique to Leeds Metropolitan is how their first internationalization strategy from 2003 stated that "the diversity of international students and responding to the diversity of home students are in fact not two agendas but one" (Jones & Killick, 2007, p. 110).

Embracing internationalization within a multicultural framework allows for better connection to local communities and their needs. Many SSAOs in our study faced challenges in internationalizing because their HEIs' missions required that they serve local, regional populations and internationalization was viewed as detracting from this because the assumption was that internationalization meant international students primarily. However, recent publications have advocated for US community college internationalization and its connection to student success and learning; therefore, institutional administrators may benefit from IaH approaches (e.g., Raby, 2016; Raby, Rhodes, & Biscarra, 2014). HEIs in Australia and the UK have begun to negotiate these seemingly contradictory missions by placing an IaH concept of "think global, act local," which allows internationalization to be a response to local and regional needs for successful participation in the global economy (Caruana & Ploner, 2010). An instructive parallel exists in that Australian and British senior managers acknowledge the "difficulties of maintaining the 'right balance' of service for local widening participation students and/or inclusion groups on the one hand (i.e., low socio-economic local students, disability students, or 'rural' and 'aboriginal' students in Australia) and international student on the other" (Caruana & Ploner, 2010, p. 46).

The Promising Practice Listen, Live and Learn (LLL) at Stellenbosch University in South Africa is a living-learning residential housing program with a main value of "embracing diversity and difference in all its forms" to advance students' active listening skills that would allow them to embrace diversity and ideological pluralism while learning how to have "reasoned disagreements and principled dissent" (para. 1). This value also incorporates Ubuntu, which encourages students to see interconnections as one's "existence is contingent upon that of different others" (para. 1). The LLL program requires that all students regularly participate in critical reflection about their engagement within the community and their own personal development as a transformative leader. The program requires that each of the houses within the LLL Village shares one meal a week together as a group and also brings in diverse speakers for lounge conversations. To demonstrate the connection to local community engagement, each house creates a project for the year that encourages student engagement in service that is meaningful to the community.

DIVERSITY AND INCLUSION CONNECTION

PROMISING PRACTICE: Listen, Live and Learn at a South African University: A milieu-based diversity and multiculturalism program— bringing diversity and internationalization home.

Institution: Stellenbosch University

Location: Stellenbosch, South Africa

Author: Birgit Schreiber, Ph.D., Senior Director, Student Affairs

Background and Context:

South African higher education, much like higher education in many other countries in the world, is positioned within an instrumentalist framework and seeks to contribute towards national and global social justice not only via broadening access to education, but also via the development of "enlightened, responsible and constructively critical citizens" (DoE, 1997, p. 9). Within this social imperative, competencies linked to diversity, multi-, inter- and trans-culturalism and internationalization are defined and universities devise a range of interventions and programs that offer opportunity to develop such competencies, often recognized in cocurricular transcripts, or defined as learning and development outcomes.

Challenges arise when such competencies are viewed as discreet skills within a skills-based framework, rather than an attribute or identity development framework, where such competencies around diversity and pluralism are viewed as part of living in a pluralist, multicultural society. The program discussed in this section seeks to expand skills-based discourses and frameworks of diversity and promotes the re-conceptualization of diversity within an immersion and milieu-based framework. Diversity, multiculturalism, and internationalization are thus part of the milieu—the lived daily living and learning context, rather than a discreet skill or a distinct competence.

The Listen, Live and Learn (LLL) program is part of the residential accommodation for students at the University of Stellenbosch, a research-intensive university at the southern tip of Africa. Stellenbosch University is one of the most highly ranked universities in Africa (Webometrics, 2015) and struggles within the South African history of divisiveness and race tensions. Stellenbosch University has 31,000 students enrolled in ten faculties, with close to 45% African, Colored and Indian students among the student population across undergraduate and postgraduate enrollment. The South African term "Colored" is a recognised category that is used to describe people of mixed descent and mixed race. This descriptive race category is required by the Department of Higher Education and Training and is one indicator used to monitor transformation. The LLL program mirrors these statistics and has 11% international students in its program.

The LLL seeks to make a critical contribution towards transformation, not only in terms of access and equity, but also in terms of developing new discourses, beyond power and positionality, beyond identity politics, and beyond the entrapment of racialized

38

DIVERSITY AND INCLUSION CONNECTION

relations. To this end, the LLL program forms a critical contribution towards sustainable transformation that spans the individual, group, and community level and brings diversity, multiculturalism, and internationalization "home," into the intimate lived experience of students, thus developing "enlightened, responsible and constructively critical citizens" who have glo-cal competencies (DoE, 1997, p. 9).

Further Description:

The Listen, Live and Learn (LLL) program focusses on senior students and accommodates these in communal houses, intentionally combining a rich diversity, such as demographics, field of study, and nationality, to maximize multicultural experiences and engagements. Currently, 28 LLL houses with 8 students per house live together and host monthly conversations (usually around a shared dinner) on a particular topic or theme, inviting allocated faculty mentors, experts, members of the public, and civic leaders to the conversation. Senior students apply to stay in LLL houses and standard residence rules apply in addition to the expectation to host themed conversations, commit to engagements around rule setting and providing a reflection at the end of the experience.

The monthly conversations are the key events that all house-members need to commit to and take part in. These are in-depth, unstructured conversations built around a chosen theme, facilitated by a faculty-mentor and usually include an invited guest. These conversations are described and experienced as evocative and immediate, address current and relevant issues, and involve the personal sharing of each student (Schreiber, Kloppers, & Cornelissen, 2016). It is through these frank discussions around themes such as racism, gender, globalization, identity, and class issues and many more, that the listening, living and learning is made real and insights and competencies are developed.

The LLL program is built on the assumption that through sharing of physically intimate living spaces, through negotiating the common challenges of student life, developing shared norms and hosting in-depth conversations with each other, that competencies are developed. Diversity, multiculturalism, and internationalization are thus vehicles for developing the very attributes that the university and this program seek to develop. While diversity may become the focus of a themed conversation, it is also that the conversation occurs within a diverse group, and is thus viewed as a key aspect that enhances the development of critical thinking, appreciation of pluralism and competencies around multiculturalism and internationalization.

The LLL program is a milieu program that seeks to extend the notion that multiculturalism is a discreet skill. Rather, it is conceptualized on constructs of "being," a self-within-the-word, where students live within a diverse social sphere and understand themselves as part of and through this diverse social world. The focus is thus not on the diversity itself, as a discreet phenomenon, but on diversity as part of living in the LLL environment as a *habitus* or milieu, where students' lives are lived, thought about, experienced, and reflected on.

The Social Change Model of Leadership (SCM) provides the theoretical conceptualization of the development of competencies around diversity and multiculturalism

DIVERSITY AND INCLUSION CONNECTION

(Dunn-Coetzee & Fourie-Malherbe, 2017). Through engagement across different nationalities, gender, race, sexual orientation, and various further categories of "othering," the critical change is achieved via the seven stages of the SCM which move from individual through group to community (Haber, 2011; Dunn- Coetzee & Fourie-Malherbe, 2017; Inkelas & Weisman, 2003).

Goals and Outcomes of the LLL Program:

The goals of the LLL are aligned to the overall transformation agenda of the university and aim to reduce stereotyping, diminish bias, as well as focus on the increase in multicultural competencies, evidenced through increased insight into stereotypes, recognition of "othering" and systemic power asymmetries (Dunn-Coetzee & Fourie-Malherbe, 2017).

The evaluation of the LLL program reveals that students who apply to live in an LLL house come with a readiness and keenness to explore and embrace plurality across "otherness." Dunn-Coetzee and Fourie-Malherbe's (2017) quantitative and qualitative evaluation of the students' experience of living in an LLL house concluded that the "LLL experience had a profound effect on the student" and that it "led to better self-understanding as well as understanding and acceptance of 'the other'" (p. 74).

The LLL program with its 28 houses spread across the university precinct homes close to 250 students, is an intentionally created listening, living, and learning space that deliberately increases diversity in interpersonal relationships, so as to create opportunity for the development of diversity competencies. Innovative is that diversity is embedded, internationalization is part of the habitus, multiculturalism is within the milieu, and not constructed as a discreet skill, but deeply engrained into the listening, living and learning experiences of the students.

Lessons Learned:

1. Milieu-based diversity experiences are effective and yield competency development.
2. Intentional contextual diversity improves competencies around diversity and multiculturalism.
3. Competencies around diversity, multiculturalism, and internationalization are closely related.
4. The LLL Program is a model for "promising practices" which can be up-scaled and emulated in a variety of settings and contexts.
5. The LLL Program is a model for inclusion of international students into the living and learning spaces of university residences which advances competency development in local students.

Media Links:

Stellenbosch University. Listen, Live and Learn [Luister, Leef & Leer]: www0.sun.ac.za/lllbeta/index.php

Webometrics (2015): www.webometrics.info/en/africa/south%20africa

DIVERSITY AND INCLUSION CONNECTION

GLOBAL SOCIAL JUSTICE THROUGH INTERNATIONALIZATION

The most commonly used definition of social justice in US student affairs addresses ensuring the equitable distribution of resources and that all societal members are safe and secure both physically and psychologically (ACPA & NASPA, 2015). This means that it is important to see how "Intercultural interactions in the context of globalization are deeply embedded in the legacy of colonization, intersecting systems of oppression, and inequitable relations of power" (Sorrells, 2013, p. 66). Within the US, this means understanding that White Supremacy as a system of power is at the core of internationalization strategies that seek to use international students for financial gain or privilege students from some countries over others through targeted recruitment plans. When "an institution most reflects the values of the dominant group in society, [it reproduces] existing patterns of privilege" rather than changing culture and climate to reflect the cultural capital of all students, not just the elite (Caruana & Ploner, 2010, p. 11). Therefore, internationalization strategies undertaken from a social justice framework allows for understanding of identities linked to power and privilege within systemic oppressive constructs of institutions and curriculum.

Student affairs practitioners committed to equity, diversity, and SJI can consider that "global and local social justice is advanced by people who see global and local others as equally human . . . [who] see how their own lives are impacted by and implicated in global inequalities and injustices" (Killick, 2017, p. 2). Internationalization offers social justice a look beyond the local community and a focus on the global level. A social justice framework offers internationalization the ethical responsibility to advocate for change for the betterment of all groups, not just those advantaged within that culture or system. Internationalization also brings national and cultural-specific context to social justice, which will be viewed or conceived differently in other countries than it is in the US. The combination of internationalization and social justice can lead to culturally inclusive and globally minded action. The importance of locating internationalization within a social justice framework in operating in a US context acknowledges some limitations of multiculturalism and international education approaches that may advocate more for tolerance rather than systemic change.

With resurgence of fearmongering ideologies around the world, a partner to exceptionalism is the dangerous companion, ethnocentrism. As discussed more in Chapter 3, exceptionalism has a "patina of cultural superiority, [which] is a pillar of US ethnocentrism" that believes in US superiority over others, including the US model of higher education as the best in the world (Ashwill & Oanh, 2009, p. 147). US exceptionalism supports many negative actions of globalization with attempts to Americanize other cultures and systems of higher education. As practitioners strive to be social justice advocates and transformative educators, more

41

work on learning and incorporating non-US frameworks, cultures, and students may avoid this (Rhoads & Black, 1995). For example, student affairs work is in a precarious position when US practitioners take the US model of student affairs into other cultural and national contexts with the goal of teaching others how to do work in a US model versus sharing resources to support their own development.

Generally, ethnocentrism is the belief that one's group is superior in its ways of thinking, being, and acting compared to other cultural or national groups. Ethnocentricity is in development models, such as King and Baxter Magolda (2005), where individuals move from ethnocentric to ethnorelative appreciation, and Bennett's (1993) Developmental Model of Intercultural Sensitivity (Spitzberg & Changnon, 2009). If unchallenged or unquestioned, ethnocentrism leads to stereotyping, discrimination, conflict, and, at times, violence (Sorrells, 2013). Individuals engage with others through socially constructed perceptions of bodies and associated identities, such as race, gender, and class, all of which are also filtered through local, national, and global understandings thereby, intercultural communication is an embodied experience.

RESISTANCE TO INTERNATIONALIZATION AND DIVERSITY

Research shows positive effects when students enroll and participate in diversity courses and programs that encourage interaction including improvements to cognitive development, reduced biases, or more tolerance toward difference. While students and colleagues may desire or demand inclusive teaching and curriculum, they can simultaneously resist because it creates significant change to personal worldviews and identities and, in doing so, creates cognitive dissonance (Higginbotham, 1996). Most students will not "voluntarily interact with those who are demographically or racially/ethnically different from themselves" (Ross, 2014, p. 871). The resistance to "cross-cultural learning is then understood as a desire for repetition, the persistent inscribing and reinscribing of what is known and taken for granted" (Jones, 2008, pp. 70–71) because it is a way for students to maintain their sense of self. If students cling to familiarity and homogeneity, then only students with previous exposure to domestic diversity or international students will engage in programs or interaction.

Pushing students to question their belief systems and ways of knowing the world causes conflict developmentally and makes it difficult to respond with critical thinking skills rather than fear, discomfort, and resistance that show up as shutting down, turning off, avoiding new information, and withdrawing (Goodman, 2011). Educators, be they student affairs or international education practitioners or faculty, may face student resistance when expanding inclusivity in curriculum and cocurriculum, especially when students hold dominant identities. Resistance looks different coming from White students and students of color (Jones, 2008; Jones, Gilbride-Brown, & Gasiorski, 2005). White students report experiencing more stress in interracial interactions, but all students may exhibit nervous behaviors like fidgeting or physically creating distance (Killick, 2017). However, it is less known how and if international students might resist intercultural curriculum but they likely employ a common resistance strategy to curriculum that is not inclusive of their experiences: silence and bodily discomfort, such as shifting in one's chair or crossing arms over the chest.

US student resistance to cross-cultural interactions focused on domestic diversity and social justice issues carries over to interactions with international students and linguistically diverse students (Jones, 2008; Leask, 2015). While resistance may be due to some indifference or lack of interest, most research shows that domestic students exhibit hostility toward intercultural groups and international peers because they believe their grades will suffer and they lack patience with language differences (Killick, 2017). For instance, graduate students from Saudi Arabia reported their US peers avoid group work with them when faculty allowed students to create their own work groups (Yakaboski, Perez-Velez, & Almutairi, 2017).

Student resistance is not solely a US trend. Even with the growth of IaH across Europe, domestic students continue to resist international classrooms and find intercultural work threatening (Harrison, 2015). Without more comprehensive integration, internationalization may promote continued inequities as only some students have access and internationalization may primarily be found in already elite pockets of academia, such as business schools. Studies in the UK have shown that intercultural competencies rarely are woven throughout academic curriculum or disciplines but most commonly, if offered at all, a separate course (Gregersen-Hermans, 2016; Jones & Killick, 2013). Like multicultural and social justice education in the US, without requiring it across the curriculum for all students, it will only be in pockets and will not reach the students who need it. Leask (2015) points out: "Internationalization of the curriculum can and should be used as a stimulus to critique and destabilize the dominant paradigms that support the status quo" (p. 12). With that, interweaving internationalization and multicultural education efforts both present a chance to advance student affairs SJI efforts.

The Promising Practice Cultural Encounters at the Chinese University of Hong Kong (CUHK), housed in the Office of Student Affairs, oversees numerous activities and programs to encourage domestic and international student interaction and learning with each other. One of the programs, the i-Ambassador Scheme, encourages non-local or ethnically diverse students to lead in promoting their culture to the university community and it promotes cultural exchange for local students to engage deeper with the multicultural local community. Students apply in groups to participate and attend a welcome gathering and one indoor and

DIVERSITY AND INCLUSION CONNECTION

one outdoor training session. Indoor sessions have included workshops on cross-cultural communication, events management, and other team builders. Outdoor sessions have included cultural tours of Kowloon City including making Thai handicrafts, tours of Sham Shui Po (a famous shopping district), and distribution of meal boxes to the homeless. In addition, students can apply for money from the Internationalization Activity Fund to design their own cultural activity for other students. Students who participate are able to record their work in the i-Ambassadors' Student Development Portfolio or receive a certificate for their internationalization activities.

PROMISING PRACTICE: Cultural Encounters at The Chinese University of Hong Kong (CUHK)

Institution: The Chinese University of Hong Kong

Location: Hong Kong, People's Republic of China

Author: Raymond Leung, Director of Student Affairs/Office of Student Affairs

Background and Context:

Hong Kong is a vibrant city and an important international financial, service, and shipping centre with particularly strong links to mainland China and the rest of the Asia-Pacific region with foreign nationals comprising 8% of the population. Higher education in Hong Kong, as with most other jurisdictions, has been evolving from a relatively closed system primarily serving the local population towards a more open and internationalized enrollment.

As a publicly funded institution, the Chinese University of Hong Kong (CUHK) serves the local community by addressing the intellectual, social, and economic needs of Hong Kong. In the 2017–2018 academic year, CUHK enrolled a total of 29,861 with 25% being non-local undergraduates and postgraduates. We have a pivotal role to play in boosting the innovative capacity of the local community, nurturing a highly skilled workforce of global thinkers and problem solvers. Building on the mission of combining tradition with modernity and bringing together China and the West, CUHK possesses a vision of nurturing students as lifelong learners and globally competent leaders.

To achieve this vision, internationalization at CUHK is always of great emphasis and has been incorporated in the University's strategic plans. In support of this strategic direction, the Office of Student Affairs (OSA) spearheads and promotes intercultural exchange and internationalization on campus through a wide spectrum of initiatives entitled "*Cultural Encounters at CUHK*":

1. Cultural Festivals—OSA organizes a cultural festival on campus based on a different theme each semester. Past themes include Islam, Africa, Latin America, Northern Europe, South and Southeast Asia. To showcase a certain culture from

44

DIVERSITY AND INCLUSION CONNECTION

diverse perspectives, each festival consists of a variety of activities, including an opening event, cultural booths, workshops, and talks/sharing sessions. The activities are open to the CUHK community and most of them also welcome the general public to join.

2. The i-Ambassador Scheme — The i-Ambassadors, undergraduate or postgraduate, local or non-local, form teams to join the scheme debuting in 2015. They receive a series of culture-awareness trainings before organizing their own cultural activities for their fellow students. The i-Ambassadors' events feature activities in four categories: Experiencing Culture, Physical Wellness, Joy of Art, and Palatable Delight.

3. CUHK Host Family Programme — OSA initiated the Host Family Programme since 2013. The non-residential programme welcomes both CUHK staff and senior local students to become hosts for the non-local undergraduate students. Hosts are encouraged to organize suitable activities throughout the year and are provided a suitable subsidy from the International Development Fund under the auspices of an Internationalization Steering Committee chaired by the President of CUHK.

Further Description:

Other than support from external organizations like consulates general, CUHK students from relevant cultural backgrounds are also involved to promote their culture. We believe intercultural competency required for global leaders could be developed through such kinds of engagements.

From receiving training to planning and executing their own activity, the students go through a process of re-discovery of their own culture, brainstorming of creative ideas, and communication with different parties. For example, the i-Ambassadors receive a series of relevant indoor and outdoor training activities, including cross-cultural communication workshops, event management workshops, circle painting workshops, cultural tours, as well as Hong Kong movies. It is a valuable opportunity for them to develop the sensitivity of culture sharing and improve their soft skills, which are essential qualities for a global leader.

By pairing up host families with non-local students, the programme offers both sides a platform to share a new culture with each other, have intercultural interaction, and ignite friendships. As such, it is believed that the participants' intercultural communication competency can be increased.

Goals and Outcomes:

Goals	Outcomes
To celebrate cultural diversity.	The positive feedback on the festivals indicates the effectiveness of creating a culturally diverse campus.
To deepen students' understanding of their own culture and other cultures.	Half of the i-Ambassadors come from regions/countries outside Hong Kong, forming an international base for organizing a wide variety of cultural activities.

DIVERSITY AND INCLUSION CONNECTION

To facilitate intercultural interaction on campus.	In 2016–2017, the i-Ambassadors were at the helm of 22 cultural events, attracting over 550 participants (148 local students and 405 non-local students), which contributed to the internationalization landscape at CUHK. The positive feedback on these activities proves the effectiveness of partnership with students.
To facilitate non-local students' adjustment to the new environment.	In the past four years, the programme has connected some 200 hosts and 300 non-local students from Asia, Europe, America, and Africa.
To enhance cultural exchange between non-local students and local students/ staff.	Some hosts joined the programme in repeated years, which is a positive recognition of the programme.

Assessment:

An evaluation is conducted to access the effectiveness of each activity/programme. Participants rate items such as programme objectives, programme design and content, intention of re-joining, etc. Many of the outcomes attained thus far are presented in the chart above under the Outcomes column.

Lessons Learned:

1. Always involve students from relevant backgrounds because they know best how to present their culture and which aspects to feature.
2. Design activity content as diversely as possible—our events are presented in both informative and informal ways so as to cater to participants' different needs.
3. Training/support from university for the students is essential, all funded by the International Development Fund stressing the importance of institutional buy-in.
4. It is critical to engage more students in taking action to promote internationalization on campus.
5. Considering manageability and easier communication within a group, the ideal host-hostee ratio is in our context 1:2 or 1:3.
6. Recruit participants as early as possible—once the international newcomers establish their social networks, they may feel less necessary to join.

Media Links:

Cultural Festivals: www.facebook.com/CUHKCulturalEncounters/

CUHK Newsletter: www.iso.cuhk.edu.hk/ebook/index.html#page=6&ui=en&lang=en&issue_id=1906

CUHK Organizes Islamic Cultural Festival to Promote Cultural Diversity: www.cpr.cuhk.edu.hk/en/press_detail.php?id=2390&t=cuhk-organizes-islamic-cultural-festival-to-promote-cultural-diversity&s=

CUHK Organises South and Southeast Asian Cultural Festival to Promote Multiple Cultures on Campus: www.cpr.cuhk.edu.hk/en/press_detail.php?id=2223&t=cuhk-

DIVERSITY AND INCLUSION CONNECTION

organises-south-and-southeast-asian-cultural-festival-to-promote-multiple-cultures-on-campus&s=

Korean Cultural Festival Promotes Korean Culture on Campus: www.cpr.cuhk.edu.hk/en/press_detail.php?id=2121&t=korean-cultural-festival-promotes-korean-culture-on-campus&s=

The i-Ambassador Scheme:
www.facebook.com/iambassadorscheme/
www.osa.cuhk.edu.hk/f/page/73/446/177.pdf

CUHK Host Family Programme:
www.facebook.com/CUHKHostFamilyProgramme
www.iso.cuhk.edu.hk/ebook/index.html#page=4&ui=en&lang=en&issue_id=1774
www.iso.cuhk.edu.hk/english/publications/newsletter/article.aspx?articleid=59900

MOVEMENT TOWARD AN INTERNATIONALIZED GRADUATE CLASSROOM

The importance of internationalizing US student affairs graduate preparation classrooms is so that all graduate students have access to develop international and intercultural competencies to support and function in a global, diverse world. Having students and/or faculty who are diverse or international will not automatically lead to a diverse and internationalized curriculum or international classroom. In fact, in line with the argument against structural diversity, "weak institutions expect that students engage themselves and assume that the educational benefits of diversity will accrue automatically from the mere presence of demographic diversity" (Chun & Evans, 2016, p. 21; Harper & Quaye, 2009). Combining global social justice and internationalization frameworks throughout the curriculum allows faculty to reimagine the possibilities of new coursework and engage with alternative knowledge traditions and ways of knowing. A framework of diversity and internationalization means that students engage in learning that involves "discovery and transcendence of difference through authentic experiences of cross-cultural interaction that involve real tasks, and emotional as well as intellectual participation" (De Vita & Case, 2003, p. 388).

Intercultural and social identity development models and theories can be helpful with analyzing xenophobic, ethnocentric, and other biased beliefs with graduate students. When evaluating learning styles, it can be useful to incorporate cultural and international considerations such as a look at national-level culture through Geert Hofstede's work on cultural dimensions and indicators of power distance index, individualism, masculinity, uncertainty avoidance, and long-term orientation (Beelen, 2007). Specific to internationalization, it is important to keep in mind that "intercultural learning needs reflection of individual and collective

47

social experiences with people from other cultures rather than the mere contact" (Otten, 2003, p. 15). Working with graduate students to analyze privilege from national and citizenship perspectives can aid them in viewing a more global system of privilege and oppression. An example from a semester seminar, "Social Justice & Intercultural Higher Education," a HESA graduate student initially felt an affinity with the other students met during the week-long experiential work in Mexico because of a shared Mexican identity (Yakaboski & Birnbaum, 2017). As the student reflected on their own privilege and power in those exchanges, they became aware that they held a US passport and citizenship and some of the students also had lived in the US but due to undocumented statuses attended an HEI in Mexico without the same opportunities as this HESA student. These can be revealing opportunities to view one's identity through a new perspective and this intercultural interaction and awareness of privilege and power will positively affect that student's decisions as a practitioner.

The design of the classroom space and norms can role model expectations of behavior about biases and stereotypes that might go unexamined, such as working with linguistically diverse students or international students, in general. In conversations of race and racism, analyzing Whiteness that includes non-US identities as well as minoritized ones is critical to removing Whiteness as a (false) neutral concept that maintains power and dominance in the classroom (Diangelo, 2006). In one observational study of a graduate research course at a university on the West coast, Diangelo found that White students assert dominance over the international Asian students and render their perspectives as irrelevant to the discussions. All the Asian students in the class were racialized, then, erased by dismissal of their contributions or not provided space through commonly used rationalizations such as language barriers or cultural preference against large class participation. To combat this, a social justice framework can assist students' development of intrapersonal skills by:

> viewing oneself in the position of the other (empathy); acting as both insider and outsider roles (consciousness to positionality); coping with problems that arise originating from intercultural encounters; and keeping flexible and open with a receptive mind, noting cultural peculiarities without either valuing them automatically or uncritically.
>
> (Stier, 2006, p. 7)

Designing assignments and discussions for students to work through these intrapersonal skills while noting behaviors in the classroom and providing readings that uncover hidden stereotypes and biases within intercultural interactions all internationalize the classroom and reduce harm.

In culturally responsive and inclusive curriculum, faculty develop a variety of teaching and facilitation skills like social justice education to improve learning

DIVERSITY AND INCLUSION CONNECTION

outcomes for all students (Otten, 2003). Therefore, similarly, in an international-ized classroom, the assignments, group work, and reflections require intentionally designed global learning outcomes to accompany diversified readings from authors outside of the US. In promoting an inclusive and international classroom, one value worth discussing is that of how the US culture prefers individualism over group membership and community. In diversity and social justice work, this can show up in attitudes that each person has opportunity, they just have to "pull themselves up by their bootstraps" and do it (Goodman, 2011). Individualism allows students to focus primarily on themselves and not on the community of the classroom or program. It allows them to think of oppression as individualistic and not a system or reflection of culture.

A final consideration for graduate preparation programs is for research to benefit from cross-pollination that connects multiculturalism and diversity to inter-nationalization and ensures the integration of these areas' theories and literature. As "graduate faculty must ensure that all graduate students enter their profession with an effective and multiculturally infused understanding of research, either as a conductor or consumer of research" (Pope et al., 2009, p. 650). Without this, any research may suffer from "cultural encapsulation," which is the lack of awareness of cultural influences in one's worldview on both the person and professional level" (Pope et al., 2009, p. 650). Within the US, the fields of inter-national education and student affairs have remained parallel, separate disciplines even though they share values and goals, but not always theories. As such, international education relies on many various models and theories related to inter-cultural competency and communication development, and student affairs relies more on multicultural competency and social justice. Both fields operate from a scholar-practitioner model, which purports that "practice, if it is reflective, and scholarship, if it is applicable, can and must become conjoined activities rather than remaining separate domains" (Streitwieser & Ogden, 2016, p. 29). With this quote in mind, it is important to share how theories and research in each can complement the other. Other research considerations are how the population is defined and by whom, the instruments used and their inherent cultural bias, the intentionality behind how the data are collected, and the use of alternate and diverse research approaches (Pope, et al., 2009). Attention to a more global research framework and literature can assist graduate researchers in conducting ethical work.

CONCLUSION

It is increasingly important to analyze internationalization efforts to ensure that the focus is not primarily or solely on numerical representation but on inclusion. The conversation in Europe around the importance of connecting international-ization to equity and access issues can be viewed through local and global lenses

DIVERSITY AND INCLUSION CONNECTION

(Atherton, 2015). The International Association of Universities (IAU) (2012) issued a call to HEIs to "revisit and affirm internationalization's underlying values, principles and goals, including but not limited to: intercultural learning; inter-institutional cooperation; mutual benefit; solidarity; mutual respect; and fair partnership" (p. 4). IAU's call concluded with expressing that institutional policy and practice should incorporate inclusive internationalization throughout and not just be symbolic or used for recruitment slogans.

Student affairs practitioners need to have knowledge, competencies, and skills to work with college students to understand global social issues and know how to frame social justice globally, and to support all students' global and intercultural competency development. These objectives cannot be left only to the realm of international education offices just as cross-cultural education cannot be left to multicultural and cultural centers. Student affairs practitioners are leaders in creating more inclusive campuses and can continue that leadership by developing global and intercultural competencies for all students and expanding multi-culturalism to be more inclusive of global diversity and cultures.

REFERENCES

American Council on Education (n.d.). *At home in the world toolkit*. Retrieved from www.acenet.edu/news-room/Pages/AHITW-Toolkit-Main.aspx

Atherton, G. (2015). Putting the international in equity. *EAIE Forum*, 38–40.

Ashwill, M. A., & Oanh, D. T. H. (2009). Developing globally competent citizens: The contrasting cases of the United States and Vietnam. In D. K. Deardorff, H. de Wit, J. D. Heyl, & T. Adams (Eds.), *SAGE handbook of intercultural competence* (pp. 141–157). Thousand Oaks, CA: Sage.

Beelen, J. (Ed.). (2007). *Implementing internationalisation at home*. EAIE Professional Development Series for International Educators, No. 2. Amsterdam, The Netherlands: EAIE.

Bennett, J. M. (1993). Towards ethnorelativism: A developmental model of intercultural sensitivity. In M. Paige (Ed.), *Education for the intercultural experience*. Yarmouth, ME: Intercultural Press.

Canadian Bureau for International Education. (2014). *Internationalization Statement of Principles for Canadian Educational Institutions*. Ottawa, Canada: Author.

Caruana, V., & Ploner, J. (2010). *Internationalisation and equality and diversity in higher education: Merging identities*. Leeds, UK: Leeds Metropolitan University.

Charles, H., Longerbeam, S. D., & Miller, A. E. (2013). Putting old tensions to rest: Integrating multicultural education and global learning to advance student develop-ment. *Journal of College and Character*, *14*(1), 47–58.

Chun, E., & Evans, A. (2016). Rethinking cultural competence in higher education: An ecological framework for student development. *ASHE Higher Education Report*, *42*(4), 7–162.

DIVERSITY AND INCLUSION CONNECTION

Cornwell, G. H., & Stoddard, E. W. (1999). *Globalizing knowledge: Connecting international & intercultural studies*. Washington, D.C.: AAC&U.

Cortés, C. E. (1998). Global education and multicultural education: Toward a 21st-century intersection. In L. Swartz, L. Warner, & D. L. Grossman (Eds.), *Intersections: A professional development project in multicultural and global education, Asian and American studies* (pp. 114–133). Washington, D.C.: Hitachi Foundation.

Cuyjet, M. J., Howard-Hamilton, M. F., & Cooper, D. L. (Eds.). (2011). *Multiculturalism on campus: Theory, models, and practices for understanding diversity and creating inclusion*. Sterling, VA: Stylus.

De Vita, G., & Case, P. (2003). Rethinking the internationalisation agenda in UK higher education. *Journal of Further and Higher Education, 27*(4), 383–398.

de Wit, H. (2016). Misconceptions about (the end of) internationalisation: The current state of play. In E. Jones, R. Coelen, J. Beelen, & H. de Wit (Eds.), *Global and local internationalization* (pp. 15–20). Rotterdam, The Netherlands: Sense Publishers.

Department of Education (DoE). (1997). White Paper 3. *A programme for higher education transformation*. Pretoria, South Africa: Author.

Diangelo, R. J. (2006). The production of Whiteness in education: Asian international students in a college classroom. *Teachers College Record, 108*(10), 1983–2000.

Dunn-Coetzee, M., & Fourie-Malherbe, M. (2017). Reflective practice promoting social change amongst students in higher education: A reflection on the listen, live and learn senior student housing initiative at Stellenbosch University. *Journal of Student Affairs in Africa, 5*(1), 63–75.

European Students' Union. (2013). *Kaunas Declaration*. Retrieved from www.esu-online.org/wp-content/uploads/2016/07/BM65_8bii_Kaunas_Declaration_ADOPTED.pdf

Glass, C. R., Wongtrirat, R., & Buus, S. (2015). *International student engagement: Strategies for creating inclusive, connected, and purposeful campus environments*. Sterling, VA: Stylus.

Goodman, D. (2011). *Promoting social justice and diversity: Educating people from privileged groups*, 2nd ed. New York: Routledge.

Gregersen-Hermans, J. (2016). From rationale to reality in intercultural competence development: Working towards the university's organizational capability to deliver. In E. Jones, R. Coelen, J. Beelen, & H. de Wit (Eds.), *Global and local internationalization* (pp. 91–96). Rotterdam, The Netherlands: Sense Publishers.

Haber, P. (2011). Peer education in student leadership programs: Responding to cocurricular challenges. *New Directions for Student Services, 133*, 65–76.

Hanassab, S. (2006). Diversity, international students, and perceived discrimination: Implications for educators and counselors. *Journal of Studies in International Education, 10*(2), 157–172.

Harper, S. R. (Ed.). (2008). *Creating inclusive campus environments: For cross-cultural learning and student engagement*. Washington, D.C.: NASPA.

Harper, S. R., & Quaye, S. J. (Eds.). (2009). *Student engagement in higher education: Theoretical perspectives and practical approaches for diverse populations.* New York: Routledge.

Harrison, N. (2015) Practice, problems and power in internationalisation at home: Critical reflections on recent research evidence. *Teaching in Higher Education, 20*(4), 412–430.

Higginbotham, E. (1996). Getting all students to listen: Analyzing and coping with student resistance. *American Behavioral Scientist, 40*(2), 203–211.

Inkelas, K., & Weisman, J. (2003). Difference by design: An examination of student outcomes among participants in three types of living-learning programs. *Journal of College Student Development, 44*(3), 335–368.

International Association of Universities. (2012). *Affirming academic values in internationalization of higher education: A call for action.* Retrieved from www.iau-aiu.net/sites/all/files/Affirming_Academic_Values_in_Internationalization_of_Higher_Education.pdf

Jenkins, T. S., & Walton, C. L. (2008). Student affairs and cultural practice: A framework for implementing culture outside the classroom. In S. R. Harper (Ed.), *Creating inclusive campus environments: For cross-cultural learning and student engagement* (pp. 87–102). Washington, D.C.: NASPA.

Jones, S. (2008). Student resistance to cross-cultural engagement: Annoying distraction or site for transformative learning? In S, R. Harper (Ed.), *Creating inclusive campus environments: For cross-cultural learning and student engagement* (pp. 67–85). Washington, D.C.: NASPA.

Jones, E. (2011). Internationalisation, multiculturalism, a global outlook and employability. *ALT Journal, 11*, 21–49.

Jones, E. (2016). Mobility, graduate employability and local internationalisation. In E. Jones, R. Coelen, J. Beelen, & H. de Wit (Eds.), *Global and local internationalization* (pp. 107–116). Rotterdam, The Netherlands: Sense Publishers.

Jones E., & Killick, D. (2007). Internationalisation of the curriculum. In E., Jones, & S. Brown (Eds.), *Internationalising higher education* (pp. 109–119). London: Routledge.

Jones, E., & Killick, D. (2013). Graduate attributes and the internationalized curriculum: Embedding a global outlook in disciplinary learning outcomes. *Journal of Studies in International Education, 17*(2), 165–182.

Jones, S. R., Gilbride-Brown, J., & Gasiorski, A. (2005). Getting inside the "underside" of service-learning: Student resistance and possibilities. In D. Butin (Ed.), *Critical issues in service-learning* (pp. 3–24). New York: Palgrave.

Killick, D. (2017). *Internationalization and diversity in higher education: Implications for teaching, learning and assessment.* London: Palgrave.

Kim, E., & Díaz, J. (2013). Immigrant students and higher education. *ASHE Higher Education Report, 38*(6), 6–170.

King, P. M., & Baxter Magolda, M. B. (2005). A developmental model of intercultural maturity. *Journal of College Student Development, 46*(6), 571–592.

DIVERSITY AND INCLUSION CONNECTION

Knight, J. (2012). Concepts, rationales, and interpretive frameworks in the internationalization of higher education. In D. K. Deardorff, H. de Wit, J. D. Heyl, & T. Adams (Eds.), *SAGE handbook of international higher education* (pp. 27–42). Thousand Oaks, CA: Sage.

Leask, B. (2015). *Internationalizing the curriculum.* New York: Routledge.

Lederman, D. (2017, November 10). Higher education's "white power." *InsideHigherEd.Com.* Retrieved from www.insidehighered.com/news/2017/11/10/head-higher-ed-research-group-calls-out-dominance-white-power

Lee, J. J., & Rice, C. (2007). Welcome to America? International student perceptions of discrimination. *Higher Education, 53*(3), 381–409.

Organisation for Economic Co-operation and Development (OECD) (2012). *Education at a glance.* Paris, France: Author.

Olson, C., Evans, R., & Shoenberg, R. E. (2007). *At home in the world: Bridging the gap between internationalization and multicultural education.* Washington, D.C.: ACE.

Otten, M. (2003). Intercultural learning and diversity in higher education. *Journal of Studies in International Education, 7*(1), 12–26.

Patel, F., & Lynch, H. (2013). Glocalization as an alternative to internationalization in higher education: Embedding positive glocal learning perspectives. *International Journal of Teaching and Learning in Higher Education, 25*(2), 223–230.

Patton, L. D. (2010). *Culture centers in higher education: Perspectives on identity, theory, and practice.* Sterling, VA: Stylus.

Pope, R. L., Mueller, J. A., & Reynolds, A. L. (2009) Looking back and moving forward: Future directions for diversity research in student affairs. *Journal of College student development, 50*(6), 640–658.

Raby, R. L. (2016). Studying community colleges: Administrator, practitioner, and scholar voices promoting international education. In B. Streitwieser & A. C. Ogden (Eds.), *International higher education's scholar-practitioners* (pp. 143–158). Oxford: Symposium.

Raby, R. L., Rhodes, G. M., & Biscarra, A. (2014). Community college study abroad: Implications for student success. *Community College Journal of Research and Practice, 38*(2–3), 174–183.

Rhoads, R. A., & Black, M. A. (1995). Student affairs practitioners as transformative educators: Advancing a critical cultural perspective. In E. J. Whitt (Ed), *ASHE reader on college student affairs administration* (pp. 407–415). Boston, MA: Pearson.

Rose-Redwood, C. and Rose-Redwood, R. (2013). Self-segregation or global mixing? Social interactions and the international student experience. *Journal of College Student Development, 54*(4), 413–429.

Ross, S. N. (2014). Diversity and intergroup contact in higher education: Exploring possibilities for democratization through social justice education. *Teaching in Higher Education, 19*(8), 870–881.

Schreiber, B., Kloppers, P., & Cornelissen, P. (2016). Department of Student Affairs (DSA) annual report. Stellenbosch, South Africa: Stellenbosch University.

Sorrells, K. (2013). *Intercultural communication: Globalization and social justice.* Thousand Oaks, CA: Sage.

Spirtzberg, B. H., & Changnon, G. (2009). Conceptualizing intercultural competence. In D. K. Deardorff, H. de Wit, J. D. Heyl, & T. Adams (Eds.), *SAGE handbook of intercultural competence* (pp. 2–52). Thousand Oaks, CA: Sage.

Stellenbosch University. (n.d.) Values Listen, Live and Learn [Luister, Leef & Leer]. Retrieved from www0.sun.ac.za/lllbeta/index.php/lll-values

Stewart, D. L. (Ed.). (2011). *Multicultural student services on campus: Building bridges, re-visioning community.* Sterling, VA: Stylus.

Stier, J. (2006). Internationalisation, intercultural communication and intercultural competence. *Journal of Intercultural Communication, 11,* 1–12.

Streitwieser, B., & Ogden, A. C. (2016). Heralding the scholar-practitioner in international education. In B. Streitwieser, & A. C. Ogden, (Eds.), *International higher education's scholar-practitioners: Bridging research and practice* (pp. 19–38). Oxford: Symposium.

Thom, V. (2010). Mutual cultures: Engaging with interculturalism in higher education. In E. Jones (Ed.), *Internationalisation and the student voice* (pp. 155–168). London: Routledge.

Usher, A., & Medow, J. (2010). *Global higher education rankings 2010: Affordability and accessibility in comparative perspectives.* Toronto, Canada: Higher Education Strategy Associates.

Valdez, G. (2016). International students: Classroom exclusion in US higher education. In K. Bista & C. Foster (Eds.), *Campus support services, programs, and policies for international students* (pp. 35–56). Hershey, PA: IGI Global.

Yakaboski, T., & Birnbaum, M. G. (2017). Case study: (Re)Blending Mayan and Mexican interculturalism with social justice in a U.S. graduate preparation program. In D. K. Deardorff & L. A. Arasaratnam-Smith (Eds.), *Intercultural competence in international higher education* (pp. 289–293). New York: Routledge.

Yakaboski, T., Perez-Velez, K., & Almutairi, Y. (2017). Breaking the silence: Saudi graduate student experiences on a U.S. campus. *Journal of Diversity in Higher Education.* Advance online publication. http://dx.doi.org/10.1037/dhe0000059

Chapter 3

Intercultural and Related Competencies for Student Affairs

In multicultural, pluralistic societies, internationalization and intercultural education offer individuals the skills to "work and live together in dignity across cultures" (Paracka & Pynn, 2017, p. 43) so they can recognize oppressions and create change in their communities. Intercultural competency development is a strategy tightly coupled with the overall internationalization of higher education, and specifically Internationalization at Home (IaH), which originated to focus on diversity and inclusion of the local campus (Deardorff & Jones, 2012). In the contexts of Australia and the UK, intercultural competency is a graduate attribute and requirement for global citizenship and career attainment at national and institutional levels (Leask, 2015). While not a part of any formalized policies at national or state levels in the US, assisting students in knowing how to begin and continue the process of intercultural learning is an important role of student affairs and international educators through partnerships with faculty (Streitwieser & Ogden, 2016).

To cultivate intercultural development, individuals foster understanding of their own identities and other cultures within and outside of their home country. Each person carries histories, oppressions, and privileges that add to "the complexity of their cultural worldviews" and it is "this 'similarity of difference' that allows us to respect the equal complexity and potential usefulness of each of our perspectives" (Bennett & Bennett, 2004, p. 150). Knowing migration, immigration, and colonization histories throughout the world helps individuals recognize the historical and social construction of privilege and oppression, and how these constructs have evolved over time, as in who has or has not been welcome depending on time and place. Student affairs practice done with an intentional awareness of the realities of cultural inequalities, difference, and marginalization can avoid exploiting culture as a resource and "othering" it within intercultural marketplaces (Sorrells, 2013). Practitioners can use a social justice framework to include equity, diversity, and inclusion by recognizing the complexity of simultaneously attending to both individual self-perception and the designations or worldviews placed upon them. It requires understanding that "Culture frames perception. It is an integrated system of learned behaviour and inscribed meaning that shapes and organises concepts and processes of identity formation" (Paracka & Pynn, 2017, p. 44). Ultimately, cultural self-awareness and in-depth knowledge of cultures are necessary first steps in intercultural competency to move beyond preconceptions, bias, and autopilot routines that limit co-creation within a shared intercultural context, to a more enlightened and nuanced knowledge of people, behaviors, and multiple paradigms, perspectives, and worldviews.

The concept of intercultural competency dates back more than 50 years in US scholarship and applies to a broad range of intercultural situations as opposed to only those abroad or those within the US (Deardorff & Jones, 2012). Intercultural competency development is a process like the lifelong journey of multiculturalism and social justice and inclusion (SJI) competencies (Cuyjet, Linder, Howard-Hamilton, & Cooper, 2016). Comparably, intercultural competency and multi-cultural competency both address awareness, knowledge, and skills (Pope, Reynolds, & Mueller, 2004). Within the context of competency development, culture references inter- or cross-cultural as subjective culture, meaning that local, global, domestic, and international diversity can all connect and combine within intercultural competency. A broader understanding of culture and inclusivity emphasizes the overlap between multicultural, intercultural, and global citizenship development. As such, this chapter discusses various related competency development theories and models that support intercultural competency and its application to US student affairs. Ultimately, this chapter defines what it means for student affairs practitioners to develop intercultural competency, through application of intercultural models and expansion of student affairs standards and professional competencies.

THE EVOLUTION OF PROFESSIONAL COMPETENCIES

Many professions espouse competencies to help practitioners develop knowledge and skills; however, it is possible to interpret competency language as something to achieve and check off rather than a lifelong learning process requiring the development of critical self-reflection skills. This checklist approach can be dangerous when dealing with culture, diversity, and systemic issues (Murray-García & Tervalon, 2017). The broad conceptualization of culture reminds practitioners that efforts to continuously understand cultural meanings and diversity is import-ant to any work at the individual level of competency development. In student affairs, multicultural education and related SJI competency development are foundational cornerstones to professional development and graduate preparation curriculum. Pope and Reynolds' (1997) theoretical model of multicultural competence is well established in the literature. A test on multicultural compe-tency was given to 100 practitioners across four areas: the awareness, knowledge,

56

INTERCULTURAL AND RELATED COMPETENCIES

and skills of multicultural competence; the degree to which student affairs practitioners held ascribed values and behavioral practices in interactions with students; differences by gender and socio-race for individuals; and the inter-relationships of the variables and degree to which self-reported multicultural awareness and knowledge predicted skills (Castellanos, Gloria, Mayorga, & Salas, 2008). Knowledge, specifically about other cultures, was most predictive of possessing multicultural skills in their study.

Globalism or global competency references another layer of knowledge, meaning awareness of issues at local, national, regional, and global levels. The format of the ACPA and NASPA (2015) professional competencies situates learning as a process where practitioners progress through foundational, intermediate, and advanced levels of knowledge, skills, and dispositions (formerly attitudes) within ten competency areas. Within these ten areas, globalism is a "point of emphasis" (formally a "thread") but not its own established knowledge area, skill set, or disposition. More specifically though, global competency in international education literature is "the acquisition of in-depth knowledge and understanding of inter-national issues, an appreciation of and ability to learn and work with people from diverse backgrounds, proficiency in a foreign language, and skills to function pro-ductively in an interdependent world community" (National Education Association (NEA), 2010, p. 1). One limitation, however, with the NEA's definition is the requirement of knowing another language. Language requirements increasingly are uncommon in the US curriculum due to many reasons, such as political push-back against any language other than English; perception of less need given the geographical nature of the US compared to regions like Europe; and the expansion of English as a global language in business and education (Duncan, 2010; Skorton & Altschuler, 2012). Even in the historical evolution of intercultural competency, there has been a long-standing debate over the inclusion of speaking another language (Deardorff & Jones, 2012). This debate persists in part because language acquisition can increase the ability for intercultural interaction and communication, as well as increase empathy in speakers by providing awareness of the challenges with operating in another language.

Both intercultural competency development and training fully developed in the US post-World War II through the 1950s and 1960s due to the increase of US citizens working abroad in governmental and corporate organizations (Arasaratnam-Smith, 2017; Pusch, 2004). The development of intercultural competency largely came out of the intercultural communication field that is inter-disciplinary across psychology, anthropology, and sociology rather than focused in education, which explains the assumption that interculturalism is primarily about cross-cultural communication (Bennett & Bennett, 2004). This is visible in NAFSA—Association for International Educators—Professional Competencies (2015) where intercultural communication is a cross-cutting competency to promote the skills and knowledge of self and others' behaviors, leadership, and

INTERCULTURAL AND RELATED COMPETENCIES

learning. One responsibility within intercultural communication is to "champion diversity, equity, and inclusion" as well as to "reflect on own culture and identity" (NAFSA, 2015, p. 37). NAFSA's cross-cutting competencies of advocacy and intercultural communication complement student affairs professional competencies to show the importance of connecting internationalization to diversity and multicultural efforts on campuses. As with multicultural competency, intercultural competency theories and models to date have all included some degree of motivation (attitudes), knowledge, skills, context, and outcomes as a lifelong learning process (see Spitzberg & Changnon, 2009 for a comprehensive review of intercultural competency models and typologies). Many international education scholars and administrators prefer defining intercultural "as the ability to communicate effectively and appropriately in intercultural situations based on one's intercultural knowledge, skills, and attitudes" (Deardorff, 2006, p. 248). Intercultural competency addresses the requirement for individuals "to expand their sensibilities, or intercultural sensitivity, with the goal of making students more comfortable in their encounters with people who think and live differently" (Olson, Evans, & Shoenberg, 2007, p. 14). Skills are the application of knowledge and attitude that show up in the ability to use language, resolve conflict, and communicate interculturally. When considering if practitioners have international or intercultural competency, there is a wide range of skills and knowledge possible and there are many frameworks and theories to draw from when looking to develop competencies (Deardorff & Jones, 2012).

However, the intercultural concept is less visible in student affairs competencies as set forth by ACPA and NASPA (2015), which have a US framework and application (Bardill Moscaritolo & Roberts, 2016). Within ACPA and NASPA's professional competencies, the most comparable competency is the recently added SJI competency to address oppression, privilege, and power relating to others, community, or local and global contexts. Similarly, Sorrells' (2013) definition of intercultural competency means that individuals "join others as allies; connect across racial, gender, ethnic, cultural, and national boundaries in intercultural alliances; and engage in intercultural activism to create and struggle for a more equitable and just world" (p. 247). Intercultural competencies tend to favor more heavily the communication aspect of engagement while multiculturalism and social justice for practitioners emphasizes how to create inclusive learning environments and change culture. Interculturalism and social justice both require a reflective and critical sense of self, and a responsibility for educating. SJI and intercultural development can be complimentary as they have shared goals of reducing harm to others, increasing understanding and appreciation of cultures, and developing inclusive learning opportunities. These definitions and configurations center primarily on the individual rather than community, thereby reflecting US and Western culture's focus on individual development (Leask, 2015) and consequently require caution in application.

58

INTERCULTURAL COMPETENCY DEVELOPMENT FOR STUDENT AFFAIRS

Professional development for those who work in student affairs often uses competency-based language, which "is sometimes conceptually equated with a set of abilities or skills and at other times a subjective evaluative impression" (Spitzberg & Changnon, 2009, p. 6). Student affairs competencies are not a linear progression, rather practitioners may work on outcomes in any of the levels and areas while working to master all of the foundational outcomes. These competencies are general enough for individuals and programs to tailor to interests and strengths. Yet, they can be so general that individuals may not have adequate guidance in what or how to develop in the area of "globalism" and its relationship to internationalization and interculturalism.

As such, in our survey, US SSAOs shared what knowledge, skills, and attitudes a "globally competent" student affairs practitioner would possess. As shown in Table 3.1, there are four main areas that US SSAOs believed that practitioners should have knowledge in: general international higher education and student affairs issues (91%); cross-cultural communication abilities (90%); culturally appropriate and diverse advising and helping skills (85%); and culturally relevant and internationally diverse programs, services, policies, and practices (77%). ACPA and NASPA competencies (2015), along with their associated rubrics (2016), for

Table 3.1 Knowledge and Skills Needed to Have Intercultural Competency

Selection of Knowledge and Skills	#	%
International issues in higher education and student affairs	80	91
Cross-cultural communication abilities	79	90
Culturally appropriate and diverse advising and help skills	75	85
Culturally relevant and internationally diverse programs, services, policies, and practices	68	77
International or global perspectives of higher education and student affairs	47	53
Cross-cultural theories	37	42
Higher education systems in other countries or global regions	36	41
Deep understanding of at least one other culture	32	36
Country-specific knowledge	30	34
Global leadership models and theories	23	26
More than one language	23	26
A degree in international studies or courses in international higher education and student affairs	4	5

INTERCULTURAL AND RELATED COMPETENCIES

SJI or student learning and development may address parts of these knowledge areas. However, neither competency area explicitly includes detailed global or intercultural frameworks or conceptualizations that would help practitioners work with individuals who may not share the same cultural identities or expand global knowledge.

Only 26% of US SSAO respondents marked knowing more than one language as necessary for intercultural competency. One implication may be that this finding expresses a devaluation of linguistic diversity within the US society in general that trickles down to the professional level. Given this book's stated importance of knowing global practices and how student affairs work occurs around the world, it may be concerning that only 41% ranked knowing about other higher education and student affairs systems as necessary to being globally competent. Other relatively lower ranked areas of knowledge needed were: knowing about specific countries (34%), or having a deep understanding of another culture (36%). Knowing about other systems of higher education or student services and knowing other cultures may increase sensitivity or empathy when working with international students, staff, and faculty.

Generally, most SSAOs in our study recognized the necessity for practitioners to have personal attributes or attitudes that foster cultural and intercultural learning. As one SSAO at a public master's comprehensive university in California said, it is preferable that staff "Understand and seek a global perspective and engage in professional development to better understand other cultures and countries in an effort to better serve all of our students (both domestic and international)." One SSAO at a liberal arts college in Massachusetts explained that practitioners need to have personal attributes that allow them the

> ability to draw connections between important events globally to important events to issues "at home" [in addition to] understanding that global competence is not "fixed" but rather always in process and evolving (e.g., we grow in our global competence and must constantly learn to maintain competence).

As demonstrated in Table 3.2, personal attributes that include understanding, respect, reflection, values, and flexibility were important to intercultural competency as student affairs practitioners.

A CRITICAL LOOK AT GRADUATE PREPARATION STANDARDS

Intercultural, global, or international competencies along with global citizenship are all increasingly common attributes or goals for undergraduate students that may be in the rhetoric of universities, programs, and faculty syllabi for undergraduate courses. Therefore, it stands to reason that these become prevalent in

60

INTERCULTURAL AND RELATED COMPETENCIES

Table 3.2 Personal Attributes of Interculturally Competent Professionals

Selection of Attributes	#	%
Respect for the uniqueness of various cultures	86	99
Understanding of one's assumptions, biases and identity through a Western/US lens	79	91
Values both cultural commonalities and differences	79	91
Open to shifting one's cultural perspectives based on context	73	84
Recognition of power and privilege based on culture	70	80
Reflection on one's place in a global world	67	77
Curiosity about other cultures or countries	66	76

student affairs graduate curriculum to prepare practitioners to work with these students and programs. Over the course of the last century, US graduate preparation, at the master's level mostly, has included both formal and informal curriculum guidance from a few sources: Council for Advancement of Standards (CAS, 2015) standards for student affairs graduate programs, Council for the Advancement of Higher Education Programs (CAHEP, 2010), and ACPA and NASPA (2015) professional competencies (DiRamio, 2013, 2014; Wright & Hyle, 2014). Student affairs programs are most commonly found at the master's level while at the doctoral level most programs are in higher education administration and there are no CAS standards for doctoral education.

CAS standards for student affairs master's level graduate programs predominantly guides the formal curriculum in the growing number of graduate degree programs. Over about 50 years of existence, CAS has updated language and now includes social justice as a possible focus area for program mission statements. In CAS, formal education includes foundational studies, professional studies, and supervised practice. Foundational studies address the desire to be interdisciplinary with fields that inform student affairs practice and it even references "international education and global understanding, including the implications of internationalization" (CAS, 2015, p. 651). International student populations, immigrant status, and national origins are all characteristics within student learning and development curriculum and as protected identities against program and services discrimination. That is the extent of the guidance or inclusion for internationalizing graduate preparation programs from CAS.

With CAS focusing primarily on student affairs, services, and development, CAHEP, a committee of the Association for the Study of Higher Education (ASHE), provides guidelines for master's programs in higher education rather than student affairs (Wright & Hyle, 2014). The five required content areas are history and philosophy, administration and leadership, economics and finance,

INTERCULTURAL AND RELATED COMPETENCIES

law, and organizational development and change theories (CAHEP, 2010). It does mention other areas including global perspectives and internationalization of higher education but does not provide details for any of the areas and is left to individual program interpretation and application, like CAS.

Following US-based standards without an explicit intercultural or global framework may challenge the ability to internationalize curriculum. All standards, as with professional competencies, reflect cultural values and historical context. CAS authors acknowledge that the main guiding principles are Western and specifically US-centric (Dean & Jones, 2014). The CAS document includes recognition of criticism "that they are too reflective of the democratic culture of U.S. higher education and therefore not inclusive enough for application to a global higher education environment . . . at this point, they remain grounded in American ideals" (CAS, 2012, p. 4). While there is international recognition of the CAS standards' usefulness, the cultural differences, for example between the US and China, result in difficulty in applying some of the CAS standards (Li, 2009). Ultimately, CAS or CAHEP standards may offer limited guidance on knowledge or competencies related to internationalization and interculturalism.

In viewing our US SSAO survey results, administrators stated that training rather than coursework is where they expect practitioners to gain global knowledge as only 5% saw a degree or coursework in international higher education or student affairs as needed. Somewhat better, in Table 6.1, 36% of these SSAOs saw international courses during graduate studies as a place to offer experience related to becoming globally competent. While a higher number, both these results pale in comparison to the high ranking of trainings and conferences outside of graduate education. Although nothing conclusive can be determined with this sample size, the findings prompt discussions about the relevance and ability of current graduate preparation curriculum as supported by professional competencies and curriculum standards, to adequately address the growing demand for globally competent student affairs graduates and practitioners. Generally during graduate study, students learn that theory and research should inform practice. However, because the current curriculum standards do not require programs to be inclusive of internationalization frameworks, intercultural theories, or international knowledge, it may not then be surprising if there is a perception that graduate programs do not offer the needed knowledge and skills to support internationalization, which is why exploring some models commonly used in international education may be helpful.

INTERCULTURAL AND GLOBAL CITIZENSHIP MODELS

Bennett and Bennett Intercultural Sensitivity

One main model for interculturalism is the Development Model of Intercultural Sensitivity (DMIS) (Bennett, 1993; Bennett & Bennett, 2004), which is often cited

62

INTERCULTURAL AND RELATED COMPETENCIES

within international education to explain individual change. DMIS recognizes cognition structure on a continuum where six stages are less about behavior and attitude and more about how individuals change their worldview from one of extreme ethnocentricity to integrated ethnorelativity. DMIS has three stages within ethnocentricity—denial, defense, and minimization—which are all about avoiding cultural differences. The ethnorelative stages of acceptance, adaptation, and integration, then, are about seeking cultural differences and eventually incorporating them into identity.

According to Bennett and Bennett (2004), in the denial stage, individuals are likely to see conversations about diversity as hostile or puzzling since they function with a worldview of their own privilege and power and see international as "other." In the defense stage, individuals protect their own cultural identities by creating an "us versus them" worldview and stereotyping other cultures. Minimization, the final stage within the ethnocentric side of the continuum, involves minimizing cultural differences by going to the core belief that humans are all the same regardless of culture. In this stage, individuals may use language of tolerance and color-blindness, but may continue perpetuating individual and dominant cultural privileges. Bennett and Bennett connect the minimization stage to William Perry's (1970) second stage of cognitive development, multiplicity, where individuals start to trust their own inner voice or personal truth; where, in the first two stages of DMIS' ethnocentrism, individuals function in Perry's dualism, or first stage.

When individuals move to ethnorelativism in DMIS, they accept that cultures are equal but different yet may still not incorporate liking or agreement. In the acceptance stage, individuals assume that their worldview is different from another's and that they may not be able to agree, therefore, differences exist unchallenged. Bennett and Bennett (2004) connect the acceptance stage to Perry's contextual relativism where individuals consider their own and others' worldviews and then use these to make decisions within the current context. The adaptation stage can only occur when individuals act outside of their cultural context, which reinforces the importance of building intentional intercultural assignments in courses or programs. At this stage, individuals display cultural empathy and act with what feels correct based on being inclusive and not because it is the right thing to do or is politically correct. The issue at hand is how to be authentic to self and to incorporate alternative behaviors that are culturally appropriate and not cultural appropriation. This stage is most like Perry's commitment in relativism where individuals integrate knowledge learned from others with their own personal reflection and identity. The final DMIS stage is integration where individuals reestablish and recreate an identity that is bi- or multicultural in its worldview. However, there can be problems that arise at this stage when individuals cannot create that new identity and get stuck between cultures and individuals may return to Perry's multiplicity when they cannot choose the appropriate cultural behavior without harm.

There are also similarities to Helm's White Racial Identity Development Model (1990) that espouses a continuum model of two overarching phases of racism and of defining a non-racist identity, to reflect cognitive developments. While DMIS is broader in its definition and approach to diversity, Helm's model uses US cultural definitions of race and ethnicity and may not be applicable to individuals who are not US born or raised. Though DMIS and White Identity Development together may combat White Supremacy in the US, which is racism towards non-White individuals and neo-nationalism where superiority is based on citizenship. This example, along with Perry's, are examples of how intercultural competency can complement theories commonly applied in student affairs work. However, there are cautions to theory application, as discussed more in Chapter 6 on re-envisioning professional development.

Deardorff's Intercultural Competence Model

Much work in the US international education field relies on the broad definition that intercultural competence is "effective and appropriate behavior and communication in intercultural situations" (Deardorff, 2006, pp. 286–287). Deardorff's research, conducted with US international education scholars and practitioners, used a consensus-building technique to develop her intercultural model and definition. Deardorff's Intercultural Competence Model includes attitudes, knowledge, skills, and internal/external outcomes. Interculturalism begins with a foundation of attitudes that include respect, openness, curiosity, and discovery. Working on attitudes is a foundation to both multicultural and intercultural competency development as they require a progression of individualized learning:

- Who am I? (knowledge of self)
- Who are we? (communal/collective knowledge)
- What does it feel like to be them? (empathetic knowledge)
- How do we talk with one another? (intercultural process knowledge)
- How do we improve our shared lives? (applied, engaged knowledge)

(Chun & Evans, 2016, p. 80)

This type of learning requires self-awareness and plenty of reflection and processing work that can be a part of student affairs graduate curriculum and professional development.

Building on intercultural attitudes, knowledge expands cultural self-awareness, culture-specific understanding, and sociolinguistic awareness. Skills pertain to the acquisition of knowledge through observation, listening, evaluating, analyzing, interpreting, and relating. Knowledge and skills interact on top of the foundation

64

INTERCULTURAL AND RELATED COMPETENCIES

of attitudes, which all then leads to desired outcomes. Outcomes are both internal and external. The attitudes, knowledge, and skills lead to the internal outcomes of flexibility, adaptability, and empathy. Whereas, with external, all the preceding components of internal outcomes display in external behaviors and communication. This is not a linear model but rather one with delicate interplay between parts, for example, attitudes of curiosity may encourage pursuit of more knowledge of another culture and then, perhaps, an experiential opportunity to develop skills. Essentially under this model, it would not be enough for higher education institutions (HEIs) to require an intercultural course or for student affairs to offer a program featuring food or a presentation from a specific culture or nation. More intentionality in learning objectives with varied ways of assessing present a clearer path to opportunities that promote intercultural learning.

Intercultural competency research and application has been a growing area in Chinese education. Recent policy documents from China's Ministry of Education have included intercultural competency development through the English language curriculum at high school and university levels (Wang, Deardroff, & Kulich, 2017). In the Promising Practice Intercultural Communication and Learning Program, Cheong Kun Lun College and Zhide College provide a practical platform for students to acquire intercultural skills and knowledge. The program uses Deardorff's (2006) model to support students' intercultural skill development. The design of the program allows students from each university in two different regions of China, to learn about the unique community of Anji, located in the Zhejiang province. Jointly, students learn about this region's economic development while also developing an understanding of differences and similarities between the different cities and cultures of Macau and Shanghai. This program promotes learning of divergent histories, colonization, and cultures within one country to reduce stereotypes and promote intercultural learning. As research on intercultural competency in Chinese contexts is emergent, assessment and research on intercultural learning for students around the world uses Deardorff's model, as shown in this practice. To expand this model, recent research has revealed attributes relevant to Chinese intercultural competency; thus, highlighting the importance of cultural context and caution in complete application of Western theories and models. The Chinese attributes related to intercultural competency fit under the same cognitive, affective (attitudinal), and behavioral modes but are reconfigured under three overarching concepts. The culturally relevant components are: *xintai* heart attitude to remain sensitive to the feelings of others; a collective we/our approach to govern the interdependency of relationships including *yin* and *yang*; and new or modern understandings of classical Chinese philosophies (Wang et al., 2017).

INTERCULTURAL AND RELATED COMPETENCIES

PROMISING PRACTICE: Intercultural Communication and Learning Program

Institution:
Cheong Kun Lun College, University of Macau
Zhide College of Fudan University

Location of Institutions:
Macau, People's Republic of China
Shanghai, People's Republic of China

Authors:
YU, Peter, Xiaoming, College Master of Cheong Kun Lun College
SUN, Sisi, Resident Fellow of Cheong Kun Lun College

Background and Context:
Established on the Hengqin campus in Macau in 2016, Cheong Kun Lun College (CKLC) is the most recent addition to the University of Macau residential college system, which started in 2014 and has now grown to a family of ten colleges. To date, CKLC consists of more than 350 students from seven different faculties—Arts and Humanities, Business Administration, Education, Health Sciences, Science and Technology, Law, and Social Sciences. Together with other residential colleges, CKLC strives to build a robust living–learning community as a foundation for implementing educational programs and activities centered around experiential learning and producing students prepared for the work and life of the 21st century. CKLC aims to establish a community that nurtures "good persons," and to enable individual students to fulfill their intellectual and personal potential. CKLC seeks to provide students with a caring environment, in which each and every student will assume responsibility for their behavior as a young adult while bringing their imagination and creativity into full play. The College expects its students to be engaged in various activities and programs that the College offers or students initiate.

On the other hand, Zhide College is one of the five residential colleges established in 2005 on the campus of Fudan University, in Shanghai, China. Its motto is: "Cultivate your uprightness, set clear goals, be decisive, and nurture your virtues" ("养正立志, 果行育德"), quoted from the *Méng Hexagram* in *I Ching* or *Book of Changes* with the meaning of encouraging people to stick to what is right, aim for the highest, be decisive and persistent, and cultivate their virtues. The College is home to 135 faculty mentors and 3,400 students from six academic schools, ranging from foreign languages, international relations, journalism, public policies, law, to sciences. As most of Zhide College students are from the humanities and social sciences, the College lays great emphasis on cultivating students' virtues and raising their social responsibilities by engaging them in research projects on social issues.

66

INTERCULTURAL AND RELATED COMPETENCIES

The Intercultural Communication and Learning Program involved a joint collaboration called "Anji Project," located in Anji County, with a population of approximately one half million, in northern Zhejiang province. Due to poor transportation, Anji has been an isolated area and many of its bamboo and tea products have been unable to be shipped out for sale. The local economy was very much undeveloped until the 1980s when China started her reform and open-door policy. Now a new highway system traversing the entire county has been completed, and it takes less than three hours to reach major cities such as Shanghai and Nanjing and less than one hour to Hangzhou, the capital city of Zhejiang province. With a booming economy and influx of tourists, Anji people are taking a sustainable development approach by developing ecology-friendly agriculture, industry, and tourism in an attempt to build a new, green community.

Anji is a success story—turning itself from a rural village into a community that combines farming, tea-production, and tourism. The impact of this social transformation is profound on the local people and institutions. The Fudan sociology department found that the Anji story would be a fascinating topic for field studies, so it worked with Zhide College to start the Intercultural Communication and Learning Program project in the summer of 2016.

Further Description:

CKLC of the University of Macau and Zhide College of Fudan entered an exchange partnership to create a joint program as an excellent learning opportunity for all students and which has been well received by the Zhide students. The Fudan students are intelligent, highly motivated, and hold a metropolitan perspective on China and world affairs. The Macau students, mostly growing up in a city known for its casino industry, are open-minded and keen on learning new things. They have a different sense of history, cultural traditions, and values. When they join hands in a field-study project, there are bound to be questions, discussions, and even debates, sparking learning opportunities of a multicultural nature. The project opens a new chapter for both students and colleges.

The Anji Project will be followed by a bilateral visit program, through which Fudan students will learn more about Macau, a Chinese city under Portuguese rule for over 400 years before returning to China in 1999 and a city whose revenues are primarily from the casino industry. The Macau students will learn more about Shanghai, a metropolitan area of 28 million people and known for its commerce, tourism, cutting-edge science and technology, and higher education. The visits will expose students to the rapid changes sweeping across China and help nurture in them the sense of leadership in the future changes.

The bilateral visit program will start next year. In February 2018, ten Zhide students will visit Macau, accompanied by ten CKLC students, for a seven-day visit. Then in the summer, 20 students from the two colleges will participate in a nine-day Anji field study, followed by a two-day visit in Shanghai. The two colleges will be responsible for the

INTERCULTURAL AND RELATED COMPETENCIES

round-trip flight tickets between Macau and Shanghai for their own students and the local expenses will be borne by the host side. Ultimately, both CKLC and Zhide will subsidize the entire Anji Project collaboratively.

Goals and Outcomes:

- Provide a unique communicative and learning experience for students from Macau and Mainland China to get to know each other.
- Break one's own cultural stereotype to better understand the other with different cultural backgrounds.
- Foster and enhance the skills to listen, observe, compare, analyze, understand, and relate.

(Deardorff, 2006)

Assessment:

Students are required to submit a report pertaining to particular aspects of cultural differences in the sweeping changes in the Anji rural area and two cities of Shanghai and Macau. The report shall include three parts—the knowledge of the specific culture (to develop a strong sense of intercultural awareness), the comparison of one's own culture and that of the host region (to better know our true selves), and lastly the skills or attitude one has learned from this program (to reflect on intercultural communication). And then students will share and exchange their personal reflections to gain a multicultural understanding.

This program is considered as a good practice of intercultural competency, as it provides students the first-hand experience by exposing them to "strange" cultures with a field study and exchange visits, where intercultural competence, knowledge of and respect for other cultures may be developed (Stier, 2006). It creates a truly experiential learning opportunity for students to develop their intercultural competency and communication skills that they might not acquire from classroom education alone.

Lessons Learned:

1. The study group should include students of various cultural backgrounds. Local students shall participate in the study group and communicate with the invited students during the whole period of the program. The program aims to engage students in developing personal respect for each other and achieving meta-reflection.
2. The program should include two or more locations to help students, already diverse, develop a comparative, multi-dimensional understanding of social issues and possible solutions in a big country like China with a large population, a long history, and complex cultural institutions.
3. A wide range of visits, activities, and workshops shall be incorporated to deepen college student interest in the program and to accommodate different learning styles.

68

Global Citizenship Development

Increasing US and world catastrophes require that higher education plays a more prominent role in developing students' commitment to honoring human dignity and supporting human rights, often using intercultural competency to promote global citizenship development (Hartman, 2015). However, most US students will not have curricular or cocurricular intercultural experiences and may graduate without preparation to navigate these changing times (Atherton, 2015; Thom, 2010). This is in contrast to Australian universities where graduate attributes include global citizenship, multicultural perspectives, and intercultural competence (Jones, 2011). Global citizenship acknowledges the interconnected nature of everything and the shift from a focus on one's own feelings and perceptions to those of others (Sorrells, 2013). Global citizenship connects to intercultural concepts through "ideas of communities of action within civic society, beyond local, national or global politics, [and] political education is inherent in notions of intercultural citizenship" (Deardorff, 2016, p. 252). The concept of global citizenship relates to the skills, knowledge, and attitudes desired of graduates who can participate fully in the global economy and labor markets. Yet, global citizenship also needs to "include affection, respect, care, curiosity and concern for the well-being of all living beings" (McIntosh, 2005, p. 23).

US student affairs has a foundation in the pragmatic perspective of John Dewey's (1964/1916) work on democratic citizenship which complements US HEIs' original establishment of public good (Reason & Broido, 2017). Additionally, democratic learning and citizenship connects to a main learning outcome of diversity work as awareness moves from self to others to support the public good and social justice issues (Chun & Evans, 2016). Therefore, educating students to be citizens within a democracy has meant that they acquire information or knowledge as well as critical reasoning and thinking skills to make good decisions for society and to operate from global, socially just frameworks (Cornwell & Stoddard, 1999). The moral and ethical call to developing global citizenship, while previously framed as more US nationalistic, is evident with the intensification of globalization and internationalization. Dewey's pragmatism has a lasting influence on US student affairs work, thus it is reasonable to understand how practitioners might be attracted to global citizenship.

In more contemporary times, democratic engagement as a form of citizenship connects to social justice work in student affairs as reflected in the Student Learning Imperative's call to address social problems of the day (ACPA, 1996; Hamrick, 1998). The work of the twentieth-century Brazilian philosopher, Paulo Freire (1970), advocates for access for all to an education of and for citizenship that will awaken people to take action. Freire calls for change in the system that Dewey was preparing students for by creating a world of individuals who work with and for those who have been and are oppressed. As global citizenship increases awareness about injustices in localities around the world, there is caution in the dominant, colonizing assumptions that can exist within the concept of global citizenship. The "global" label "can too easily be coopted into serving neo-colonial, neo-imperial or even neo-patriarchy systems that deliberately globalize neoliberal ideologies which de-legitimate the needs and aspiration of marginalized populations" (Abdi, Shultz, & Pillay, 2015, p. 3). A contributor to this problem is that a common means to achieving global citizenship is through education abroad or other travel. Without a focus on IaH, travel to promote global citizenship education often involves the usual north to south and west to east privileged directions, educating students from already privileged identities or already advanced positions, or capitalizing on locations marketed as exotic (Killick, 2015).

As such, reframing to address these concerns offers "responsible global citizenship" as:

> The sense of attitudes and values—mindset and mindfulness—a way of thinking about ourselves and others, awareness of how our actions affect others, respect and concern for their well-being, and a commitment to certain types of action to address world problems.
>
> (Leask, 2015, p. 60)

As many of these points highlight, it is easy to see the benefits of promoting global citizenship when done ethically and with reciprocal relationship building. Increasingly, HEIs reference preparing students to be global citizens in mission statements and strategic plans (Green, 2012; Leask, 2015). However, as many scholars point out, global citizenship has been adopted without consideration of what it means to embody this concept, much less how to achieve it, and without consideration for who all it excludes (Abdi, 2015). Having intercultural alliances for social justice, which are "sites where cultural differences, positionalities, and issues of power and privilege are negotiated, translated, and potentially transformed," as a foundation can counter some concerns in global citizenship work (Sorrells, 2013, p. 241). Ultimately, as HEIs continue to leverage the concept of global citizenship, student affairs practitioners can lead the way in developing intercultural competencies to function in a responsible manner that avoids neo-colonizing practices and is less individualistic and more community focused.

The Promising Practice from Centennial College in Toronto, Canada, showcases global citizenship in an ethical and responsible manner that pays attention to historical and local context. Centennial College has been an award-winning leader in inclusive internationalization as recognized with the Canadian Bureau of International Education (CBIE) Board of Directors Award for Comprehensive Internationalization in 2014 and the Colleges and Institutes Canada (CICan) awards for Indigenous Education Excellence and Internationalization Excellence in 2016. Centennial College's Statement of Diversity includes an institutional commitment to global citizenship and social justice through acknowledging individual and systemic biases that contribute to marginalization along with resolving First Nations equity issues. In 2006, Centennial College launched the Signature Learning Experience (SLE) program as a promise to students that their educational journey at Centennial College would prepare them for employment in their fields of study, and for their role as global citizens and professionals in an evolving global economy. The SLE is a distinctive educational experience that integrates the principles of global citizenship, SJI, and equity through four core components:

- GNED 500: A required General Education course, Global Citizenship: From Social Analysis to Social Action explores the nature of diversity and discrimination in society and builds global citizenship and equity competencies in every student.
- Embedding/Integrating Global Citizenship and Equity (GCE) into Curriculum: The integration of GCE learning outcomes in all schools at both program and course levels.
- GCE Student Portfolio: The portfolio is a collection of artifacts that demonstrate learner's growth with GCE concepts and ideas over the course of their program.
- Faculty and Staff Training: Professional development opportunities for members of the college community related to GCE, which include Global Citizenship and Equity Learning Experiences or GCELEs.

(Razack & Arman, forthcoming)

As such, the Promising Practice, Global Citizenship & Equity Learning Experiences (GCELE), is one of Centennial's Signature Learning Experiences. The GCELE program applies critical service learning where students develop, in collaboration with community groups, global projects to address social issues through a social justice framework inclusive of Indigenous concepts. While some of the programs offered to students through the GCELE do involve international travel, they still fit with IaH because experiential learning is part of the required program and there are local Ontario-based programs working with high school girls and women in the local Indigenous communities and with the organization Habitat for Humanity.

PROMISING PRACTICE: Global Citizenship & Equity Learning Experiences

Institution: Centennial College

Location: Toronto, Canada

Authors:

Yasmin Razack, Director of Global Citizenship Education & Inclusion
Neil Buddel, Dean of Students

INTERCULTURAL AND RELATED COMPETENCIES

Background and Context:

Service learning develops individuals and communities in the spirit of charity; however, critical service learning (CSL) elevates global citizenship where "the goal is to deconstruct systems of power so that the need for service and the inequalities that create and sustain them are dismantled" (Mitchell, 2008, p. 50). Thus, CSL establishes the foundation for the Global Citizenship and Equity Learning Experiences (GCELE) at Centennial College, located in Toronto serving approximately 22,000 full-time students and 19,500 part-time students. Centennial College has been recognized as a leader in internationalization for its award-winning work to actively integrate global citizenship, social justice education, equity and inclusion. The College's Book of Commitments and Academic Plans detail how students and staff actively engage with learning that promotes citizenry in the global sense through a recognition that we must all be aware of our use of the world's resources and our impact on diverse communities.

Developed in 2009, GCELEs reflect Centennial's enduring commitment to advance positive social change in collaboration with historically marginalized, underserved, and underrepresented communities toward an egalitarian, inclusive, and socially just world. Further, and in reverence of Canada's Indigenous citizens' relational ontology and epistemology, the centerpiece of the GCELEs facilitates students' deconstruction of individual and social power, privilege, and oppression toward *wigoshiwin*—that all things living are connected and interdependent and, therefore, worthy of respect and inclusion.

Centennial believes in the transformative power of GCELEs to the extent that the governing board has committed to making GCELEs accessible—they are fully funded at no cost to students. GCELEs are global CSL projects that allow students to participate in thoughtfully organized learning experiences that work to advance the social justice goals of the partnering community organizations within each respective destination. Since the first GCELE in the Dominican Republic in 2010, over 740 students, faculty and staff participated in 58 social justice projects around the world focusing on issues as diverse as sustainable farming practices in Cuba, community health initiatives in Honduras, advancing early childhood education in Ghana, developing a global interactive multi-platform communications project to build greater awareness of LGBT+ issues, and working collaboratively to advance the skills of high school girls and women from Indigenous communities in Ontario, to name a few. GCELEs are both local and global to offer service learning projects that are accessible to diverse student populations.

Faculty participants are selected to guide, support, and facilitate the Project Learning Outcomes and the GCE Learning Outcomes of the GCELE through the development of facilitated activities pre-departure, during the GCELE project, and sustainability initiatives post-arrival (i.e. reflective practice circles, the crafting of blogs, the assigning of research to students/staff on the country destination that will increase the knowledge of the country's history, socio-political context, economy, Indigenous knowledge).

INTERCULTURAL AND RELATED COMPETENCIES

The intention of each GCELE is to examine both the historical precedents of social problems and the impact of their personal action/inaction in maintaining and transforming those social issues; as a result, GCELE staff lead deeply introspective, challenging, and provocative reflective practice sessions before, during, and after each experience.

Goals and Outcomes:

Internationalization has been misconstrued as a revenue stream for post-secondary institutions. At its core, internationalization is about disruption—challenging social, economic, cultural, political, and psychological structures toward an equitable society. As a result, and within the post-secondary realm, internationalization is the "intentional process of integrating an international, intercultural or global dimension into the purpose, functions and delivery of post-secondary education, in order to enhance the quality of education and research for all students and staff, and to make a meaningful contribution to society" (de Wit & Hunter, 2015).

With a focus on developing power-and-privilege-conscious global citizens, with a responsibility to respect and elevate conditions for inclusion and interconnectedness, GCELEs, as embedded and accessible learning experience at Centennial College, substantively contribute to core tenets of internationalization. Stated differently, GCELEs create conditions for inclusion *vis à vis* individual transformation: "when we are no longer able to change a situation, we are challenged to change ourselves" (Frankl, 2006, p. 2).

The goals of the GCELEs are to advance social justice initiatives outlined by the local/global community partner or organization. Students, staff, and global community partners collaboratively work together to deepen their knowledge and critical thinking of global issues, advance personal development and global employability skills, heighten awareness on the impact of historical inequities, and participate in global citizenship activities that significantly contribute to positive social change.

The GCELEs goals are derived from Centennial College's broader Social Justice Framework and Global Citizenship and Equity learning outcomes, which are as follows:

- Identify one's roles and responsibilities as a global citizen in personal and professional life.
- Identify beliefs, values, and behaviours that form individual and community identities and the basis for respectful relationships.
- Analyze issues of equity at the personal, professional, and global level.
- Analyze the use of the world's resources to achieve sustainability and equitable distribution at the personal, professional, and global level.
- Identify and challenge unjust practices in local and global systems.
- Support personal and social responsibility initiatives at the local, national or global level.

INTERCULTURAL AND RELATED COMPETENCIES

Assessment:

A research study completed by Centennial College's Centre for Global Citizenship Education and Inclusion used a mixed methods approach for data collection from three GCELE cohorts (Razack & Arman, forthcoming). In total, 248 students within 23 GCELE Projects from 2013–2014 participated in the research study. Participants completed two online surveys (one survey before departure and one just under three months after they returned) that measured their self-perceptions and attitudes toward various elements of social justice, global inequity, global citizenship, inclusion, social responsibility, and critical service learning.

All students were also invited to participate in a one-hour focus group discussion to share their perspectives six months after the experience to further reveal the sustainability of critical service learning goals. Students were required to write blogs before, during, and after participating. This research selected two repeat bloggers from each GCELE Projects. In total, 56 out of 219 blog posts by students were selected for analysis.

The self-esteem of students increased by 18% in the post-experience survey compared to pre-departure survey data. The capacity to work with other people and within the team increased by 25% and the acceptance of people from diverse cultures increased by 24%. Data from this research project demonstrated that the GCELEs were effective in offering a transformative learning experience through a critical service learning model consistent with the spirit of internationalization.

Most of the students (67%) mentioned in post-survey group discussions, and also in blog posts written after the experience, that they would like to volunteer with social change organizations. Furthermore, the research indicated that blogging is an effective tool to increase student engagement in local/global critical service learning experiences.

In this recent GCELE research project:

- 82% of participants indicated that participation in a GCELE enhanced their knowledge of other cultures.
- 78% of participants reported that participation in a GCELE raised their awareness of social issues.
- 73% of participants shared that participation in a GCELE helped them to connect with diverse local/global communities.

Lessons Learned:

1. To have impactful critical service learning, integrating a social justice methodology, addressing power through an equity lens and equalizing capital through an equitable funding model supported by organizational inclusive leadership are key component.
2. How transformative learning outcomes can be actualized on critical service learning experiences though reflective practices.
3. The GCELEs demonstrated how students were able to deepen and apply key equity principles through experiential education.

74

Media Links:

Global Citizenship and Equity Learning Experiences: www.centennialcollege.ca/about-centennial/college-overview/signature-learning-experience/global-citizenship-and-equity-learning-experiences/

Global Experience Blog: https://centennialglobalexperience.com/

CONCLUSION

The rising backlash against diversity and cosmopolitanism makes intercultural and global citizenship development even more critical today for current and future generations. Given the findings from our SSAO survey and the lack of guidance in US student affairs professional competencies, graduate preparation curriculum requires paradigmatic, content, and pedagogical revisions to be inclusive of intercultural and global citizenship models. Student affairs professional competencies and graduate curriculum standards, as currently written for a US audience, offer little guidance in these more inclusive revisions. As such, intercultural competency theories and global citizenship development are theoretical models to help advance "globalism" for professional competency development and in practitioners' work with students to advance their world understanding and skill sets. Using intercultural competency and global citizenship development can help advance students' critical thinking and reflection skills and knowledge or awareness of global social justice and equity issues. These additions would offer a more integrated approach to student development as "global learning is consistent with a holistic approach to student development because it frames students as global citizens" (Charles, Longerbeam, & Miller, 2013, p. 51). Intercultural competency and global citizenship development are not offered as replacements to any current models used, rather supplements to shift into more internationalized development for practitioners, cocurriculum, and services that offer everyone access to inclusive programs and spaces that honor various ways of knowing the world and experiencing culture.

REFERENCES

Abdi, A. A. (2015). Decolonizing global citizenship education. In A. A. Abdi, L. Shultz, & T. Pillay (Eds.), *Decolonizing global citizenship education* (pp. 11–26). Rotterdam, The Netherlands: Sense Publishers.

Abdi, A. A., Shultz, L., & Pillay, T. (2015). Decolonizing global citizenship. In A.A. Abdi, L. Shultz, & T. Pillay (Eds.), *Decolonizing global citizenship education* (pp. 1–9). Rotterdam, The Netherlands: Sense Publishers.

American College Personnel Association. (1996). *The student learning imperative: Implications for student affairs.* Washington, D.C.: Author. Retrieved from www.myacpa.org/files/acpas-student-learning-imperativepdf

INTERCULTURAL AND RELATED COMPETENCIES

American College Personnel Association—College Student Educators International (ACPA) and The National Association of Student Personnel Administrators—Student Affairs Administrators in Higher Education (NASPA). (2015). Professional competency areas for student affairs practitioners. Washington, D.C.: Authors.

American College Personnel Association—College Student Educators International (ACPA) and The National Association of Student Personnel Administrators—Student Affairs Administrators in Higher Education (NASPA). (2016). *ACPA/NASPA professional competencies rubrics*. Washington, D.C.: Author. Retrieved from www.naspa.org/images/uploads/main/ACPA_NASPA_Professional_Competency_Rubrics_Full.pdf

Atherton, G. (2015). Putting the international in equity. *EAIE Forum*, 38–40.

Arasaratnam-Smith, L. A. (2017). Intercultural competence: An overview. In D. K. Deardorff & L. A Arasaratnam-Smith (Eds.), *Intercultural competency in higher education: International approaches, assessment and application* (pp. 7–18). New York: Routledge.

Bardill Moscaritolo, L., & Roberts, D. (2016). Global competencies for student affairs. In K. Osfield, B. Perozzi, L. Bardill Moscaritolo, & R. Shea (Eds.), *Supporting students globally in higher education* (pp. 109–126). Washington, D.C.: NASPA.

Bennett, J. M. (1993). Towards ethnorelativism: A developmental model of intercultural sensitivity. In M. Paige (Ed.), *Education for the intercultural experience*. Yarmouth, ME: Intercultural Press.

Bennett, J. M., & Bennett, M. J. (2004). Developing intercultural sensitivity. An integrative approach to global and domestic diversity. In D. Landis, & J. M. Bennett (Eds.), *Handbook of intercultural training* (pp. 147–165). Thousand Oaks, CA: Sage.

Castellanos, J., Gloria, A. M., Mayorga, M. M., & Salas, C. (2008). Student affairs professionals' self-report of multicultural competence: Understanding awareness, knowledge, and skills. *NASPA Journal, 44*(4), 643–663.

Charles, H., Longerbeam, S. D., & Miller, A. E. (2013). Putting old tensions to rest: Integrating multicultural education and global learning to advance student development. *Journal of College and Character, 14*(1), 47–58.

Chun, E., & Evans, A. (2016). Rethinking cultural competence in higher education: An ecological framework for student development. *ASHE Higher Education Report, 42*(4), 6–170.

Cornwell, G. H., & Stoddard, E. W. (1999). *Globalizing knowledge: Connecting international & intercultural studies*. Washington, D.C.: AACU.

Council for the Advancement of Standards in Higher Education (2012). *CAS professional standards for higher education* (8th ed.). Washington, D.C.: Author.

Council for the Advancement of Standards in Higher Education (2015). *CAS professional standards for higher education* (9th ed.). Washington, D.C.: Author.

Council for the Advancement of Higher Education Programs. (2010). *A commitment to quality: Guidelines for higher education administration and leadership preparation programs at the masters degree level*. Las Vegas, NV: Author.

Cuyjet, M. J., Linder, C., Howard-Hamilton, M. F., & Cooper, D. L. (Eds.). (2016). *Multiculturalism on campus: Theory, models, and practices for understanding diversity and creating inclusion*, 2nd ed. Sterling, VA: Stylus.

de Wit, H., & Hunter, F. (2015). The future of internationalization of higher education in Europe. *International Higher Education, 83*, 2–3.

Dean, L. A., & Jones, G. M. (2014). The council for the advancement of standards in higher education and the role of standards in professional practice. In S. Freeman, L. S. Hagedorn, L. Goodchild, & D. Wright (Eds.), *Advancing higher education as a field of study: In quest of doctoral degree guidelines* (pp. 93–109). Sterling, VA: Stylus.

Deardoff, D. K. (2006). Identification and assessment of intercultural competence as a student outcome of internationalization. *Journal of Studies in International Education, 10*(3), 241–266.

Deardorff, D. K., & Jones, E. (2012). Intercultural competence: An emerging focus in international higher education. In D. K. Deardorff, H. de Wit, J. D. Heyl, & T. Adams (Eds.), *SAGE handbook of international higher education* (pp. 283–303). Thousand Oaks, CA: Sage.

Deardorff, D. K. (2016). Key theoretical frameworks guiding the scholar-practitioner in international education. In B. Streitweiser & A. C. Ogden (Eds.), *International education's scholar-practitioners: Bridging research and practice* (pp. 247–264). Oxford: Symposium.

Dewey, J. (1964/1916). *Democracy and education: An introduction to the philosophy of education.* New York: Macmillan.

DiRamio, D. (2014). Professional competencies and standards of practice: The student affairs perspective from the Student Affairs Administrators in Higher Education, College Student Educators International, and Council for the Advancement of Standards in Higher Education. In S. Freeman, L. S. Hagedorn, L. Goodchild, & D. Wright (Eds.), *Advancing higher education as a field of study: In quest of doctoral degree guidelines* (pp. 77–92). Sterling, VA: Stylus.

Duncan, A. (2010). Education and the language gap: Secretary Arne Duncan's remarks at the foreign language summit speech. Retrieved from www.ed.gov/news/speeches/education-and-language-gap-secretary-arne-duncans-remarks-foreign-language-summit

Green, M. F. (2012). Global citizenship: What are we talking about and why does it matter? *International Educator, 21*(3), 124–127.

Hamrick, F. A. (1998). Democratic citizenship and student activism. *Journal of College Student Development, 39*(5), 449–459.

Hartman, E. (2015). Global citizenship offers better solutions. *International Educator, May/June*, 74–79.

Helms, J. E. (Ed.). (1990). *Black and white racial identity: Theory, research and practice.* Westport, CT: Praeger.

Frankl, V. (2006). *Man's search for meaning.* Boston, MA: Beacon Press.

Freire, P. (1970). *Pedagogy of the oppressed*. New York: Continuum.

Jones, E. (2011). Internationalisation, multiculturalism, a global outlook and employability. *ALT Journal*, *11*, 21–49.

Killick, D. (2015). *Developing the global student: Higher education in an era of globalization*. London: Routledge.

Leask, B. (2015). *Internationalizing the curriculum*. New York: Routledge.

Li, J. (2009). A study of student affairs administration professional preparation in Chinese higher education (Doctoral dissertation). University of Southern California, Los Angeles, CA.

McIntosh, P. (2005). Gender perspectives on educating for global citizenship. In N. Noddings, (Ed.), *Educating for global awareness* (pp. 22–39). New York: Teachers College Press.

Mitchell, T. D. (2008). Traditional vs. critical service-learning: Engaging the literature to differentiate two models. *Michigan Journal of Community Service Learning*, *14*, 60–65.

Murray-García, J., & Tervalon, M. (2017). Rethinking intercultural competence: Cultural humility in internationalising higher education. In D. K. Deardorff & L. A Arasaratnam-Smith (Eds.), *Intercultural competency in higher education: International approaches, assessment and application* (pp. 19–31). New York: Routledge.

NAFSA—Association for International Educators. (2015). International Education Professional Competencies. Washington, D.C.: Author

National Education Association. (2010). *Global competence is a 21st century imperative*. Washington, D.C.: Education Policy and Practice Department. Retrieved from www.nea.org/assets/docs/HE/PB28A_Global_Competence11.pdf

Olson, C., Evans, R., & Shoenberg, R. E. (2007). *At home in the world: Bridging the gap between internationalization and multicultural education*. Washington, D.C.: ACE.

Paracka, D. J., & Pynn, T. (2017). Towards transformative reciprocity: Mapping the intersectionality of interdisciplinary intercultural competence. In D. K. Deardorff & L. A Arasaratnam-Smith (Eds.), *Intercultural competency in higher education: International approaches, assessment and application* (pp. 43–52). New York: Routledge.

Perry, W. G. (1970). *Forms of intellectual and ethical development in the college years: A scheme*. New York: Holt, Rinehart, and Winston.

Pope, R. L., & Reynolds, A. L. (1997). Student affairs core competencies: Integrating multicultural awareness, knowledge, and skills. *Journal of College Student Development*, *38*(3), 266–277.

Pope, R. L., Reynold, A. L., & Mueller, J. A. (2004). *Multicultural competence in student affairs*, 1st ed. San Francisco, CA: Jossey-Bass.

Pusch, M. D. (2004). Intercultural training in historical perspective. In D. Landis, J. M. Bennett, & M. J. Bennett (Eds.), *Handbook of intercultural training*, 3rd ed. (pp. 13–36). Thousand Oaks, CA: Sage.

Razack, Y., & Arman, S. (forthcoming). A closer look: Examining the impact of Global Citizenship and Equity Learning Experiences (GCELEs). *Journal of Global Citizenship & Equity Education*.

Reason, R. D., & Broido, E. M. (2017). Philosophies and values. In J. H. Schuh, S. R. Jones, & V. Torres (Eds.), *Student services: A handbook for the profession*, 6th ed. (pp. 39–55). San Francisco, CA: Jossey-Bass.

Skorton, D., & Altschuler, G. (2012, Aug 27). America's foreign language deficit. *Forbes*. Retrieved from www.forbes.com/sites/collegeprose/2012/08/27/americas-foreign-language-deficit/#616008b7382f

Sorrells, K. (2013). *Intercultural communication: Globalization and social justice*. Thousand Oaks, CA: Sage.

Spitzberg, B. H., & Changnon, G. (2009). Conceptualizing intercultural competence. In D. K. Deardorff, H. de Wit, J. D. Heyl, & T. Adams (Eds.), *SAGE handbook of intercultural competence* (pp. 2–52). Thousand Oaks, CA: Sage.

Stier, J. (2006). Internationalization, intercultural communication and intercultural competence. *Journal of Intercultural Communication, 11*, 1–12.

Streitwieser, B., & Ogden, A. C. (2016). Heralding the scholar-practitioner in international education. In B. Streitwieser, & A. C. Ogden, (Eds.), *International higher education's scholar-practitioners: Bridging research and practice* (pp. 19–38). Oxford: Symposium.

Thom, V. (2010). Mutual cultures: Engaging with interculturalism in higher education. In E. Jones (Ed.), *Internationalisation and the student voice: Higher education perspectives* (pp. 155–165). London: Routledge.

Wang, Y., Deardorff, D. K., & Kulich, S. (2017). Chinese perspectives on intercultural competence in international education. In D. K. Deardorff & L. A. Arasaratnam-Smith (Eds.), *Intercultural competence in international higher education* (pp. 95–109). New York: Routledge.

Wright, D. A., & Hyle, A. E. (2014). Council for the advancement of higher education programs' master's degree guidelines for higher education administration programs. In S. Freeman, L. S. Hagedorn, L. Goodchild, & D. Wright (Eds.), *Advancing higher education as a field of study: In quest of doctoral degree guidelines* (pp. 111–123). Sterling, VA: Stylus.

Chapter 4

Organizational Alignment of Student Affairs for Internationalization

The internationalization process aligns higher education with a more globally focused vision by creating formal strategic plans, implementing organizational or divisional strategies, or incorporating international goals and learning objectives. Internationalization activities have become more common across US institutional types, from research universities to community colleges. At the institutional level, internationalization is a strategic process "of integrating an international, intercultural, or global dimension into the purpose, functions, or delivery of post-secondary education" (Knight, 2003, p. 2). Internationalization efforts often require organizational change, which may be "institution-wide, or in practices and regulations associated with specific areas of programming, or in something as broad as organizational identity" (Hudzik, 2015, p. 38). The latter point is one of the larger organizational change components, that of an alteration to identity and culture.

Parsons and Söderqvist's (2005) model of institutional internationalization views organizations functioning within and through five stages. In the "zero" (first) stage, internationalization is a marginal activity, where a few individuals engage in activities associated with status building or specific activities. The second stage, "student mobility," acknowledges internationalization as a means to an end related to mobility programs like education abroad. Most US institutions are in these two earlier stages depending on institutional type, size, resources, and location. Larger research or well-funded HEIs may be in the third stage, which is "curriculum and research internationalisation." In this stage, faculty are the drivers of internationalization through research and curriculum revisions. Most continental European HEIs reach this stage with Internationalization of the Curriculum. In the fourth stage, "institutionalisation of internationalisation," HEIs strategize through structure and policies; development of networks, partnerships, and strategic alliances; connection between internationalization and multiculturalism; and the creation of internationalization managers or Senior Internationalization Officers (SIOs). The fifth stage is "commercialising the outcomes of internationalisation"

81

ORGANIZATIONAL ALIGNMENT

where the goals are export of education, franchising education services, and joint or strategic alliances. This stage model of internationalization is not linear or sequential, but shows that internationalization processes and strategies are continuous efforts built upon itself. For example, some US institutions are appointing SIOs, with aspirations to move beyond this second stage and/or to assist faculty in internationalizing the curriculum. Student affairs divisional work can fit into these stages of internationalization at any of the points but likely is at the student mobility stage unless strategic efforts institutionalize practices throughout the division.

How student affairs as a profession in the US, broadly, and how specific student affairs divisions across institutions will embrace this identity shift to encompass a global perspective while continuing to incorporate the essential local aspects is still undetermined. Student affairs is known as being "very internally focused" and "adopting a global perspective . . . runs counter to a strong aspect of the overall culture of student affairs" (Love & Estaneck, 2004, p. 177). Missing from many conversations about internationalization are what strategies and frameworks student affairs practitioners can use to progress personally and professionally. IaH offers a "both and" approach where internationalization can be undertaken at any, some, or all of these levels: individual, departmental, divisional, and institutional. The IaH framework stresses changing the "at home" campus' focus to inclusively integrate all students and re-envision student affairs work through a global lens.

SSAOs, divisions, departments, and practitioners can all build capacity through guiding global concepts and initiatives that will position student affairs in a central role with internationalization. Vision statements, values, and underlying assumptions can help solidify an international mindset and set up staff for success over the long term. Many aspects of internationalization may already be present and operating within an institution or division of student affairs, and collaborative programs and services likely already span multiple areas to support diversity and multiculturalism. With that, divisions can create synergy for internationalization by building on these collaborations with academic affairs, international education, and cultural center colleagues. To build capacity, SSAOs can leverage resources and support services through these partnerships, and revising hiring and on-boarding practices for staff. This chapter provides examples of strategic development, collaboration or partnerships, structural and service support, and human resources to intentionally integrate student affairs work with internationalization efforts.

STRATEGIC DEVELOPMENT TO INTEGRATE INTERNATIONALIZATION

Organizational documents, such as vision statements, policies, and strategic plans, are overt declarations of the focus and values of HEIs that convey deep and lasting meaning for institutions as they guide overall objectives and operations.

ORGANIZATIONAL ALIGNMENT

Leaders in internationalization at HEIs in Western Europe cite the importance of separate strategic plans for internationalization rather than having it only incorporated into the institution's overall strategy (Engel, Sandström, van der Aa, & Glass, 2014). Staff at institutions with formalized internationalization strategies believed they possessed the skills and knowledge to advance internationalization, whereas staff elsewhere did not. Not having internationalization as an institutional strategy caused institutions to lag behind in policy and activity. One reason many institutions, such as those in the European Higher Education Area (EHEA), are remarkably more advanced in internationalization relates back to the 1990s when the first planning documents and European Policy Statements related to the European Union SOCRATES/ERASMUS programs were released (Parsons & Söderqvist, 2005). As European HEIs have had several decades to revise and implement internationalization plans, they have had time to invest in resources, hire trained internationalization managers and policy developers, and work with faculty to revise curriculum and programs. While the EHEA is a drastically different context compared to the US in terms of internationalization policy, laws, and incentives, European HEIs do offer many examples for strategic development at the organizational level.

The Hague University of Applied Sciences' (THUAS) 2014 Institutional Strategic Plan, "Global Citizens in a Learning Society," aligns internationalization as the way to achieve their vision of becoming the "*most* international institution of its kind in The Netherlands by 2020" (p. 1). The plan is an integrated approach that centers on student learning and global citizenship to reflect the mission of applied universities to prepare students with attention to training and career preparation. In developing their internationalization plan, THUAS recognized that Dutch students are less likely than their European peers to travel outside of the country for educational experiences and, thus, an IaH approach would help all students have intercultural development before graduating. THUAS' Compass model, see Figure 4.1, adapts Elsbeth Jones' (2013) integrated internationalization of ten elements for centering students in the internationalization process. The ten elements include:

- Rationale and strategy for internationalization links to HEI vision and values.
- Governance, leadership, and management all communicate and report on internationalization strategies.
- Internationalization of the formal curriculum for all students through content, pedagogy, assessment and learning outcomes.
- International campus culture and informal curriculum reflects IaH strategies for an international and multicultural HEI.
- Student diversity means students are active participants and valued for their identities and what they bring to campus.

THUAS Compass:
Critical elements of Internationalisation

1. Rationale and policy or strategy for internationalisation
- An effective and comprehensive policy or strategy for internationalisation linked to the university's vision and values is clearly communicated.
- Is understood by academics and support staff at all levels across the institution as well as academic committee, the Governing Body and external stakeholders.

2. Governance, leadership and management
- Importance and relevance of internationalisation is recognised by the Supervisory and Executive Board and all management, and demonstrated as such across the institution
- Explicit in all key university policies and strategies, incorporated into planning processes, aligned and delivered through normal line management routes
- Key areas to include are positioning and profiling, learning and teaching, research strategies, human resources policy, assessment, subsidies (local, national and international) and facilities

3. Internationalisation of the formal curriculum for all students
- University-wide strategy is translated to internationalized curricula and learning outcomes across the institution – global perspectives and intercultural communication
- Content, pedagogy, assessment processes and graduate outcomes
- Varied international mobility opportunities support the internationalised curriculum e.g. academic study abroad, work placement, group study tours, international volunteering and service learning, demonstrably linked to the desired internationalized learning outcomes and curricula
- Intercultural learning opportunities in multicultural classrooms, within the local community and during internships in multicultural workplaces
- Build international reputation in the field of applied research.

4. International campus culture and informal curriculum for all students
- An international and multicultural campus culture is evident, well established within the international region of The Hague, including student union clubs, societies and informal gatherings
- Forms the basis of the informal curriculum for all students
- International aspects of university life are celebrated regularly through events, displays and activities which support internationalisation at home
- Students are trained to make full use of the international campus culture to deepen their intercultural competencies

5. Student diversity
- Vibrant diverse international and multicultural student community as active participants in (off) campus life.
- Students valued for the way in which they enrich the classroom and campus culture.

6. Guidance and support for students outside the classroom
- Effective systems and services provide support to support internationalisation, including

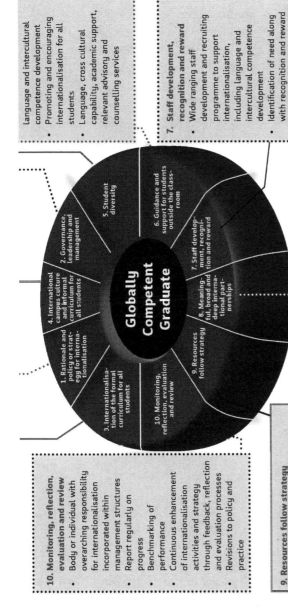

Figure 4.1 Global Citizens in a Learning Society. Internationalization at THUAS 2015–2020

ORGANIZATIONAL ALIGNMENT

- Guidance and support for students outside the classroom to ensure effective systems and services.
- Staff development, recognition and reward for all staff to support internationalization.
- Broad and deep international partnerships to offer students meaningful opportunities and to benchmark institutional performance.
- Resources follow strategy to reflect commitment and ensure delivery of internationalization strategies.
- Monitoring, reflection, evaluation and review through an SIO type position or group of people to ensure oversight and reporting.

THUAS recognized the need to craft a bottom-up and top-down approach to internationalization to support their goal of graduating global citizens. Their approach supports the stance that:

> A guide for internationalized strategic development is the belief that, it is important to present internationalization as issue-oriented, reflective of real world issues, and inclusive of domestic diversity concerns. It is not sufficient to emphasize the benefits of internationalization in terms of personal growth (as study abroad is often viewed).
>
> (Olson, Evans, & Shoenberg, 2007, p. 30)

The integrated internationalization approach places students as the beneficiaries to this process and the purpose of engaging in internationalization efforts to achieve wider goals of global citizenship not padding institutional budgets. At THUAS, student diversity as one of ten components to internationalization avoids emphasizing structural diversity measures that would fail to automatically improve students' satisfaction or integrate student community (Spencer-Oatey & Dauber, 2015). The THUAS model aims to produce global citizenship skills in all students throughout curriculum as internationalization is a compulsory part of all academic programs. However, there should not be too much reliance on strategic planning and associated documents, as plans "often serve to institutionalise existing behaviour" (Parsons & Söderqvist, 2005, p. 15) rather than change organizational identities, culture, or strategies. Therefore, a positive approach remembers that "an internationalization plan or strategy is hardly ever a blueprint; it's more of a developing conversation, an iterative process of meaning-making where creative solutions emerge over time from a series of significant and intentional conversations" (Nolan, 2015, p. 34).

In our study of US SSAOs, the connection or alignment between internationalization and institutional vision and mission may be symbolic in nature, rather than through intentional or coordinated practice or implementation as with THUAS. Of the survey respondents, 62% of SSAOs indicated that the mission statement of their institution included international goals, see Table 4.1.

ORGANIZATIONAL ALIGNMENT

Table 4.1 Documents Inclusive of International Goals/Activities

	Institution includes internationalization (%)	Student Affairs Division includes internationalization (%)
Yes	62	46
No	28	47
Unsure	9	7

If institutions prioritized or included internationalization in their mission, vision, or strategic plan, then student affairs divisions were more likely to mirror, reflect, and support those broader internationalization sentiments, as shown in Table 4.2. For those institutions, whose missions did not include international goals or activities, SSAOs were more likely to report internationalization as a low or medium priority. SSAOs at institutions with a low or medium priority for internationalization overall often cited this as a barrier because there was no commitment or resources from the institution.

Table 4.2 Prioritization of Internationalization

Respondents Reporting Prioritization of Internationalization	Not a Priority (%)	Low Priority (%)	Medium Priority (%)	High Priority (%)	Total Responses (%)
For the institution	2	14	42	42	100
For the student affairs division	9	24	48	19	100
For the student affairs professional staff	12	29	47	12	100

SSAOs believed that top-down prioritization was necessary to develop an internationalized student affairs division. To achieve the greatest effectiveness with internationalization efforts, multiple levels of stakeholder involvement within HEIs from various functional and academic areas across the institution is best. One SSAO in New York offered this advice: "It is much like any change management issue, it takes multiple messages, a champion, support from above, and time!" Similarly, an SSAO in New Jersey shared: "There has to be institutional commitment to internationalizing the campus across curricular and cocurricular programs." When student affairs division level documents such as mission, vision, or strategic plans did not include internationalization then, not surprisingly, SSAOs reported low priority levels compared to when it was a medium priority then student affairs division documents reflected internationalization to some

87

minor degree. Important to note is that for some SSAO respondents, the term or concept of internationalization was not something they saw reflected in or a part of their student affairs divisions.

Additionally, a few SSAOs interpreted their student affairs mission as connecting to diversity work because internationalization means the support all students' need to foster a campus culture inclusive of international students. An SSAO at a small private university in Ohio reported that their student affairs divisional documents include "Diversity and Inclusion [as] declared learning domains for student affairs, and Globalism is one of our targeted student competencies within it." Another SSAO shared the values of their North Carolinian private university: "One of our values is cultural competency, which we define as including behaviors and attitudes that enable staff and students to work respectfully and effectively across diverse cultures, languages, socioeconomic status, race-ethnic background, religion, gender, and sexual orientation." These examples represent a strategy where SSAOs incorporated internationalization with diversity efforts.

Policies reflect values of organizations and often require revisions or new creations when shifting organizational identity to be more inclusive and international. Handbooks and manuals share formal and informal policies meant to help guide students and practitioners through ethics and the bureaucracy of institutional, divisional, and academic-related guidelines or procedures. They carry within them cultural and institutional values and often unwritten beliefs that can manifest in stereotypes and biases for non-majority students or linguistically diverse students. Often there are high level, and even unreasonable, expectations and assumptions placed on international students studying in countries where academic English is the language of instruction. The language "problem" often ascribed to international students follows deficit thinking and requires intercultural and linguistic training. As Killick (2015) says, "Linguistic imperialism is rife on our campuses" (p. 134) and without intercultural support efforts, classroom and cocurriculum spaces are not inclusive for all learners and students. For example, in one study, staff in a student services office instructed a Saudi graduate student that they were not allowed to call to set up an appointment but rather had to come in person. The student perceived this was due to their accent and being a non-native English speaker (Yakaboski et al., 2017). Shifting the onus of responsibility to the dominant group is "academic equity, as language dominance acts considerably on the balance of power . . . " (Killick, 2015, p. 136). In the case of the Saudi student, offices can set up online appointment systems along with clearly communicated policies listed online, detailing what and why. Knowledge about language and accents and how to be inclusive without isolating can be components of divisional and departmental trainings to change culture and support service delivery while ensuring organizational policies do not place extra burden on diverse students.

ORGANIZATIONAL STRUCTURE AND CAPACITY BUILDING

There are countless ways to conceptualize modern student affairs organizations with models ranging from out-of-classroom-centered to student-centered (Manning, Kinzie, & Schuh, 2014) or management models, such as a revenue source for auxiliaries to a direct supervision model for smaller institutions (Ambler, 2000). These models all reflect varieties in student affairs organizational structure based on a wide range of criteria and reasons including functions, institutional history, or leadership preferences. In other countries, such as China and Belize, student affairs areas typically are organized under a department or an office. And in other cases, there is no specific or necessarily intentional organizational alignment of student affairs programs and services. In Finland, at the University of Jyväskylä, for example, there is no student affairs division but many components work together to support student development and learning within an internationalized university. The typical structure of US student affairs divisions offers a natural platform for synergy and collaboration within the division; however, the very nature of large organizations often creates structural silos.

In the search for efficiency, bureaucratic methods for delivering information and aligning work segments people and areas, which leads to literal and figurative divisions of the whole. Separation has been visible with higher education diversity work in that often it is "fragmented and localized within particular programs . . . these approaches are typically characterized by a lack of intentionality and even negligence and do not transcend departmental or program boundaries to address the needs of diverse students across the institution" (Chun & Evans, 2016, p. 20). Having internationalization or international activities centralized in international education offices or academic affairs divisions can create separation from student affairs divisions who may not experience integration and engagement in these efforts. Part of the separation between student affairs and internationalization seems to be the perception that internationalization is an academic venture and not one for the cocurriculum. Often SSAOs held the perception that internationalization taskforces were academic-only focused rather than holistic, as shared by an SSAO in North Carolina, who said that student affairs is "consistently left out; it is a faculty planning and taskforce." Further, involvement on the committees connected back to increasing international student enrollment numbers.

Many organizations in the European Higher Education Area began the process of internationalization by having a centralized, individual office responsible for the task. However, as internationalization became mainstreamed in Dutch universities, for example, many institutions have decentralized efforts while still maintaining central services offices and creating new administrative positions to support internationalization outside of international education and services offices (Yakaboski, 2017). While this is good symbolism for support of internationalization, it has given way to a more diffuse approach that involves many units and people across the

ORGANIZATIONAL ALIGNMENT

institution. An administrator at an HEI in Utrecht said: "there can't be one office on campus that has responsibility for internationalization . . . But you have created the environment, the ecosystem to actually sustain it and grow it . . . It [internationalization] should be everywhere" (Yakaboski, 2017, p. 15). However, a decentralized approach requires great attention to communication and culture within the structure. In a review of Harvard and Yale universities' attempts at decentralized internationalization, when there was less institutional planning, the model tended to be more opportunistic, growing out of isolated initiatives rather than intentional coordination or connected to structural goals (Edwards, 2007).

For the US SSAOs in our survey, organizational structure and issues, such as the location of internationalization or international services and the HEIs geographical location, were all stated as barriers. For most institutions, centralizing internationalization efforts with international student services led to perceptions of efforts being siloed rather than shared across campus and within student services. Quite directly some saw internationalization as out of their organizational responsibility because the student affairs division did not have direct oversight for international services. Often even if internationalization was a high priority for the institution, it was low for student affairs in part due to the separation. Even at a university in Colorado where the SSAO reported high prioritization of internationalization at all levels, the perception of silos prevailed. The SSAO highlighted:

> The International Services Office reports outside of Student Affairs—we have to work much harder to build collaborations, keep them informed and they us. That the campus does not have a clear senior administrator with leadership responsibilities for international—we are working to improve and address that with the Provost's office.

The organizational separation led to concerns over communication and the availability of resources for those outside of the organizational line of command and role for internationalization. A few institutions had moved or were moving toward a separate chief international/internationalization officer, detached from, but connected to, international services, to coordinate and communicate efforts across campus.

In Australia and Europe, internationalization has become much more mainstreamed through SIOs' leadership and management of HEIs in both administrative and academic staff (Murray, Goedegebuure, van Liempd, & Vermeulen, 2014). SIOs are less common in US HEIs, therefore it may be up to SSAOs to fulfill some of this leadership. Australian and European SIOs view their role as facilitators of key priorities including building institutional relationships by serving in leadership roles as coordinators of internationalization with attention to communication, structure of work, and strategic objectives. US SIOs share that "greater

90

integration/coordination of campus resources" would positively impact their ability to increase the university's engagement in internationalization (Koehn, Deardorff, & Bolognese, 2011, p. 340). With the scarcity of institutional resources as a clear barrier to internationalization, leveraging available, internal resources can be essential for achieving internationalization goals. This leaves SIOs and other senior administrators with a main task of collaborative relationship building to enhance internationalization (Nolan, 2015). Yet in our study, only 40% of SSAOs reported that they had regular interaction with their institution's SIO. For the other 60%, interaction was occasional to not at all.

It is important for student affairs practitioners to ensure participation on these committees or even to be leaders in the process when possible. Many institutions have committees and taskforces to address internationalization, which can help increase the level and breadth of commitment of the university community. Ward (2016), on behalf of ACE, stated that:

> while student affairs professionals are critical to implementation of internationalization goals, institutions do not always turn to student affairs leaders when planning for internationalization . . . Nevertheless, involving the senior student affairs leader from the start can help to avoid costly missteps during implementation.
>
> (p. 5)

Paradoxically, just under half of the SSAOs in our survey reported that their institution had an internationalization group and under a third indicated there was no formal committee or taskforce. Within those HEIs with a committee, few SSAOs reported student affairs divisional representation on institutional internationalization committees, and of those who did, there was little active engagement. Participation mainly was in the form of one representative to advise on international student related issues and topics.

Another way student affairs practitioners and SSAOs can collaborate with academic affairs to achieve internationalization goals is through cross-departmental assessment, evaluation, and research partnerships. Research and collaboration were important to the leaders at the 2014 Global Summit on Student Affairs and Services, held in Rome, Italy, in that they supported efforts to build capacity by doing research both independently and collaboratively (Perozzi, Giovannucci, & Shea, 2016). Although there are plenty of professional association activities in the US, one idea from a Colorado-based SSAO was that their student affairs division created an internal conference. Their "professional development team has made this [internationalization] a priority for training and we have expanded our student development conference to include a deeper focus on international student development research." Requiring a bit more structure and planning is that part of The Hague University of Applied Sciences internationalization

ORGANIZATIONAL ALIGNMENT

strategies they created an internationalization research group, called International Cooperation, that consists of members intentionally selected from various departments and divisions on campus to develop assessment, evaluation, and research projects based on what needs the university has related to understanding or improving internationalization and intercultural learning (Jos Walenkamp, personal communication, 2015, 2017). This group costs the university little more than some time reassignment for the coordinating faculty member, yet the benefits are substantial with regular campus publications using data from their collective projects. For example, they have published on topics of students' acquisition of international competencies (Heijer, Walenkamp, & Hoven, 2015), and world citizenship (Walenkamp, 2013). THUAS' example is one that US student affairs divisions could implement rather simply, as they are likely already conducting assessment projects and could expand to collaborating with faculty across campus who may share research agendas and are interested in applied research.

The Promising Practice from Fudan University, China, showcases how one university undertook a series of initiatives to involve practitioners in the internationalization process of student affairs. The Opening-Up of Student Affairs Initiative is broad and involves practitioners at many levels, exposing them to new paradigms of program and service delivery for students. Fudan seeks to be in alignment with national ideology by looking outward and focusing programs, such as exchanges on senior leaders, while providing vision and experience for newer practitioners via internships and conferences, which take place locally. Fudan also partners with the city of Shanghai and works closely with the Shanghai Moral Education Development Center on their strategies. Practitioners created a research program to develop Chinese applicable practices and advance theory and research in the region, while also working to network practitioners to enhance their professional development.

PROMISING PRACTICE: The "Opening-Up" of Student Affairs Initiative

Institution: Fudan University

Location: Shanghai, People's Republic of China

Authors:
Jin Xu, Director, Student Affairs Office, Fudan University, China
Dun Mao, Senior Student Affairs Officer, College of Foreign Language and Literature, Fudan University, China

Background and Context:
In the national conference on higher education in 2016, China's President, Xi Jinping, addressed the importance for Chinese universities to internationalize and gain a global

ORGANIZATIONAL ALIGNMENT

perspective while maintaining Chinese characteristics (Xinhua news agency, 2016a). Chinese characteristics is a common expression from Chinese officials, which indicates that theory and practice should adapt to unique Chinese conditions. According to the President, college students should "understand the trends of development of China and the world, the Chinese characteristics and international comparison, their responsibilities and mission, ambitions and hard work." Additionally, the Chinese central government issued a state policy regarding the Opening-Up of education in the new era, to emphasize international communication and collaboration in higher education and foster a better environment to promote global cooperation (Xinhua news agency, 2016b). Thus, while Chinese characteristics and embodying global perspectives are the educational visions of many Chinese universities, methods to speed up the process of internationalization have become the challenge in China's higher education.

Founded in 1905 and located in Shanghai, Fudan University is considered one of the best Chinese universities. More than 13,000 undergraduate students and 19,000 postgraduate students study on campus. Among these students, 3,000 are from overseas countries. As one of the most internationalized universities in China, Fudan partners with 152 overseas colleges and institutions. In 2015, the University sent 2,728 students abroad for exchanges and received 2,362 international students; both are leading numbers among universities in mainland China. However, new challenges emerge when more students go abroad and the local campus gains more diversity. For example, how to handle situations when students face risk moments; what is the mechanism to get in touch with them when an emergency happens; how to solve the campus issues when cultural backgrounds are varied? Thus, priorities of the Student Affairs Office are:

- To expand the international vision.
- To have a better understanding of the diversification on campus.
- To enhance the intercultural competency.

Goals and Outcomes:

In 2014, Fudan's Student Affairs Office (SAO) started an opening-up initiative, including conducting research, establishing international networks, and organizing conferences.

1. **Conducting comparative research.** Academic research in relevant fields, such as higher education, social science, and management, has been a vital part of China's student affairs profession. Many student affairs officers are university administrators who teach at the same time. In 2014, Fudan's SAO carried out a research program themed "Theories and Practices: The Internationalization of Student Affairs." One hundred and thirty Chinese student affairs professionals joined the program, which was organized into seven sub-themes, including student residential life, university and parents' partnership, extra-curricular activities and student leadership, international student affairs, campus risk moment management, study outcome evaluation, and student campus engagement. It was the major research operation in Fudan's student affairs field from 2014 to 2015. In the same year,

ORGANIZATIONAL ALIGNMENT

we published *International Student Affairs Professionalization Handbook* (6 volumes), translated from English to Chinese.

2. **Setting up the International Student Affairs framework.** We established connections with international organizations such as NASPA and the International Association of Student Affairs and Services (IASAS). The University signed a working memorandum with NASPA in 2016, and jointly built a Sino-USA Student Affairs Network (SUSAN) as the cooperative mechanism. It was the first agreement signed by a Chinese university with another international professional association. This memorandum includes facilitating communication between universities from the US and China, designing and implementing international projects, creating exchange staff programs to improve intercultural competency, etc. A shadowing exchange project and five training programs have been developed under the SUSAN network.

3. **Organizing international conferences on student affairs.** Starting in 2015, Fudan University hosted an international conference on student affairs to be held every two years. The purpose is to investigate the professional advances in relevant fields and to promote equal-footed dialogue among the international student affairs community. More than 150 participants, including student affairs vice presidents and senior practitioners from China and abroad, attended the 2015 conference, themed "Professionalization of Student Affairs and International Collaboration," which included workshops, panels, sub-forums, and roundtable discussions (Shengqing, Zhongni). It also created a platform for in-depth cooperation. The theme of the 2017 conference was "Global Perspectives on Student Learning and Development" and had more than 100 student affairs officers participate in the event (Fudan SAO, 2017).

Assessment:

Fudan's opening-up initiative was the leading international program of student affairs in China's higher education from 2014–2017 as most of Fudan's student affairs officers have participated in the initiative. Fudan University and the Shanghai educational commission funded programs under this initiative. As a result, we saw:

1. Significant growth in international exchange of student affairs practitioners. In 2016, five of Fudan's student affairs officers participated in NASPA's annual conference, and 53 student affairs officers went to universities and institutions in America, Australia, and Asia for a short-term visit or long-term internship. These numbers will continue to grow once more international projects are carried out.

2. Intercultural competency has become an important research topic for Fudan's student affairs area. These studies on intercultural competency could be used to provide advice for policy making and direct the student affairs daily practices in China.

3. Promotion of international collaboration through organizing conferences, exchanging staff, and building a cooperative framework has led to Fudan developing

ORGANIZATIONAL ALIGNMENT

relationships with 30 other universities in the student affairs field, and signing cooperative packages with different partners.

Lessons Learned:

Fudan has chosen the path to internationalize its student affairs profession, and has gained insight and perspective through this innovative initiative and process.

1. Learn from one another. The platform (conferences, networks, or visitings) could be varied; however, it always helps to start the dialogue.
2. Stable mechanism is essential. Once you establish the connection, it is vital to set up regular meetings, online calls, and so on, to execute the projects.
3. Combine practice and research. The professional student affairs practice requires theoretical support and theories reflective of practical experience.

In the context of globalization and campus diversification, Fudan's case clearly shows that the student affairs profession has encountered more and more multicultural circumstances, which requires theoretical support of intercultural competency and cross-national cooperation. As international vision remains one of the core values of the University's education, Fudan will continue its cross-national collaborations to solve the upcoming challenges and contribute to the student affairs professionalization under the context of globalization.

STUDENT SUPPORT AND SERVICES

A part of organizational structure and capacity building relates to the specific student support services and activities that fall under specific divisions and reporting structures. The US SSAOs reported that fewer than 45% of their divisions had direct supervision of international services, as shown in Table 4.3. The majority of surveyed HEIs separated out international education services from

Table 4.3 International Services Supervised by the Student Affairs Division

International and Internationalization Efforts	#	%
International student advising	30	45
International student and scholar services	28	42
International admissions	25	38
International recruitment	23	35
Study/education abroad	20	30
English language program/courses	14	21
Other international function	24	36

ORGANIZATIONAL ALIGNMENT

student affairs and had them report through academic affairs, thus creating a real and perceived barrier to collaboration and cross-divisional support or connection.

The SSAOs saw that providing services for international students as an informal or indirect way of supporting campus internationalization. The SSAO data shows that divisions need to re-envision how to work together to avoid pitfalls of divided functions and services. European institutions that excel at internationalization support a culture of internationalization through collaboration and infusing internationalization into everyone's work rather than isolating out services.

In addition to structural supervision of international services, about a quarter of our surveyed US SSAO respondents referenced and used the word "support" when discussing what internationalization meant for their division. Support most often referenced travel or mobility-related programs such as exchange, education abroad, and recruitment of international students. Other associated programs included those for international students such as orientations, visa and travel logistics, and/or programs for domestic students to increase global understanding and knowledge or to interact with international and culturally diverse students. If internationalization or international goals were present at any level (institutional, student affairs, or taskforce), then SSAOs reported being more engaged in providing services or support for international students. The most noticeable difference was at the institutional level. For HEIs that had internationally focused missions, 51% of SSAOs reported engaging in most of the activities listed in Table 4.4 compared to only 21% if their institutions did not have internationalization as a part of their mission.

While international students may not require more services than domestic students, they access them in different ways (Ward, 2015). International students report lack of awareness about the purpose and helpfulness of some support services offered on college campuses while staff are frustrated with their lack of use or how they try to use the services (Roberts & Dunworth, 2012; Yakaboski, Perez-Velez, & Almutairi, 2017). For Australian HEIs that have seen growth in

Table 4.4 Student Affairs Division/Staff Engagement in International Activities

Selection of activities	#	%
Hiring international students as student employees	68	71
International programs or speakers for students, staff, and faculty	62	65
International service learning trips	52	54
International admissions or recruiting	31	32
International branch campuses	7	7
Other	8	8

ORGANIZATIONAL ALIGNMENT

international student numbers, research shows expectations and satisfaction of services provided vary between students and staff with students wanting more support transitioning into the community and practitioners wanting students to engage with campus more (Roberts & Dunworth, 2012). A main barrier to international students' use of support services remains related to practitioners' lack of awareness of cultural differences and openness to non-native English speakers.

Student affairs divisions and related offices are integral stakeholders in providing services to international students and fostering a sense of belonging and inclusion with campus and the local community. Most institutions include international education and services that specifically assist international students with immigration-related issues and services, if not more. If international students encounter difficult times, they may have less familiarity with and comfort using existing services. Yet there is great potential and opportunity already in place, if students perceive services as interculturally inclusive. In the US, college or student unions can be critical places of partnership to support inclusive, diverse, and international programming and service provisions (Yakaboski & Perozzi, 2014). Many international student populations have diverse food and nutritional needs that vary from US students' expectations (Alakaam, Castellanos, Bodzio, & Harrison, 2015). College or student unions, dining halls, and retail food services can design menus that incorporate students into the planning of meals and recipes or food preparation such as for Halal and kosher meals. Student affairs can work to ensure institutional food providers offer daily religious and special (non-Christian) holiday menus and options and flexible meal plans. These decisions can be requirements in any request for a proposal (RFP) bid for new food vendors and providers and would go a long way in supporting students and an inclusive culture.

Incorporating IaH into all events rather than labeling specific ones as "international" may fix a common problem where domestic students often assume international events or programs are meant for international students and not them. There is a balance needed between creating inclusive spaces and services that support all student identities and when those identities are "othered" and segregated (Killick, 2015). International students and scholars currently at an institution can be great local resources to offering global and intercultural learning opportunities when done appropriately, meaning not assuming they are the expert on their home countries history, politics, religion, etc., but rather to share their personal experience and perspective (Ward, 2015). The primary areas supporting internationalization, international education, multicultural and cultural centers, academic affairs, and student affairs can all work closely together to support global learning outcomes.

In an award-winning example of providing educationally rich environments for students, the Promising Practice of Global Lounges from Nottingham Trent University (NTU) in the United Kingdom provides support for all students. These comfortable and well-resourced lounges serve multiple functions for international

97

ORGANIZATIONAL ALIGNMENT

and domestic students and NTU staff and faculty. The educational focus of the lounges is in alignment with the university's Connecting Globally strategy. The activities of the Global Lounges are overseen by the Global Student Experience (GSE) team comprised of practitioners and student employees. NTU's Global Lounges offer support to domestic and international students and staff by providing two convenient locations to meet, and offering a wide range of programs, cultural sharing, and internationalization advice.

PROMISING PRACTICE: NTU's Global Lounges

Institution: Nottingham Trent University

Location: Nottingham, United Kingdom

Author: Cheryl Rounsaville, Global Student Experience Manager, NTU Global*

Background and Context:

Nottingham Trent University (NTU) is a British HEI located in the East Midlands area of England. The University offers bachelors, master's, and doctoral degrees in a range of disciplines across four campuses. It has more than 28,000 students of which approximately 3,000 are international and European Union students. NTU has been ranked among the top 800 universities in the world according to the QS World Rankings and received the top rating of five stars for internationalisation.

NTU's Connecting Globally strategy, one of five university ambitions, states our commitment to internationalising the student experience for all students. The University aims to nurture global citizens by providing a chance for all students to internationalise their learning through a range of off-campus and on-campus international opportunities. Many of the on-campus opportunities/events/activities take place in, or are organized by, our award-winning Global Lounges, including our annual (university-wide) Global Week celebration.

Established in 2013, NTU's Global Lounges are focal points for our diverse range of international activities and opportunities and are multi-functional hubs that offer all NTU students and staff the opportunity to engage in internationalisation initiatives. The Global Lounges are located at NTU's City site and Clifton campus. The City site is in the center of the city of Nottingham, and the Clifton campus is about 20 minutes from the City site on the outskirts of Nottingham. The Global Student Experience team within NTU manage the Global Lounges and serve exchange students, international and EU students, UK home students, and NTU staff. In 2016, the Global Lounges won two NUS-UKCISA Internationalisation Awards for Excellence in International Student Support, and Innovation in Internationalising the Student Experience.

Further Description:

The Lounges provide international students with personal and social support, and opportunities for integration. They are unique events spaces that host a variety of cultural

98

ORGANIZATIONAL ALIGNMENT

events, workshops, and social gatherings to provide numerous opportunities for our international students to share their cultures and meet other students from around the world. Once a week, for example, the City Global Lounge holds a Global Community Lunch, a social event where students have an opportunity to socialize with other students from around the world. The attendance at this lunch is anywhere from 150–200 students per week and is funded by the University to ensure all students have access to an international learning experience. The Lounges also provide a safe and comfortable space for international students to relax between/after classes.

Throughout the year, we work with our international students to develop cultural events where these students have the opportunity to showcase their cultures to other students. Our cultural events have included Chinese New Year, Diwali, Eid, Kurdish New Year, Nigerian Independence Day, and American Thanksgiving. We provide funding and logistical support, while the students determine how to run the event and what activities to have. In addition, every year the Lounges organize Global Week, a celebration of the diversity at NTU through art, music, dance, sport, and food. We celebrate a different world region from which our students come (including the UK and Europe) every day of Global Week. Students are encouraged, supported, and funded by the Global Lounges to develop cultural stalls to showcase their cultures to other students and staff. This event takes place across our three main campuses. This year we were delighted that students from 53 countries engaged with the programme.

The Lounges employ students from different regions of the world to act as Global Lounge Assistants (GLAs), which are similar to student ambassadors. The GLAs provide a friendly face for students using the Lounges and are responsible for introducing students during events to promote an international community. We also employ a student placement, usually an international postgraduate student, whose focus is increasing student engagement. The GLAs and student placement posts also give international students an opportunity to obtain some work experience.

Information sessions are held in the Lounges with various support departments from within the university (e.g., Student Services, Students' Union, Careers & Employability) to inform international students about the resources available to them. Outside of these sessions and on a daily basis, the Lounges do a lot of signposting or referring students to various university services.

The Lounges are also places for UK students to be inspired to learn more about global issues. This year we introduced weekly Language Cafes at City and Clifton where students and staff can practice speaking other languages. The Cafes have been well received by students interested in other languages and the English table has been particularly popular with international students wanting to improve their English language skills. While engaging home students still remains a challenge for the Global Lounges we have seen an increasing number of these students at our events. During Global Week 2017, we were pleased to find that more than half of the students who attended the celebrations were home students!

ORGANIZATIONAL ALIGNMENT

Goals and Outcomes:

- Create an inclusive and welcoming international community at NTU where all students and staff feel valued regardless of national or ethnic origin.
- Offer opportunities for all students to internationalise their learning, broaden their cultural perspectives, develop cross-cultural skills, and become true global citizens.
- Provide support to staff to internationalise their own experience and curriculum to help their students become global citizens.

To achieve these goals, the Lounges offer many on-campus opportunities, events, and activities to all students and staff that promote internationalisation, cultural sharing, and the development of an international community. All events are free and open to all students and staff so that no one is limited from accessing them. The mission of the Lounges not only includes the development of extra-curricular international opportunities, they are also responsible for supporting our International Mobility team to promote off-campus (but often built into the curriculum) international opportunities such as study abroad, exchange, work placements abroad, and international volunteering projects. Each Lounge has a resource corner for students who want to participate in these off-campus opportunities that provide more information on our international partnerships, the various overseas programs, and funding available to students, as well as a range of travel guides for students to learn about their potential country of study. The Global Lounge is open all year but most events and activities take place in term-time.

The Global Lounges work with teams from across the University such as the International Development Office (international student recruitment office), International Student Support Services (visa advising), the Students' Union, Careers & Employability, International Volunteering, the Mobility (study abroad) team, and many academic departments. These partnerships are critical in supporting international students as well as providing an international learning experience for UK home students. We collaborate with International Student Support Services on the key events and activities for international students during the University's welcome week at the beginning of the academic year.

Staff are welcome to attend all Global Lounge events and we also promote staff opportunities for internationalising their experience such as those offered through the Erasmus+ programme. We hope that staff will bring these experiences back to the classroom as part of the curriculum and share the experiences with their students, encouraging them to have their own international experiences. The Global Student Experience Manager also provides support to staff through offering advice on various ways to internationalise their curriculum because NTU's Connecting Globally strategy requires all curriculum to be internationalised.

Assessment:

Our international students tell us these opportunities to share their cultures with the support of the Global Lounges makes them feel welcomed and valued.

100

ORGANIZATIONAL ALIGNMENT

The Lounges have had a positive impact on international students who now feel they have a place at the university where they can find personal and social support, or just go to hang out and relax. One student said: "The Global Lounge is an enrichment to the experience of Uni, bringing with it a Global Integration of people, communities, countries and the world!"

Before the Global Lounges we had no central space to highlight international opportunities or create an international community. Since they opened in 2013, interest in all things international has increased with more interest in student mobility and our cultural/social events. After nearly four years we now have a thriving space that welcomes more than 10,000 students each year to our events and activities.

The work of the Lounges in partnership with our Mobility team has led to a 10% increase in uptake in study abroad this academic year and increased uptake of language learning, summer schools, and other international opportunities.

Lessons Learned:

1. Student engagement is key to the success of these kinds of initiatives and is something that needs to be worked on all year round not just immediately before an event—this refers to both getting students to lead events/activities but also to having student ambassadors/student placements who focus on engaging other students.
2. Make on-campus international events free for all so that access is not limited for students—international students are particularly price conscious and may not engage if they have to pay to participate—and this means you need a healthy budget to work with.
3. Prioritise student-led, student organised, and student-focused events and activities.
4. Relationship building with colleagues across the University is critical to achieving the goals of these kinds of initiatives.

Media Links:

NTU Global Lounge Webpages:

www4.ntu.ac.uk/current_students/while_here/global_lounge/index.html
www.ntu.ac.uk/university-life-and-nottingham/student-life/life-outside-lectures/ntu-global-lounges
https://ntuglobalweek.com/
(Global Week is an annual event organized by the Global Lounges)

NTU Global Lounge Social Media Sites:

www.facebook.com/NTUGlobalLounge/
https://twitter.com/ntugloballounge?lang=en
www.instagram.com/ntugloballounge/

*NTU Global is NTU's international office and has a remit for all aspects of internationalisation except international student recruitment in the traditional sense.

101

NEW STAFF HIRING, ON-BOARDING, AND ORIENTATION

A final component to supporting internationalization at the divisional or organizational level of student affairs includes leveraging human resources to build high-performing teams that focus on global perspectives and world challenges. Bringing new employees into organizations is a critical task and an opportunity to recruit and hire those with experience and/or ideas that align with globalism and have an interest in internationalization (Parsons & Söderqvist, 2005; Taylor, 2010). Developing job descriptions to include international and intercultural knowledge, skills, and attitudes is a structural decision that can help shift organizational culture. While every job may not focus largely on supporting internationalization strategies, implementing international education, or direct work with international students, all jobs can reflect the ability to collaborate and understand global trends, support internationalization strategies, and promote self and students' intercultural development. Job and position requirements can highlight the importance of international and intercultural experiences whether they be local or global in nature and the need for practitioners to pursue intercultural development. Ultimately, without hiring practitioners who are sensitive to interculturalism and supportive of international perspectives, internationalization efforts or programs success will be limited.

If recruiting non-US staff, it is good to keep in mind that educational and experiential backgrounds will vary and this is a benefit that adds new perspectives. Non-US applicants may not have educational backgrounds like those of US student affairs practitioners. With a master's degree in higher education and/or student affairs increasingly a preferred minimum qualification, this can limit the pool of non-US applicants. Student affairs practitioners in many countries come to their roles from the faculty ranks or have worked in other sectors of the economy, such as hospitality, counseling, or health (Perozzi, Seifert, & Bodine Al-Sharif, 2016), which is underscored by the diversity of the Promising Practices authors' bios showcased in this book. It is difficult for non-US individuals to obtain a degree in student affairs administration as very few graduate programs exist globally and are not likely to be necessary outside of the US.

Many of those working in student affairs in the US have an advanced degree in HESA or a related field, which shapes the way in which they view the world. These graduate preparation programs have influenced practitioners' paradigms for many years, and set the foundation for the work that they do, which further supports the need to internationalize graduate preparation curriculum. In the global community of student affairs practice, options abound for graduates to enter careers in the US or to take on roles in student affairs in other countries either as ex-patriots or nationals. For example, Roberts (2015) suggests that the influence of Western education globally has created a desire in some areas, such as the Middle East, to hire US student affairs practitioners to provide leadership at various levels in their organizations, while fostering and supporting domestic employees.

102

ORGANIZATIONAL ALIGNMENT

Working as an ex-patriot outside of one's home country can be a valuable experience for practitioners yet requires a high level of intercultural competency.

Unless hired into an international education office, most new staff members may not have the opportunity to continue implementing internationalization or developing their intercultural competencies. Practitioners may yearn for intercultural experiences and seek programs that can help them develop related skills. Therefore, the time for socialization and training occurs after hiring new staff when there is a critical period to familiarize them with the values and culture of a student affairs division and department (Davenport, 2016; Tull, Hirt, & Saunders, 2009). On-boarding and orientation programs can be a valuable place to incorporate international and intercultural exposure for all staff members regardless of functional area or position as any person may have contact with students and require the support necessary to operationalize institutional and division goals and the societal need for global citizens. The University of California, Berkeley, has developed a robust on-boarding process, taking place over time, at multiple levels within their organization. Part of the on-boarding process can be sharing division and departmental documents, which is why it is important to include internationalization or intercultural development within goals, program mission statements, or value statements. Supervisors understanding these documents and philosophies, and how to incorporate them into staff training or individualized professional development plans, is equally important.

CONCLUSION

In this rapidly changing global society, SSAOs, practitioners, and faculty play a more prominent role in supporting an internationalized vision that aligns the academic mission of higher education with global learning. While many US SSAOs recommended, or stressed, the importance of top-down or presidential-level prioritization of internationalization, there is evidence that student affairs divisions are still doing good work in incorporating internationalization within their own division, given limited additional resources for this purpose. Institutional prioritization matters, but it is not a game stopper as divisions still provide essential services related to internationalization, such as providing basic programs and services, and supporting student engagement. Student affairs can work on internationalization in a systematic or intentional manner. As multicultural and cultural centers have long been collaborating to create meaningful cultural experiences, these practitioners make ideal partners in changing the system to be more intercultural. Student affairs historically has been a frontrunner in advocating for student changes and needs, this pattern can continue in the areas of internationalization and intercultural development through collaboration and partnerships.

Diffuse alignments across various HEI divisions and departments, combined with the complexity of stakeholders and leadership roles among faculty, staff, students, and community members, can create challenges to coordinating efforts

103

and communication across institutions. Student affairs can be a major player in internationalization by understanding and leveraging the structure of the division or area, and by strategically aligning with areas outside of the functional core, especially those areas working with key elements of internationalization and diversity. Working across divisions, particularly with students and academic affairs, is critical, as internationalization is an organization-wide process, and necessarily cuts across many boundaries and structural alignments. Moving past the more routine programs and services for both international and domestic students to dynamic services and activities that embrace learning and practice intercultural competency is what transforms organizations to powerful supporters of a global agenda. Institutionalizing these concepts within organizational structures can be one of the most impactful ways to embed internationalization into the fabric of campus culture, increasing access to the skills and knowledge necessary to thrive in a global marketplace and society.

REFERENCES

Alakaam, A. A., Castellanos, D. C., Bodzio, J., & Harrison, L. (2015). The factors that influence dietary habits among international students in the United States. *Journal of International Students*, *5*(2), 104–120.

Ambler, D. (2000). Organizational and administrative models. In M. J. Barr, M. K. Desler, & Associates (Eds.), *The handbook of student affairs administration* (pp. 121–133). San Francisco, CA: Jossey-Bass.

Chun, E., & Evans, A. (2016). Rethinking cultural competence in higher education: An ecological framework for student development. *ASHE Higher Education Report*, *42*(4), 6–170.

Davenport, Z. R. (2016). Recruiting, selecting, supervising, and retaining staff. In G. S. McClellan & J. Stringer (Eds.), *The handbook of student affairs administration*, 4th ed. (pp. 389–410). San Francisco, CA: Jossey-Bass.

Edwards, J. (2007). Challenges and opportunities for the internationalization of higher education in the coming decade: Planned and opportunistic initiatives in American institutions. *Journal of Studies in International Education*, *11*(3/4), 373–381.

Engel, L., Sandström, A., van der Aa, R., & Glass, A. (2014). *The EAIE barometer: internationalisation in Europe*. Amsterdam, The Netherlands: EAIE.

Fudan's student affairs office. (2017). 复旦大学 2017 学生工作国际研讨会举行 [Fudan University 2017 International Seminar on Student Work Held]. Retrieved from http://news.fudan.edu.cn/2017/0609/43957.html

Heijer, J., Walenkamp, J., & Hoven, R. F. M. (2015). *Study or internship abroad and the acquisition of international competencies*. The Hague, The Netherlands: Haagse Hogeschool/The Hague University of Applied Sciences, Research Group International Cooperation.

Hudzik, J. (2015). *Comprehensive internationalization: Institutional pathways to success*. New York: Routledge.

Jones, E. (2013). The global reach of universities: Leading and engaging academic and support staff in the internationalisation of higher education. In R. Sugden, M. Valania & J. R. Wilson (Eds), *Leadership and cooperation in academia: Reflecting on the roles and responsibilities of university faculty and management* (pp. 161–183). Cheltenham, UK: Edward Elgar.

Killick, D. (2015). *Developing the global student: Higher education in an era of globalization*. New York: Routledge.

Koehn, P. H., Deardorff, D. K., & Bolognese, K. D. (2011). Enhancing international research and development-project activity on university campuses: Insights from U.S. senior international officers. *Journal of Studies in International Education*, *15*(4), 332–350.

Knight, J. (2003). Updated definition of internationalization. *International Higher Education*, *33*, 2–3.

Love, P. G., & Estaneck, S. M. (2004). *Rethinking student affairs practice*. San Francisco, CA: Jossey-Bass.

Manning, K., Kinzie, J., & Schuh, J. H. (2014). *One size does not fit all: Traditional and innovative models of student affairs practice*, 2nd ed. New York: Routledge.

Murray, D., Goedegebuure, L., van Liempdt, H., & Vermeulen, M. (2014). *Leadership needs in international higher education in Australia and Europe: Final report of a Delphi study*. Amsterdam, The Netherlands: EAIE.

Nolan, R. W. (2015). The senior international officer—an advocate for change. In G. W. Merkx and R. W. Nolan (Eds.), *Internationalizing the academy: Lessons of leadership in higher education* (pp. 23–36). Cambridge, MA: Harvard UP.

Olson, C., Evans, R., & Shoenberg, R. E. (2007). *At home in the world: Bridging the gap between internationalization and multicultural education*. Washington, D.C.: ACE.

Parsons, C., & Söderqvist, M. (2005). *Managing internationalisation in higher education*. EAIE occasional paper 18. Amsterdam, The Netherlands: EAIE.

Perozzi, B., Giovannucci, G. L., & Shea, R. (2016). *The global dialogue*. In K. Osfield, B. Perozzi, L. Bardill Moscaritolo, and R. Shea (Eds.), *Supporting students globally in higher education* (pp. 21–42). Washington, D.C: NASPA.

Perozzi, B., Seifert, T., & Bodine Al-Sharif, M. A. (2016). Staffing for success. In D. Roberts & S. Komives (Eds.), *Enhancing student learning and development in cross-border higher education: New directions for higher education* (pp. 93–103). San Francisco, CA: Jossey-Bass.

Roberts, P., & Dunworth, K. (2012). Staff and student perceptions of support services for international students in higher education: A case study. *Journal of Higher Education Policy and Management*, *34*(5), 517–528.

Roberts, D. C. (2015). Internationalizing higher education and student affairs. *About Campus*, *20*(2), 8–15.

Shengqing, Zhongni 盛情,钟妮. (2015). "全球化背景下的学生工作专业化与国际合作国际研讨会在我校举行"全球化、跨文化、专业、发展、合作成高频用词 [The international conference on student affairs, themed Professionalization of Student Affairs and

International Collaboration, successfully held at Fudan University]. Retrieved from http://news.fudan.edu.cn/2015/0609/39187.html

Spencer-Oatey, H., & Dauber. D. (2015). *How internationalized is your university? From structural indicators to an agenda for integration.* GlobalPAD Working papers. Retrieved from www.warwick.ac.uk/globalpadintercultural

Taylor, J. (2010). The management of internationalization in higher education. In F. Maringe, & N. Foskett (Eds.), *Globalization and internationalization in higher education: Theoretical, strategic and management perspectives* (pp. 97–108). London: Continuum.

The Hague University of Applied Sciences/ Haagse Hogeschool. (2014). Global Citizens in a Learning Society. Internationalisation at THUAS 2015–2020 Strategic Plan. The Hague, The Netherlands: Author.

Tull, A., Hirt, J. B., & Saunders, S. A. (2009). *Becoming socialized in student affairs administration: A guide for new professionals and their supervisors.* Sterling, VA: Stylus.

University of California, Berkeley. (2017). Onboarding. Retrieved from http://sa.berkeley.edu/ld/onboarding

Walenkamp, J. (2013). *Looking over the dunes: A conference on educating world citizens.* Haagse Hogeschool/ The Hague University of Applied Sciences, Research Group International Cooperation.

Ward, H. H. (2015). *Internationalizing the co-curriculum: Part one: Integrating international students.* Washington, D.C.: ACE. Retrieved from www.acenet.edu/news-room/Documents/Intlz-In-Action-Intlz-Co-Curriculum-Part-1.pdf

Ward, H. H. (2016). *Internationalizing the co-curriculum: Part three: Internationalization and student affairs.* Washington, D.C.: ACE. Retrieved from www.acenet.edu/news-room/Documents/Intlz-In-Action-Intlz-Co-Curriculum-Part-3.pdf

Xinhua news agency. (2016a). 全国高校思想政治工作会议交流发言摘登 [National conference on ideological and moral education in China's University]. Retrieved from www.moe.edu.cn/jyb_xwfb/s6319/zb_2016n/2016_zb08/201612/t20161208_291276.html

Xinhua news agency. (2016b). 中办国办印发《关于做好新时期教育对外开放工作的若干意见》坚持扩大开放 做强中国教育 [Opinions on education opening-up in the new era]. Retrieved from www.moe.edu.cn/jyb_xwfb/s6052/moe_838/201605/t20160503_241658.html

Yakaboski, T., Perez-Velez, K., & Almutairi, Y. (2017). Breaking the silence: Saudi graduate student experiences on a U.S. campus. *Journal of Diversity in Higher Education.* Advance online publication. http://dx.doi.org/10.1037/dhe0000059

Yakaboski, T., & Perozzi, B. (2014). Globalization and college unions. In T. Yakaboski, & D. M. De Sawal, (Eds.), *The state of the (college) union: Contemporary issues and trends: New Directions for Student Services* (pp. 79–90). San Francisco, CA: Jossey-Bass.

Yakaboski, T. (2017). Perceptions of international educators and professionals: A consideration of Dutch internationalization efforts using neo-institutional theory to understanding mainstreaming pressures. Paper presented at annual conference of the Consortium of Higher Education Researchers, Jyväskylä, Finland.

Chapter 5

Student Engagement and the Cocurriculum

Even with the internationalization of US higher education gaining prominence, only about 56% of institutions emphasize global student learning outcomes and internationalizing academic curriculum, and these are more common at research universities (American Council on Education (ACE), 2017). The National Survey of Student Engagement (NSSE) survey statistics show that one in five first-year students in the US do not plan to take any courses that focus on global trends or issues (Kinzie, Helms, & Cole, 2017). Further, only half of all US seniors report having taken a course on global trends or issues or on non-US regions or countries. Based on the first year of data from NSSE's global learning module, US students gain only a very basic level of global learning through their academic careers. However, "global engagement—which includes five items related to discussing international topics, attending global events, and planning programs—has the strongest positive relationship with the composite measure of global gains" (Kinzie et al., 2017, para. 13). The connection between continued exposure to global learning and engagement is good news for the work of student affairs. Internationalization at Home (IaH) of the cocurriculum includes how faculty and practitioners work with all students in programs that drive interactions and intercultural development, and to what extent all students engage in cocurricular opportunities, such as formal leadership programs, student employment, and inclusive programming.

However, internationalizing the cocurriculum can be more challenging than the internationalization of the curriculum itself as it presents these unique challenges:

- Cocurricular programs often influence, and are influenced by, institutional culture, which is deeply engrained and can be slow to transform.
- The cocurriculum encompasses a wide range of services and programs, making it difficult to identify where and how to direct internationalization efforts.

STUDENT ENGAGEMENT AND THE COCURRICULUM

- Student participation in cocurricular activities is almost always voluntary, and levels of engagement vary.
- Without attendance records, academic credit, or grades, it can be difficult to assess student learning as a result of participation in cocurricular programs.

(Ward, 2015b, p. 2)

Even with these challenges, internationalization of the cocurriculum offers important experiential learning "where students encounter cultural" others, "navigate shared space, learn to manage conflict, calibrate their moral compasses, and test their leadership skills" (Ward, 2015b, p. 2) with benefit in the overlap of internationalization and diversity and social justice and inclusion (SJI) learning outcomes.

Student affairs practitioners regularly apply the principles of engagement as "the time and effort students devote to activities that are empirically linked to desired outcomes of college and what institutions do to induce students to participate in these activities" (Kuh, 2009, p. 683). Environments in which students feel supported to practice and apply key learning principles, and partner in the learning process can foster engagement. Students can acquire essential intercultural competencies through internationalized cocurriculum that includes global learning outcomes. Decades of research show that US majority students receive benefits of increased persistence and greater academic success through meaningful engagement and involvement (Astin, 1984; Kuh, 2009; Kuh, Kinzie, Schuh, Whitt, & Associates, 2011; Pascarella & Terezini, 2005). However, as more recent research has shown, students from diverse backgrounds benefit from engagement and involvement to varying degrees. Many other countries do not yet have research on their own student populations to determine if deep engagement in cocurricular programs has similar benefits. Some organizations like NSSE are working closely with institutions outside of the US to develop culturally appropriate tools to measure student learning and engagement.

Cocurricular programs can be intentional about including internationalization and intercultural development so that students develop a wide range of relevant skills and abilities to be competitive in a global economy. Learning outcomes for the workforce, commonly called "soft skills" in Europe and elsewhere, include teamwork, leadership, creativity, and the ability to communicate effectively cross-culturally, which can increase the "employability" of college graduates (Cinque, Perozzi, Bardill Moscaritolo, & Miano, 2017). This chapter discusses inclusive opportunities for intercultural competency development through cocurriculum programs of student leadership, global citizenship, employment, and inclusive programming to enhance the global learning outcomes for all students.

108

STUDENT LEADERSHIP

Leadership programs are common in student affairs worldwide because they provide opportunities to "teach students to anticipate with curiosity how encounters with diverse identities will strengthen their capacity to solve problems" (Glass, Wongtrirat, & Buus, 2015, p. 40). Formalized leadership roles in student government and student organizations, or opportunities with student activism, can assist students in attaining an increased understanding of intercultural competence along with other important leadership skills. In the US, student government, student organizations, and leadership programs often fall under the functional area of student affairs, where practitioners can apply a student development framework in advising and supporting (Whipple & O'Neill, 2011). Campus-based leadership opportunities are popular cocurricular activities for both domestic and international students alike (Glass et al., 2015).

At Tshwane University of Technology in South Africa, leadership development is a centerpiece of their student engagement strategy, where they coordinate different programs for students that partner with the local Pretoria community (Gugulethu Xaba, personal communication, 2015). Leadership programs allow faculty and practitioners to design intentional interactions and discussions between international and domestic students within the program. The Pontificia Universidad Javeriana in Bogotá, Colombia, offers students a structured program, Liderazgo Ignaciano, focused on transformational leadership with 14 sessions to build peer-to-peer relationships and personal leadership skills to assist them in their community projects (Reyes, 2017). Another example comes from the Promising Practice at Duke Kunshan University (DKU) in China, where their Student Leadership Development Program centers on the key intercultural concepts and skills of global consciousness and civic responsibility. DKU students engage in multiple modalities, like group work and mentorship, while recognizing both Eastern and Western approaches to leadership through various workshops.

PROMISING PRACTICE: Student Leadership Development Program

Institution Name: Duke Kunshan University

Location: Kunshan, Jiangsu Province, People's Republic of China

Authors:
Howard S. Wang, Associate Dean & Adjunct Professor of Education, Student Affairs
Jia Zheng, Residence Life Officer, Student Affairs

Background and Context:
University students go through different "tasks" while developing their identity, including developing competence, managing emotions, moving through autonomy to independence,

STUDENT ENGAGEMENT AND THE COCURRICULUM

developing purpose, and establishing mature interpersonal relationships (Chickering & Reisser, 1993). The "90s generation" of Chinese students mostly come from "one-child families" with unique characteristics, including being sociable, contrary to popular belief that Chinese students demonstrate weak social skills. However, they have weak or no self-identity, have difficulty managing conflicts or stress, tend not to compromise yet find it difficult to say "no" to parents, and are not ready for hardship due to a lack of clear understanding of what "success" is (Wong, 2016).

Duke Kunshan University (DKU) is a joint-venture liberal arts university with partnership between Duke University and Wuhan University, located in Kunshan, Jiangsu Province, China. The mission of DKU is to prepare students for professional, intellectual, and societal leadership roles across the globe, with one of the educational principles of "pluralism, tolerance and a willingness to engage with and learn from others in preparation for living, working and leading—effectively and ethically—in an inter-connected, multi-cultural world" (para. 2). DKU currently has 175 students, with four graduate degree programs and a semester-long program—Global Learning Semester Program. The Global Learning Semester is designed for undergraduate students cur-rently enrolled in other accredited institutions in China and around the world, generally in their second or third year of undergraduate studies, with a minimum GPA (grade point average) of 3.0 or a ranking in the top 25% of their class.

Responding to this generation of undergraduate students' developmental needs, a one-semester long pilot program called the Student Leadership Development Program was designed by the Office of Student Affairs at DKU to help students explore self-identity, establish personal goals, and develop leadership knowledge and skills to succeed in the dynamic global context. Sixteen Global Learning Semester students were selected through applications and interviews, with 15 Chinese students from universities in China and 1 Brazilian student from a US university. The students ranged from sopho-more to senior and not all are in formal student leadership positions, but are all interested in enhancing skills and exploring identities as "leaders" through the program.

Further Description:

The components of the Leadership Program include workshops, experiential learning activities, mentorship, full-day leadership training, two-day outdoor challenge, review sessions, and a group project. Each student must attend 7 mandatory workshops, and is encouraged to attend several optional ones. Workshops spark conversation among students on intercultural competence in the context of leadership. Workshops include "Leadership in Different Cultural Contexts," "Western" vs "Eastern" Leadership Styles, "Women's Leadership" and several others. Conceptions of good leadership differ across cultures. In China, good leadership means "benevolence, dignified/aloof but sym-pathetic," whereas in the US, good leaders are those who "empower and encourage subordinates; or are bold, confident, and risk-oriented" (Plaister-Ten, 2017, p. 5). The women's leadership panel discussions provide a platform for students to discuss gender differences in the context of leadership, including the differences between men and women. The program also introduces students to "ethical leadership" through case

110

STUDENT ENGAGEMENT AND THE COCURRICULUM

studies where students learn about the definitions of ethical leadership, why we need ethical leadership, and how to be an ethical leader who can not only "think into a way of action" but more importantly, "act into a way of thinking" (Gentile, 2010).

Each student must complete at least 10 hours of one or more activities such as initiating or serving in officer roles in clubs and organizations, volunteering at campus events or community service agencies, serving as student leaders in residential life, or working as student interns. The student identifies one or two of the five listed areas (see below in "Goals and Outcomes") to improve upon, under the guidance of a mentor. Mentors are selected from current faculty and senior administrators from DKU and are from diverse backgrounds, including both Chinese and US. In addition, mentees participate or observe mentor's work, such as a project the mentor is involved in, a staff meeting that the mentor is attending, or a field trip led by the mentor. During discussion with mentors on issues of leadership, students are exposed to different experiences and perspectives that inspire them to reflect on their own culture and opinions.

For the group project, the program facilitator deliberately groups students with different cultural backgrounds together, including Chinese with US, Northern China with Southern China, etc. A full day of training is provided for students to work in their assigned groups and complete different tasks together. At the end of the training, students reflect on the group dynamics and learn about how to collaborate with individuals from different cultural backgrounds. This program concludes with an awards/closing banquet event in which all participants receive completion certificates issued by the university as well as at the Global Learning Semester Closing Ceremony.

Goals, Outcomes, and Future Plans:

The program aims at preparing emerging leaders who contribute to the DKU campus, communities, and future global contexts. The program integrates with students' overall experiences and provides an opportunity beyond the classroom for students to grasp skills and competencies that are essential in the 21st century work force, including:

- Self-management (self-awareness, goal setting, time- and stress-management).
- Social and civic responsibility (commitment to social issues, community service, service learning).
- Leadership competence (decision-making, problem-solving, communication, collaboration).
- Professionalism (team spirit, conflict resolution, ethics).
- Diversity and global consciousness (intercultural competence).

With the establishment of the Undergraduate Degree Program in 2018, we are planning to expand the program to one year as part of the first-year experience. We hope the sophomore leadership students can play the role of "mentors" for first-year students, and can have equal say in how the program should be designed and implemented to further develop their leadership skills as well as supporting first-year student leadership development. With the expansion of the program, we are also looking at turning it into a one-unit course in the future.

111

STUDENT ENGAGEMENT AND THE COCURRICULUM

Assessment:

Pre-assessment questionnaires and one-on-one interviews were completed with each student and post-assessment questionnaires and one-on-one interviews with individual students will be conducted after completion of the program to assess students' learning outcomes. Pre-and post-assessment are completed for each workshop and training to find out students' learning outcomes. Mid-semester and end-of-semester review sessions are conducted, and reflection papers are used for students to reflect on their leadership experiences. Meetings with mentors collect feedback on their mentorship experience and suggestions to improve the program.

Lessons Learned:

1. The one-on-one, face-to-face mentorship component is the highlight of the program. Preference from mentees or mentors should be taken into consideration when matching mentees with mentors. A current focus is to improve the mentor selection process, training for mentors, and whether to consider having a "one mentor and two mentees" model when the number of student participants increases or adopt the "board of mentors" model in which one student has a number of mentors. The latter may give mentors less pressure, but may not achieve the close relationship established through one-on-one mentorship.

2. Commitments from mentors vary. Among the current 14 mentors, the majority of them are willing to meet with the students on a regular basis. However, some mentors are far too busy to meet with their mentees. So, some have to rely on online interaction, which is less effective compared with face-to-face communication. When we have more students participating in the leadership program in the future, we will need to recruit more mentors both internally and externally and also need to take into account the commitment level of the mentors.

3. It is beneficial to have both international and Chinese students in the leadership program. It provides students the opportunity to work with individuals from diverse cultural backgrounds and expose them to different perspectives, ideas, and values and equips them with intercultural competence and interpersonal communication skills for future study and work, as well as increasing self-awareness and identity. Marketing must be both broadened and targeted in the future to attract more international students.

4. The pilot program is one semester long and all the components are squeezed into four months. This puts pressure on students, mentors, and administrators in completing the program successfully. Once we have the four-year undergraduate program, the leadership development program should expand to one-year for first and second-year students.

Media Links:

Housing and Residence Life: https://dukekunshan.edu.cn/en/student-life/residence-life

Kunshan Student Ambassador Council (KSAC) 昆山杜克 KSAC on WeChat

STUDENT ENGAGEMENT AND THE COCURRICULUM

Leadership participation can help international students make sense of their experiences with local diversity, their own identities, and create a sense of belonging and inclusion. Old Dominion University in Norfolk, Virginia, created an International Student Advisory Board to advocate to senior administrators on behalf of international students and their related concerns (Glass et al., 2015). International student advisory boards or student councils can vary by the composition of members, responsibilities, reporting structure, decision-making authority or programming responsibilities, all dependent upon which model fits the organizational needs and culture (Ward, 2015a). In the US, college unions have offered students leadership roles on advisory boards that can be inclusive of international students and have learning outcomes that reflect intercultural communication for all involved (Yakaboski & Perozzi, 2014).

Throughout student affairs, support of student organizations and groups comes from student activities, residence life, and college unions, to name a few. Many SSAOs in our study reported that they advise international student clubs and organizations and occasionally domestic students engage in these clubs or organizations. Student organizations often serve as support to incoming international students, as in this example from an SSAO at a public research university in Washington:

> Student Publications supervises a new Mandarin radio station and it is paying off in many ways. Not only do they help educate and orient Chinese students, it also assists with recruitment throughout parts of China. It's still small, but it is paying large dividends . . . for the school and the students involved.

Since student organizations exist worldwide, they can be a platform to work with students on intercultural skill development that may positively impact academic performance and achievement (Hawkins, 2010). Many of the Promising Practices showcased throughout this book incorporate opportunities for domestic and international students to develop programs for their peers or use student organizations to advance advocacy and cultural education.

In the US, participation in student government develops leaders' competencies and skills as well as self-esteem and confidence (Whipple & O'Neill, 2011). Outside of the US, student union representatives, elected by their peers, function a bit more independently and politically than US student government at most HEIs. All these experiences develop leadership skills and networks to gain employment, sometimes in government, nonprofits, and corporate advancement after graduation. Unlike the terms student or college unions that are common in the US, student union outside of the US more often references student body governance with connection to national politics such as in Kenya (Yakaboski, 2011; Yakaboski & Birnbaum, 2013). During their tenure, UK student union representatives work with university administrators and government officials to advocate for academic

113

STUDENT ENGAGEMENT AND THE COCURRICULUM

and wellness issues on behalf of the student body in addition to planning social events or engaging in lobbying (Brooks, Byford, & Sela, 2015). In a study on student leadership in Nigeria, students are relegated to decision-making about other students rather than institutional level decisions (Oni & Adetoro, 2015). Comparably, in Germany, the local Studentenwerk, which functions independently from the university, supports students through social, housing, and cultural services to help them successfully maintain study status and wellness (Oste, 2009). In another example from the National Union of University Students in Finland, students lobbied to oppose legislation that would introduce tuition fees in the Finnish higher education system where previously no students paid tuition fees (Weimer, 2015). These examples are a few that reflect student government positions to address student welfare issues like dining, housing, and health, sometimes in collaboration with student support practitioners and faculty.

Working with student leaders across HEIs globally includes developing and supporting their involvement in campus and community activism. Compared to counterparts around the world, US student leaders have less of a historical and structural connection to politics compared to how student unions around the world function. However, the surge of student activism in the US points to the need for increased cultural and intercultural competencies and the need to understand social issues through a global social justice lens. The Occupy Wall Street Movement is one example. It spread to HEI campuses across the US with student protests and sit-ins against the establishment not recognizing the varied socioeconomic situations of different segments of the US population (Rhoads, 2016). Also, the Black Lives Matter movement, while not originating on HEI campuses, has seen involvement from students with campus protests around the world and faculty creating new curriculum to address issues (Rhoads, 2016). Similarly, students in South Africa, with the Twitter handle #FeesMustFall, protested increases to higher education fees, first, at institutions that primarily served Black students who suffered most from lack of funding and, then, spread across the country (Moja, Luescher, & Schreiber, 2015). At Tshwane University of Technology, practitioners have been integral as liaisons between students and senior-level institutional officials in efforts to help students understand fiscal realities while relaying social realities of students' demands to administrators (Gugulethu Xaba, personal communication, 2015). These tensions among students play out in countless ways, and practitioners help students make sense of the issues and conflicts to process them in the most productive ways that lead to growth and understanding (Birgit Shreiber, personal communication, 2016).

Student affairs practitioners most frequently interact with students outside of the classroom, and manage situations that result from government action, institutional policy, and social unrest. In response to historical student activism in the Chilean higher education system and government, practitioners at Pontificia Universidad Católica de Chile created the showcased Promising Practice Leader-

114

STUDENT ENGAGEMENT AND THE COCURRICULUM

ship and Student Activism program to support and educate student leaders. The program supports both elected student leaders and volunteer leaders of social projects. It uses a project-based learning methodology where students incorporate theory and experiential learning to work on social problems within their communities while developing leadership skills including team and self-management.

PROMISING PRACTICE: Leadership and Student Activism Development

Institution: Pontificia Universidad Católica de Chile

Location: Santiago & Villarrica, Chile

Authors:
María Soledad Cruz, Director University Life/Student Affairs
Priscila Gallardo, Students Representative Leaders Coordinator/Student Affairs
Ivonne Moraga, Students Social Leaders Coordinator/Student Affairs
William Young, Director of Student Affairs/Student Affairs

Background and Context:

In Chile, there has been a tradition of creating spaces in universities where students can express their voice. In the 1960s this reached its peak when student presence had great bearing on the reforms made to the university system. By the end of the 1980s, students once again exerted political pressure during the dictatorship. In 1997, a large student mobilization of secondary and higher education students formed, the first since the return to democracy in 1989, demanding greater quality and participation in the educational projects of their institutions. This resulted in many institutions generating greater interest, especially from student affairs, in communication and the creation of opportunities for participation.

The Pontificia Universidad Católica de Chile (UC) is a private, non-profit, internationally recognized university founded in 1888, with the goal of being an institution that integrates academic excellence and education inspired by Christian doctrine. It has 24,446 undergraduate students and 4,075 graduate students, with campuses located in the Chilean cities of Santiago and Villarrica. In UC's Institutional Development Plan (2015–2020) it is clear that "The commitment that the university has is not only with forming competent professionals in their fields of study . . . We are aware of this challenge and we will continue making efforts so that our graduates are recognized as people with an integral development [of students] . . . " (p. 17). The relevance of developing an active university life is recognized, for example, through social activities, participation in pastoral work and student leadership, among others.

The Division of Student Affairs (DAE) seeks to contribute to the integral formation of students and watch over the quality of life of its students, framed in UC's guiding

115

STUDENT ENGAGEMENT AND THE COCURRICULUM

documents. The DAE supports these institutional goals through the development of support services, promotion, and prevention, in the field of health, sports, and university life, in the curricular and cocurricular activities as well as the extra-curricular.

The Student Leadership Area, part of the DAE, was created in response to the sociocultural changes that Chile experienced in the early 2000s, which had an important impact at the university level. Our objective is to implement a program to develop competencies for our integral education programs for undergraduate and graduate students. In this particular program, we work with two kinds of leaders: those who are democratically elected by their peers and leaders of different social projects. These students use different areas in university engagement, mainly topics of political and social interest, to strengthen the public commitment of the university in response to Chile's needs and problems. We understand leadership as a process of collaborative action through which students acquire and/or strengthen skills that allow them to make decisions and take actions to achieve their own objectives and those of the collective. This process allows students to promote changes in their social environment, positioning themselves as an agent of positive change in their context.

Our model of leadership training for social change uses the project-based learning methodology (PBL), as we put students at the core of their learning, empowering from the practice of their volunteer initiatives and/or social activism, the application of the theoretical contents they have learned. This methodology allows students to be the creator of their own learning, that is, it makes them an active element in what they are building and the educator becomes a facilitator of that process. In this scheme, students actively participate in solving a problem, identifying learning needs to investigate, learn, and solve problems (Unión Europea y Ministerio de Educación Cultura y Deporte de España, 2002).

Goals and Outcomes:

The Student Leadership Area seeks to implement an education and development program of competencies in university leadership, where the specific goals are:

- Identify current student leaders.
- Generate education and meeting opportunities that allow us to improve the management of our leaders and the promotion of networks.
- Capture and enhance the good practices that are developed in the academic and administrative units, through which students develop leadership.
- Strengthen student leadership and instances of university participation aligned to the Education Project and the UC Development Plan.

The PBL is expressed as a guiding methodology for the ongoing work that the area carries out with the student. It begins with developing an initiative of community involvement as a volunteer or policy management. The student must go through a teaching–learning process contained in a training program with advising, which includes different workshops associated with the level of knowledge and development of the students themselves in

116

STUDENT ENGAGEMENT AND THE COCURRICULUM

their role as leaders. The training program has a duration of one year and is implemented by the professionals in the Student Engagement and Student Leadership Area.

In the case of social leaders, they are mentored in subjects like project design, management of financial resources, volunteer management, time management, competitive funds, individual counseling, among others, depending on their seniority as a leader, they correspond to different activities.

For the elected representative student leader, actions are taken even prior to their choice, aimed at knowing their concerns and establishing a collaborative communication. Once students are elected, the Representatives Summit is held, a space for dialogue, collaborative work among all the student representatives as well as directors and university authorities (3 days off campus). They receive training on topics such as university history, inclusion and diversity, sexual assault prevention, support, and reception of students, warning signs of emotional suffering, and wellness and sports. They also receive training in planning and development of their own projects and promotion of teamwork. This creates an opportunity for dialogue with key agents of the institution on areas of infrastructure, economic management, academic development, etc., which makes it possible for representative leaders to be constantly contributing to institutional development projects in a collaborative way. Mentoring has milestones that allow for the evaluation of the management itself as the learning that each student has managed to develop in this process exercising their role in the proposed program.

Assessment:

We mainly evaluate management indicators that evaluate the efficiency and effectiveness of the objectives set out in the training program. We use various types of evaluation indicators by percentage of:

- Projects applied to by students.
- Student funded projects.
- Economic resources delivered to each project financed.
- Attendance in training and/or educational workshops.
- Training and/or educational workshops implemented.
- Satisfaction of services delivered.

In 2015, a qualitative study was carried out regarding the learning reported by students who were student representatives during that year and who participated in the program's activities. Among the main areas of learning reported are self-management regarding time management; organization and management of multiple responsibilities; involvement and commitment; teamwork; management of conflicts and setbacks; prioritize work with authorities; argue assertively; and revaluation and endowment of meaning to the policy.

It is important to mention that we are currently working on developing evaluation indicators for learning that are institutionally validated, by means of a cocurricular certificate (cocurricular transcript).

117

STUDENT ENGAGEMENT AND THE COCURRICULUM

Lessons Learned:

- Programs need a theoretical model and a learning methodology that legitimizes leadership training, combining personal and group work activities, with permanent practical application (meaningful learning).
- Services should be differentiated between leadership categories, since the focus of interest responds to the different profiles of leadership and educational paths of the students.
- Communication with students is another crucial element; it should be fluid, while keeping in mind the relational limits of the bond. Staff in charge of the programs have a formative role, mainly mediator or facilitator.
- The university must create spaces so that leaders and student groups can get to know each other, relate to each other, get feedback, and actively bond, thus creating a sense of belonging and supporting their learning. In this sense, combining the spaces for participation with formal spaces of collaborative learning, with clear learning goals and evaluation of those same goals, it becomes transcendental to give continuity and consistency to the leadership programs.

In addition, we wanted to highlight some good practices and relevant players associated with them:

Best Practices	Key Players
1. Recognize the development cycles of the different leaderships and generate differentiated strategies of formation and accompaniment, through the application of the PBL methodology.	The recognition of the development cycles of different leaderships should be promoted from: ▪ Student Affairs Department ▪ Student Government ▪ Academic Units.
2. Mentor and mediate situations of emerging political activism using dialogue as the methodology and problem-solving as the main tool.	The process of mentoring in situations of emergent activism is done collaboratively between: ▪ Student Affairs Department ▪ University authorities ▪ Student Government ▪ Academic Units.
3. Support and mentor the development of initiatives of student leaders that respond concretely to the needs and problems of the country, in an innovative way and with positive social impact.	The process of mentoring the development of initiatives can be promoted from: ▪ Student Affairs Department ▪ Student Government ▪ Academic Units.

Media Links:

Hechos y cifras [Facts and figures]: www.uc.cl/es/la-universidad/campus

Plan de Desarrollo [Development Plan]: www.uc.cl/plan-de-desarrollo

Liderazgo estudiantil [Student leadership]: http://vidauniversitaria.uc.cl/liderazgoe
studiantil/

Líderes UC [Leaders at UC Facebook]: www.facebook.com/groups/20359560314
1453/?fref=ts

Vive la UC [Live UC University Facebook page]: www.facebook.com/vivelauc/?fref=ts

INCLUSIVE, INTERNATIONALIZED PROGRAMMING

Many student affairs practitioners specialize in inclusive programming, particularly in functional areas like cultural and affinity centers, student activities, residence life, and others. However, internationalized programming may be more limited. Between the 2012 edition and the 2017 edition of the *Mapping Internationalization on US Campuses* survey, the number of HEIs offering international festivals or events as part of the cocurriculum increased from 58% to 71% (ACE, 2012, 2017). Yet, these festivals are most often organized by, or in partnership with, international education. In our study, as many as 90% of SSAOs reported collaboration with international services/education offices or with academic affairs on international festivals and celebrations, often employing food as a central programmatic element. An SSAO at a private research university in Illinois described successful program collaboration as "combining academic activities in programs, including faculty, and the ever-important food." International weeks and festivals can no doubt be powerful experiences; however, reaching deeper issues and critical discussions that lead to developing intercultural competence is far more difficult and complex, requiring significant collaboration and partnership.

Cultural festivals and international weeks or days are common cocurriculum programming around the world. At Rhodes University in South Africa, practitioners create partnerships to support programs, events, and seminars to advance IaH and intercultural learning through the cocurriculum (Chapter 1 Promising Practice). Their programs that specifically target the inclusion of international students include "an international parade organized with the local community; multicultural 'Africa Ball' celebrating the continent's diversity; international student participation in service-learning and community engagement programmes; campaigns like 'Know Africa' or 'Reject Zenophobia'" (Quinlan, 2015, p. 19). Or as part of the Promising Practice Cultural Encounters at the Chinese University of Hong Kong (Chapter 2), the Office of Student Affairs organizes cultural festivals every semester with rotating themes and cultural foci as shown in the Korean festival (2015), Southeast Asian festival (2016), and Islamic festival (2016).

Peer programs via student mentors, ambassadors, or buddies are common within an IaH framework as they promote friendship and encourage cross- and intercultural interaction (Ward, 2015a). Other less widespread programs at US institutions are buddy programs that pair domestic and international students (at 34% of US HEIs), language partner programs (at 27%), and those within residence life to promote domestic and international student integration (at 25%) (ACE, 2017). In our study, an SSAO at an urban baccalaureate college in the Northeast explained how partnerships between departments help to "implement an international student ambassador program with international students and domestic students who have studied abroad to encourage greater understanding of other cultures." However, peer programs require careful planning and implementation to avoid common pitfalls that decrease the authenticity of the program for international students, such as paying domestic students or offering other types of incentives for participation (Beelen, 2007). Additionally, a minimum of six months is desirable for pairs to work together to begin seeing any benefits of cross-cultural work (Leask & Carroll, 2011).

Some formalized academic and student affairs collaborations offer an academic component where students can expand their intercultural learning outside of the classroom. The University of South Australia (UniSA) created interventions to internationalize the cocurriculum and reward intercultural engagement through an online peer-mentoring system where international and domestic students, enrolled in the same course, are paired together before arrival (Leask, 2009). Staff created a learning guide, "What do I call you?—An introduction to Chinese, Malay and Hindu names," that was provided during workshops with staff and with domestic students who serve in peer mentor or ambassador programs. Or at the private Universidad Popular Autónoma del Estado de Puebla in Mexico, an undergraduate certificate, Certificado de Competencias Interculturales, develops intercultural competence using comprehensive and theory-based initiatives (Fabregas Janeiro, Lopez Fabre, & Nuño de la Parra, 2013). To receive the certificate, students need to have an intermediate knowledge of an additional language to Spanish, take two courses related to international themes, pass an online course titled "Viviendo en una Sociedad Diversa" [Living in a Diverse Society], participate in at least three months of an international experience, and volunteer at least 100 hours each working with the international education office. Some international residence hall programs, organized as living-learning communities, require students to enroll in credit-bearing coursework together or participate in other programming and activities (Ward, 2015a). The Promising Practice Listen, Live and Learn at Stellenbosch University (Chapter 2) highlights students living together in on-campus housing and engaging with each other on topics of racism, gender, identity, classism, and globalization, all the while developing intercultural competencies.

Finally, student organizations and college or student unions play a key role in advancing internationalization and diversity efforts through informal cocurricular

STUDENT ENGAGEMENT AND THE COCURRICULUM

cultural events, social and language-based interaction programs, and many other programmatic efforts that engage students in both planning and participation of the activities. At Leeds University in the UK, the Global Café has students meet to practice English and better understand British culture. These efforts, when combined with institutional commitment and structure to merge internationalization and diversity efforts, led international students at these institutions to comment that they believe these "measures are designed to ensure that, not only are they treated as equals, but they are made to 'feel at home'" (Caruana & Ploner, 2010, p. 78). However, a common limitation to any of these programs, like in international student organizations, is the lack of domestic student involvement where many international-themed clubs, societies, or associations have students interacting with peers from their own and other countries more so than domestic students.

ON-CAMPUS STUDENT EMPLOYMENT PROGRAMS

The demographic reality of US students today is that most work while attending HEIs, with 43% of full-time, undergraduate students working part time and 86% of part-time students working while in college (National Center for Education Statistics, 2017). On-campus employment increases students' academic success especially when incorporated within student development frameworks while off-campus employment and working more than 30 hours per week decreases academic performance (Perna, 2010; Perozzi, 2009). Therefore, on-campus student employment is a way to both develop leadership skills and support academic performance when employment includes intentionally designed learning environments to influence students' development, cognitive skills, and intellectual growth (Padgett & Grady, 2009). A goal for student affairs areas that employ students is to make the employment experience more than just a job by demonstrating the connections between student roles and responsibilities, and the larger picture of how skill development fits into their academics, career, as well as local and global communities.

On-campus employment can include significant intercultural learning opportunities and outcomes through the education or training program associated with the employment program, through the planned diversity of students and their intentional interactions, and by bringing to the fore the educational and employment backgrounds of diverse employees (Perozzi, Seifert, & Bodine Al-Sharif, 2016). The process of fostering diverse environments and being overt with learning outcomes for intercultural competence that connect to broader HEI missions and vision is key to providing a connected experience for students (Perozzi, Kappes, & Santucci, 2009). Employing students in meaningfully constructed roles with overt learning outcomes, together with methods for teaching and measuring the outcomes, can be a powerful high-impact activity (Kuh, 2009). Similar to what

121

STUDENT ENGAGEMENT AND THE COCURRICULUM

faculty do with internships, supervisors can hold regular meetings with student staff using guided reflection to discuss what they are learning on the job, and the connection back to their degrees and career goals. The ability to infuse the outcomes into learning platforms associated with the employment role is essential so that students can learn, experience, and practice the desired outcomes. Having realistic methods for measuring student acquisition of key outcomes for intercultural learning is the final and most critical step (Lane & Perozzi, 2014; Perozzi, 2009).

For international students, on-campus employment positively impacts persistence and enhances their experience of US culture (Di Maria & Kwai, 2014). While US government regulations make it difficult for international students to work off-campus, policies allow them to work directly for their educational institutions. This provides a platform for student affairs to hire international students, allowing them to learn from and contribute to their host institutions. Student affairs offices can partner with international student services to learn about federal visa and work authorization requirements and how to recruit students through their networks. Of the US SSAOs in our survey, 71% reported the importance of hiring international students into undergraduate employee positions and as graduate assistants. Hiring international students for campus positions not only assists in their intercultural connections and sense of belonging but also offers domestic students and staff the opportunity to meet and interact with international students.

By leveraging the employment platform, practitioners can help students acquire cultural competency skills to improve their overall employability profile by offering flexible and relevant development opportunities. Weber State University (2017) in Ogden, Utah, embraces student employment by defining learning outcomes for students, which includes global diversity, and then uses various methods to teach those outcomes throughout the academic year. Weber State hosts a conference-style program in late August for hundreds of employees, where targeted programs focus on learning outcomes, including global diversity. Representatives from the International Student and Scholar Center routinely present sessions during the start-of-school training program. After that, students can avail themselves of additional programs related to global competence throughout the year via the GetSET (Get Student Employee Training) program. GetSET kicks off during the start-of-school training, and then an online learning management system guides the rest of the program throughout the year, including recorded videos, presentations, and upcoming events student employees can participate in to qualify for rewards while learning about global diversity and other key learning elements.

In another case, the Promising Practice from the American University of Kuwait is an example of a culturally adapted, culturally focused, and locally relevant student employment program where practitioners help students understand

122

STUDENT ENGAGEMENT AND THE COCURRICULUM

the potential benefits of working on campus. The program markets meaningful employment opportunities to students in a country where there are limited options for traditional college-aged students.

PROMISING PRACTICE: Student Employment Program

Institution Name: American University of Kuwait

Location: Salmiya, Kuwait

Authors:
Tadd Kruse, Assistant to the President for Institutional Planning & Effectiveness Office of the President, American University of Kuwait
Bader Al-Sayed Ahmed, Coordinator of Student Clubs & Student Employment Office of Student Life, American University of Kuwait

Background and Context:
Kuwait is a small, oil-rich Arabian gulf nation-state and a modest Islamic nation with conservative values and strong family ties. The legal age to drive is 18 years, and adults do not typically move out of the family home until married. The limited opportunities for most young persons to gain work experience includes reasons such as government subsidies to nationals, university scholarships, and familial expectations. Additionally, most of the population are expatriates who occupy jobs that would typically be filled by young adults or unskilled workers. For HEIs, one common priority is to prepare students academically, but also to support their success as new professionals. On-campus student employment is an excellent way for students to gain skills and income as they prepare themselves for the workforce, especially within a society with limited employment opportunities.

The American University of Kuwait (AUK) is a small, liberal arts institution located in Salmiya, one of Kuwait's most modern retail areas, with an annual fall enrollment of approximately 2,500 students. AUK is the only liberal arts university in Kuwait and one of approximately ten private institutions of higher learning in Kuwait. The Student Employment Program (SEP) at AUK provides students with opportunities to play integral roles in university operations by supporting departmental services, and, ultimately, meeting campus needs. Student employment is a vital and cost-effective supplement to supporting professional staff and provides students with the acquisition of professional skills. Originally, the assumption was that local youth held an unwillingness to work; however, this since has proven to be inaccurate, as the number of applications and participation rates for the program have been significant. The first year, 10 different departments employed 27 students. By 2016–2017, the program employed 137 students supporting 27 administrative and academic departments across campus. Over the years, approximately a quarter or fewer of employed students have been Kuwait nationals and those employed are often among the highest performing students on campus both as employees and student leaders.

123

STUDENT ENGAGEMENT AND THE COCURRICULUM

Further Description:

AUK's SEP, founded within the Division of Student Affairs in 2004 and structured in 2005, has continued to develop both in participation and structure by taking a student-centered approach derived from various student development theories. The SEP structure follows a combination of institutional human resources practices with modified components based on a review of other student employment and internship programs. Having structure, yet allowing departmental flexibility, creates a supportive, streamlined, and sustainable process. The program is entirely internally operated, managed, and funded, needing limited resources. Program processes and components mirror professional expectations and real-world work settings with varying position levels based on responsibility, and offer training, recommendations, and an end of service letter. The SEP program integrates into AUK's student information system to allow hiring departments to manage their needs directly while requiring standardized structure and mandatory components, such as applications, hiring letters, evaluations, and timesheets to support the overall program. Each year at the Annual Student Awards night, each department recognizes the top performing individuals for their outstanding work efforts.

The SEP program is an internally developed, sustainable, replicable, and culturally adapted program. AUK's SEP has been presented at several regional conferences since 2012, to highlight program strengths, structures, and regional application. Regional colleagues found these presentations very helpful and "as the foundation for a complete restructuring of our program." AUK's SEP provides a comprehensive (from application to termination), de-centralized process for hiring built upon a standardized information systems base. Utilizing a foundational yet extensive infrastructure, the program serves to promote consistency and standardization of the program across more than 20 academic and administrative offices annually. This structure, conveyed through online systems and program handbooks, was developed intentionally, and put in place during the early years of the institution as "tools and resources for supervisors" to support and streamline activities towards effectiveness (Burnside, 2017, p. 18).

The strengths of AUK's program include a decentralized structure (streamlined inter-departmental interactions); entirely paperless and accessible at any time (reductions in time and effort); wage and position system (merged with the institutions and established a position structure); cost reduction (overall program is managed as part of the duties of one employee); strong foundation for student employees (positive feedback from former student employees with full-time jobs shows benefits); and program does not require specialized advertising (program is promoted through orientation, limited web sources, and past success via word of mouth).

Goals and Outcomes:

The SEP enhances students' educational experience by providing opportunities to establish meaningful connections with the AUK community through employment placement in campus offices. The program offers three levels of employment status based on the required skills or experience for the role. Specific duties may vary from a general

124

STUDENT ENGAGEMENT AND THE COCURRICULUM

front-desk worker in the library or other office, to more specialized work as a peer tutor or student designer. Through these placements, students gain experiences that not only bolster their resumes and acquire the necessary skills to enhance their employability, but also embrace the value of different cultures and how to effectively interact within a diverse community. Learning outcomes for the program emphasize the primary objectives and benefits to students and the institution. Students participating in the program will:

- Learn the basic skills required to be a successful employee in a professional market (cognitive).
- Be more comfortable when dealing with situations and the steps necessary to resolve issues (cognitive & affective).
- Conduct themselves in a more professional and appropriate manner (behavioral).
- Understand the standards of professional workplace behavior (cognitive).
- Demonstrate the ability to independently resolve situations and be more autonomous in the workplace (affective).

Assessment:

The program coordinator reviews the program annually and meets with direct supervisors to evaluate current program figures and discuss the overall program. The coordinator assesses any complaints/suggestions received from other departments or student feedback. The Student Employment Manual is reviewed and updated annually.

Additional focused assessment practices have taken place through an annual meeting with all hiring departments at the start of the fiscal year to review issues, challenges, and successes. During a few select years, focus groups were utilized for soliciting feedback for both hiring departments and student employees. In 2015, a survey was distributed to students on student employment training and needs for a training program. Consideration for a centralized training program, beyond that provided within the hiring department itself, to support the overall development of participating students is still under review.

Lessons Learned:

1. A comprehensive, structured, and systematic approach to supporting on-campus student employment is needed to meet student needs and balance departments' varying requirements.
2. Student employment programs support comprehensive student development by engaging students in standard recruitment, training, and employment practices.
3. Via the program's structure, specific activities and life skills are acquired by students as manifested through the hiring practices (i.e., applications, resumes, interviews), office training (i.e., customer service, communication, collaboration), and performance evaluations (i.e., managing feedback, accountability, critical thinking).
4. A sustainable program requires technology and collaboration with multiple departments to offer a fully online program and process for students, faculty, and staff.

Media Links:

AUK Student Employment: www.auk.edu.kw/student_affairs/sl_student_employment.jsp

ASSESSMENT OF INTERCULTURAL LEARNING

Practitioners in the US will be familiar with the ongoing assessment movement born out of demand for accountability, public dissatisfaction and mistrust of the learning outcomes of higher education, and the demand for employment after graduation (Upcraft & Schuh, 1996; Schuh, Biddix, Dean, & Kinzie, 2016). Solid assessment practice, which is "any effort to gather, analyze, and interpret evidence which describes institutional, departmental, divisional, or agency effectiveness" (Upcraft & Schuh, 1996, p. 18) requires practitioners ensure their departmental goals and learning outcomes align with those of the academic mission of the institution they serve and support (De Sawal & Yakaboski, 2014). Global learning increasingly is an area that practitioners are interested in assessing, especially when measuring individual students or specific programs, such as service learning or residential living-learning communities (Schuh et al., 2016). As more HEIs include or reference internationalization, diversity, SJI, globalism, and other related concepts, practitioners can use this opportunity to revise or create new goals and vision statements with related global and intercultural learning outcomes and associated measurements.

Overall, student affairs divisions, likely in partnerships with academic affairs and the international education office, will want to regularly assess their international student experience and intercultural development for all students. At the institutional or program level, five key principles provide a foundation to assessing intercultural competency:

- The "define principle" references the importance of being specific about what the terms global citizenship, internationalization, and intercultural competency mean in the institutional context.
- To prioritize means selecting which elements are most important to assess and developing learning outcomes.
- Align the important elements of intercultural assessment, such as learning outcomes, goals, activities, and measurements, which is required for quality assessment.
- With those pieces specified, then identify direct and indirect evidence for collection.
- Lastly, use the information and analysis for improvement and begin the cycle again.

(Deardorff, 2017)

STUDENT ENGAGEMENT AND THE COCURRICULUM

To assess intercultural competency requires a shift from pre- and post-measurements to ones that can measure process-oriented learning that occurs more in group work or service learning. Intercultural and global learning assessment requires using multiple varied assessment tools and methods.

As "student learning remains at the heart of Interationalisation at Home," there are a multitude of common or accepted assessment tools in existence (Deardorff, 2015, p. 13). However, individualized global learning, connected to intercultural competency, has no clear way to measure when or if competency has been achieved and no best or one way to assess, but it is important to use a variety of qualitative and quantitative approaches (Deardorff, 2006). Some tools are the Organisation for Economic Cooperation and Development's Programme for International Student Assessment (PISA) in the European Higher Education Area, or the Collegiate Learning Assessment in the US. Intercultural outcome assessments can include formal reflections and informal self-evaluation of students' participation in a cross-national partnership or group (Yefanova & Johnstone, 2015; Yefanova, Woodruff, Kappler, & Johnstone, 2014). Practitioners must "consider whether to adopt, adapt, or devise alternative assessment or evaluation tools from other countries or cultures" or not (Chen & Mathies, 2016, p. 89).

CONCLUSION

Student affairs can be a leader in internationalization by incorporating global student learning outcomes throughout the cocurriculum. Programs, activities, leadership opportunities, and student employment are all ways in which students can interact and engage with global and intercultural concepts. Helping students learn and develop as global citizens is a shared responsibility for all those working in higher education. Students' academic majors and career aspirations may drive their goals, but practitioners can support these varied directions through shared, yet individualized, learning that allows for exploration to address local and global social issues within their communities. Results from the NSSE (2017) global learning module show the importance of student exposure to global learning immediately upon entering the institution, or better yet, before arriving to campus to ensure that they take advantage of opportunities throughout the years. The cocurriculum supports learning and the practice of concepts that are learned elsewhere, particularly in the classroom, and brings them together with learning outcomes appropriate for individual contexts. Specific methods and programs are already common in supporting student learning around global and intercultural issues.

Encouraging student engagement in their own academic experience in intentional ways has positive outcomes for students and HEIs. Engagement opportunities that foster intercultural growth and development is positive for international and home students alike. Environments that support student empowerment, and allow students to assume significant leadership responsibilities and help educate and expose other students to global issues and contexts, are necessary. Leadership roles that help students acquire the soft skills necessary to bolster employability, and be competitive in a global workforce, are often found, or can be created, in student affairs areas. Student employment generally can be a significant way in which student affairs practitioners directly and meaningfully impact students. Being such a natural platform for regular feedback, frequent interaction, and one-on-one attention, the employment environment can be pivotal, especially because US-based international students have limited work options. Student employees can also reach other students and act as ambassadors for the intercultural nature of programs and services. Student affairs can leverage and enhance current leadership and programs to assist students in developing as global citizens. The type of assistance required by students and institutions will necessarily vary by cultural nuance, but ultimately, practitioners are seeking culturally relevant outcomes that help students learn and grow, and that move institutions forward in productive and healthy ways.

REFERENCES

American Council on Education. (2012). *Mapping Internationalization on U.S. Campuses: 2012 Edition.* Washington, D.C.: Author.

American Council on Education. (2017). *Mapping Internationalization on U.S. Campuses: 2017 Edition.* Washington, D.C.: Author.

Astin, A. W. (1984). Student involvement: A developmental theory for higher education. *Journal of College Student Personnel*, *25*(4), 297–308.

Beelen, J. (2007). *Implementing internationalisation at home.* Amsterdam, The Netherlands: EAIE.

Brooks, R., Byford, K., & Sela, K. (2015). The changing role of students' unions within contemporary higher education. *Journal of Education Policy*, *30*(2), 165–181.

Burnside, O. (2017). Beyond the paycheck: Transforming the student employment experience. *Leadership Exchange*, *15*(3), 16–20.

Caruana, V., & Ploner, J. (2010). *Internationalisation and equality and diversity in higher education: Merging identities.* Leeds, UK: Leeds Metropolitan University.

Chen, P. D., & Mathies, C. (2016). Assessment, evaluation, and research. In D. Roberts & S. Komives (Eds.), *Enhancing student learning and development in cross-border higher education* (pp. 85–92). San Francisco, CA: Jossey-Bass.

Chickering, A. W., & Reisser, L. (1993). *Education and identity*, 2nd ed. San Francisco, CA: Jossey-Bass.

Cinque, M., Perozzi, B., Bardill Moscaritolo, L., & Miano, S. (2017). *Trends in higher education: Employability, competencies, and global civic engagement.* Brussels, Belgium: EucA.

STUDENT ENGAGEMENT AND THE COCURRICULUM

De Sawal, D. M., & Yakaboski, T. (2014). Preparing the college union for the future through assessment, evaluation, and research. In T. Yakaboski, & D. M. De Sawal (Eds.), *The state of the (college) union: Contemporary issues and trends. New Directions for Student Services* (pp. 91–98). San Francisco, CA: Jossey-Bass.

Deardorff, D. K. (2006). Identification and assessment of intercultural competence as a student outcome of internationalization. *Journal of Studies in International Education*, *10*(3), 241–266.

Deardorff, D. K. (2015). Myths and principles. *EAIE Forum: Internationalisation at Home*, 12–13.

Deardorff, D. K. (2017). The big picture of intercultural competence assessment. In D. K. Deardorff & L. A. Arasaratnam-Smith (Eds.), *Intercultural competence in higher education: International approaches, assessment and application* (pp. 124–133). New York: Routledge.

Di Maria, D. L., & Kwai, C. K. (2014). *Developing an international student retention strategy: Theory to practice.* Washington, D.C.: AIEA.

Duke Kunshan University. (2017). Mission Statement. Retrieved from https://duke kunshan.edu.cn/en/about/mission-statement

Fabregas Janeiro, M. G., Lopez Fabre, R., & Nuño de la Parra, P. (2013). Building intercultural competence through intercultural competency certification for undergraduate students. *Journal of International Education Research*, *10*(1), 1–8.

Gentile, M. C. (2010). *Giving voice to values: How to speak your mind when you know what's right.* New Haven, CT: Yale UP.

Glass, C. R., Wongtrirat, R., & Buus, S. (2015). *International student engagement: Strategies for creating inclusive, connected, and purposeful campus environments.* Sterling, VA: Stylus.

Hawkins, A. (2010). *Relationship between undergraduate student activity and academic performance.* College of Technology Directed Projects. Paper 13. Retrieved from http://docs.lib.purdue.edu/techdirproj/13

Kinzie, J., Helms, R. M., & Cole, J. (2017). A glimpse of global learning: Assessing student experiences and institutional commitments. *Liberal Education*, *103*(2). Retrieved from www.aacu.org/liberaleducation/2017/spring/kinzie_hclms_cole

Kuh, G. D. (2009). What student affairs professionals need to know about student engagement. *Journal of College Student Development*, *50*(6), 683–706.

Kuh, G. D., Kinzie, J., Schuh, J. H., Whitt, E. J., & Associates. (2011). *Student success in college: Creating conditions that matter.* San Francisco, CA: Jossey-Bass.

Lane, T., & Perozzi, B. (2014). Student engagement and college unions. In T. Yakaboski, & D. M. De Sawal (Eds.), *The state of the (college) union: Contemporary issues and trends: New directions for student services* (pp. 27–38). San Francisco, CA: Jossey-Bass.

Leask, B. (2009). Using formal and informal curricula to improve interactions between home and international students. *Journal of Studies in International Education*, *13*(2), 205–221.

129

STUDENT ENGAGEMENT AND THE COCURRICULUM

Leask, B., & Carroll, J. (2011). Moving beyond "wishing and hoping": Internationalisation and student experiences of inclusion and engagement. *Higher Education Research & Development*, *30*(5), 647–659.

Moja, T., Luescher, T.M., and Schreiber, B. (2015). Equity and social justice in higher education. *Journal of Student Affairs in Africa*, 3(2): v–xii.

National Center for Education Statistics. (2017). *College student employment*. Retrieved from https://nces.ed.gov/programs/coe/pdf/coe_ssa.pdf

Oni, A. A., & Adetoro, J. A. (2015). The effectiveness of student involvement in decision-making and university leadership: A comparative analysis of 12 universities in southwest Nigeria. *Journal of Student Affairs in Africa*, *3*(1), 65–81.

Oste, D. (2009). Germany, Deutsches Studentenwerk. In R. Ludeman & Associates (Eds.), *Student affairs and services in higher education: Global foundations, issues and best practices* (pp. 214–216). Paris, France: UNESCO.

Padgett, R., & Grady, D. (2009). Student development and personal growth in employment. In B. Perozzi (Ed.), *Enhancing student learning through college employment* (pp. 31–45). Bloomington, IN: ACUI.

Pascarella, E. T., & Terezini, P. T. (2005). *How college affects students: A third decade of research*. San Francisco, CA: Jossey-Bass.

Perna, L. (2010). *Understanding the working college student: New research and its implications for policy and practice*. Sterling, VA: Stylus.

Perozzi, B. (2009). *Enhancing student learning through college employment*. Bloomington, IN: ACUI.

Perozzi, B., Kappes, J., & Santucci, L. (2009). *Learning outcomes and student employment programs*. In B. Perozzi (Ed.), *Enhancing student learning through college employment* (pp. 67–84). Bloomington, IN: ACUI.

Perozzi, B., Seifert, T. & Bodine Al-Sharif, M. A. (2016). Staffing for Success. In D. Roberts & S. Komives (Eds.), *Enhancing student learning and development in cross-border higher education: New directions for higher education* (pp. 93–103). San Francisco, CA: Jossey-Bass.

Plaister-Ten, J. (2017). Leading across cultures: Developing leaders for global organizations. *Transpersonal Leadership Series: White Paper Four*. New York: Routledge.

Quinlan, O. (2015). South Africa: Small steps in the right direction. *EAIE Forum: Internationalization at Home*, 17–19.

Reyes, C. P. (2017). Escenario de participación de estudiantes: Liderazgo y participación estudiantil panel [Student participation scenario: Student leadership and participation panel]. Presentation at I Congreso Internacional de Asuntos Estudiantiles, Bogotá, Colombia.

Rhoads, R. A. (2016). Student activism, diversity, and the struggle for a just society. *Journal of Diversity in Higher Education*, *9*(3), 189.

Schuh, J. H., Biddix, J. P., Dean L.A., & Kinzie J. (2016). *Assessment in student affairs: A guide for practitioners*. San Francisco, CA: Jossey-Bass.

Unión Europea y Ministerio de Educación Cultura y Deporte de España (2002). Competencias para la inserción laboral, Guía para el profesorado [Competencies for transitions from higher education into the workplace: Guide for teachers]. Retrieved from https://tomillo.org/wp-content/uploads/2016/12/Guia_para_el_Profesorado_866.pdf

Upcraft, M. L., & Schuh, J. H. (1996). *Assessment in student affairs: A guide for practitioners*, 1st ed. San Francisco, CA: Jossey-Bass.

Ward, H. H. (2015a). *Internationalizing the co-curriculum: Part one: Integrating international students*. Washington, D.C.: ACE. Retrieved from www.acenet.edu/news-room/Documents/Intlz-In-Action-Intlz-Co-Curriculum-Part-1.pdf

Ward, H. H. (2015b). *Internationalizing the co-curriculum: Part two: Global and intercultural education in the co-curriculum*. Washington, D.C.: ACE. Retrieved from www.acenet.edu/news-room/Documents/Intlz-In-Action-Intlz-Co-Curriculum-Part-2.pdf

Weber State University. (2017). Career services 50/50 employment funding program. Retrieved from https://apps.weber.edu/wsuimages/careerservices/50–50%20Policies%20and%20Procedures.pdf

Weimer, L. (2015). Student union resistance in Finland. In M. Klemenčič, S. Bergan, & R. Primožič (Eds.), *Student engagement in Europe: Society, higher education and student governance*. Strasbourg, France: Council of Europe Publishing.

Whipple, E. G., & O'Neill, K. B. (2011). Student activities. In N. Zhang & Associates (Eds.), *Rentz's student affairs practice in higher education*, 4th ed. (pp. 359–395). Springfield, IL: Charles C. Thomas Publisher.

Wong, H. C. J. (2016). Adversity training for Chinese university students. In D. C. Roberts & S. R. Komives (Eds.), *Enhancing student learning and development in cross-border higher education*: *New directions for higher education* (pp. 41–47). San Francisoo, CA: Jossey-Bass.

Yakaboski, T. (2011). Student centers in Kenya: A shift from living rooms to business offices. *ACUI Bulletin, 79*(3), 26–32.

Yakaboski, T., & Birnbaum, M. G. (2013). The challenges of student affairs at Kenyan public universities. *Journal of Student Affairs in Africa, 1*(1&2), 33–48.

Yakaboski, T., & Perozzi, B. (2014). Global student union. In T. Yakaboski & D. M. De Sawal (Eds.), *The state of the (college) union: Contemporary issues and trends: New Directions for Student Services* (pp. 79–90). San Francisco, CA: Jossey-Bass.

Yefanova, D., & Johnstone, C. (2015). *Maximising the educational impact of international students*. EAIE Forum: Internationsation at Home, 9–11.

Yefanova, D., Woodruff, G., Kappler, B., & Johnstone, C. (2014). *The study of the educational impact of international students in campus internationalization at the University of Minnesota: Phase 1*. Retrieved from https://global.umn.edu/icc/documents/15_EducationalImpact-IntlStudents.pdf

Chapter 6

An Internationalized Context for Professional Development

Being a student affairs practitioner in the US means "lifelong professional development, professional identity, serving one's profession, and mentoring others" (Arminio & Ortiz, 2017, p. 378). The requirement for lifelong learning is due, in part, to the complexity of issues, constantly changing technologies, and evolving student demographics, which create the need for diverse frameworks (Komives & Carpenter, 2016). In the US, professional development frequently comes in the form of graduate preparation degrees, professional conferences, mentorship programs, field experiences or internships, and graduate assistantships. Graduate preparation programs expose practitioners to a wide array of theories, literature, and research all to support current and future practice. Many of these methods and programs are available to practitioners outside of the US, such as professional associations, workshops, and mentoring programs, but formalized degree programs are rarely a part of the professional development paradigm (Perozzi, Seifert, & Bodine Al-Sharif, 2016). Instead, practitioners develop innovative, local, or regional programs to support the work of student affairs as demonstrated through the Promising Practices in this chapter.

Practitioners require continuous professional development to enhance knowledge, skills, and competencies to support diverse student populations, foster inclusion, institutionalize the benefits of campus diversity (Pope, Mueller, & Reynolds, 2009), and implement inclusive internationalization strategies. As such, the question to student affairs practitioners is, "why are all educators not 'international educators' equipped to work effectively with multicultural cohorts?" (Killick, 2017, p. 24). Professional development can assist internationalizing learning despite how current conceptualizations of US student affairs professional competencies and graduate curriculum standards do not require internationalization, and specifically interculturalism. Practitioners who work outside of the US or who work in international education regularly use intercultural competence and communication skills, and this can be more of the norm for those working across functional areas in higher education institutions (HEIs). Student affairs

133

divisions and departments can emphasize various aspects of professional development with global outcomes in mind by extending multicultural and social justice and inclusion (SJI) competency development programs and other training.

Many student affairs professional associations and graduate preparation programs rely on international travel as the primary way to develop global and intercultural competency within professional development (Ward, 2016). A few individual institutions have used travel-required programs, such as Michigan State University's residence education and housing staff visiting China to develop their understanding of the growing Chinese student population (Ward, 2016). In Europe, HEIs have relied on the European Commission and Erasmus programs to support and fund staff mobility to promote intercultural development. Even within our study of US SSAOs, travel remained the dominant idea for how to support intercultural professional development. However, some HEIs are recognizing the need to shift more toward an Internationalization at Home (IaH) approach for training and professional development, because while it is easy to applaud increased international mobility programs, they can be costly, time consuming, and inaccessible to many for a variety of reasons.

SSAOs and student affairs supervisors can shift away from the assumption that international travel or experiences are necessary for global learning and intercultural professional development. In keeping with an IaH framework, professional development activities that partner with faculty, international education, cultural centers, and local community organizations can all offer more open access to intercultural competency development. This chapter reviews ideas for how student affairs divisions, graduate preparation programs, and practitioners can increase intercultural competency and international knowledge by expanding and building on the overlap of diversity and internationalization, reevaluating the application of common student development theories, learning about the expanse of global professional development activities, and building campus-based opportunities to reach most staff.

CAPITALIZE ON THE OVERLAP BETWEEN DIVERSITY AND INTERNATIONALIZATION

An important caveat in designing professional development opportunities is to ensure they incorporate an inclusive approach to diversity and internationalization. A common challenge within the US context is that practitioners may see internationalization and diversity efforts as in competition for resources, attention, and time. For example, from our survey, an SSAO in Illinois discussed competing priorities where internationalization was a high priority for senior administrators but not for student affairs, and, conversely, diversity training were high priority for student affairs. An SSAO at a public HEI in Massachusetts stated that staff with intercultural competency have "diversity experiences that have enabled them to be more competent at understanding other cultures (language, sense of time, 'politeness' from other perspectives, etc." This SSAO "encourages staff to attend events sponsored by [the international office]" and offers "discussion groups and presentations at staff meetings with international educators." Partnering and collaborating with multicultural or cultural centers on campus and with cultural organizations in the local community are ways to promote inclusive training opportunities for practitioners.

Stressing internationalization and diversity's overlaps also assists with another common challenge of staff viewing international-related activities as more work rather than as a part of the existing workload. One SSAO at a public associate's college in New York saw the challenge of internationalization resulting from staff not understanding,

> that international students aren't an "add-on" to their responsibilities and that inclusion/diversity also means thinking of our international student population. This is new to many of the staff at our institution who have been in place a very long time and have not been professionally active on a national or global scale.

Many other SSAOs in our study echoed this idea of reframing internationalization and international students not as add-ons or afterthoughts but as part of the responsibilities of supporting the entire student population and being inclusive. Reframing diversity to be inclusive of international populations and reframing internationalization to be inclusive of US and global diversity are solid foundations for professional development in student affairs.

The Promising Practice Embedding Cultural Competence in Student Affairs: An Australian Perspective offers a great demonstration of merging intercultural development and local diversity efforts. In accordance with the University of Sydney's mission in creating and developing leaders of the future, the university has embarked upon producing students, graduates, leaders, researchers, and teachers who are able to engage in dialogue respectfully, within a personal reflection frame. This approach is relevant for all global leaders, and addresses the objectives of the "Wingara Mura—Bunga Barrabugu, the University-wide strategy for Aboriginal and Torres Strait Islander education, research, participation and engagement" (para. 3). The University of Sydney established the National Centre for Cultural Competence (NCCC) to change campus culture and engage the whole institution in embracing cultural competence to promote respect for all 160 cultural groups represented in the University of Sydney's staff, faculty, and student populations. Additionally, the work of the NCCC has direct benefits to Sydney's Aboriginal and Torres Strait Islander staff and students in creating a safer space and increasing awareness on campus of the impact of 200 years of colonization (Jordi Austin, personal communication, 2017). The NCCC offers five online

INTERNATIONALIZED PROFESSIONAL DEVELOPMENT

training modules on cultural competence for students, staff, and faculty including self-discovery and recognizing and challenging racism. Also, the NCCC trains faculty in how to develop culturally responsive teaching and pedagogical practices and classroom environments.

PROMISING PRACTICE: Embedding Cultural Competence in Student Affairs: An Australian Perspective

Authors:
Juanita Sherwood, Acting Deputy Vice Chancellor, Indigenous Strategy and Services
Jordi Austin, Director, Student Support Services

Institution Name: University of Sydney

Location: Sydney, New South Wales, Australia

Background and Context:
The University of Sydney is a large, comprehensive, research-intensive university with a current student profile of more than 65,000 students, of which more than 33% are international. More than one third of our students are higher degree (master's by coursework or research). We have the highest intake of Higher Degree by Research (HDR) students annually in the country. The University consistently is ranked in the top 100 universities globally on multiple indicators, and has the highest ranked graduate outcome rating in the country, and 4th globally.

Nationally, our Aboriginal and Torres Strait Islander peoples (hence forth Australia's First Nations peoples) comprise 2.8% of the national population, however, traditionally have been underrepresented in tertiary education; a direct result of colonial policy that continues to influence the circumstance of Australia's First peoples. While the University has one of the highest rates of retention and success for First Nations students, we recognize that a comprehensive and sustained approach to cultural competency will increase the attraction, retention, and success of all First Nation staff and students.

The University is embarking upon an ambitious and whole-of-institution approach to cultural competency, being led by the National Centre for Cultural Competence (NCCC) at the University. The University aims to support the growth of collective, collaborative communities that respect and value the oldest living cultures in the world, Australia's First Nations peoples, who have maintained and sustained the oldest continent for some 95,000 years. This depth of Indigenous knowledge systems associated with a deep connection to country is unique and critical to the well-being of our planet and the entire human race.

Our University has embraced the opportunity to be open to and deepen its philosophies of inclusion and embracing all knowledge systems. The essential framework for scaffolding this knowledge development starts with the recognition that Australia has a Black history. Most Australians have not grown up with a balanced notion of this

136

INTERNATIONALIZED PROFESSIONAL DEVELOPMENT

story, rather they have been taught that James Cook, an Englishman, discovered Australia in 1770. The NCCC framework focuses upon the unpacking of the colonial stories, and unlearning histories that silenced the 200 years plus of not so peaceful settlement. We explore these stories by supplying the critical context often excluded in explaining the circumstances of our unfinished business in Australia. We ask students and staff to reflect upon how the stories of discovery and victory over the noble but dying savage influenced their ways of knowing Australia's First Nations peoples. The unpacking of long-held notions of "Western truth" can be quite unsettling. This unsettling is, however, the vital step toward being enabled to critically reflect.

Growing our capacity and capabilities in critical reflection and cultural competency provides both students and all university staff with the tools to develop openness and respect for their own circumstances, and to engage skillfully with global diversity. This journey requires all members of the University community to undertake personal critical reflection, along with unconscious bias and cultural competence training. However, to ensure that Student Support Services (SSS) staff are equipped to best assist students on their own cultural competence journey, we are required to adapt the University program at the local level. Faculty and staff have responded to the invitation to participate in the University Cultural Competence journey, and many conversations and training have taken place. There is now a rich partnership with the NCCC, and next steps are being undertaken to embed cultural competency conversations in all student services programs, policies, and support pathways.

To ensure coverage within the SSS staffing complement, professional development days have been set aside to allow staff to complete five online modules exploring cultural competency under the banner of "Know your world, See my world." These modules have been developed by the NCCC and are self-paced, with links to online and other resources, materials, and points of reflection. All SSS staff have been required to complete the modules, which is built into the induction and on-boarding for new staff. The SSS staff have also undertaken the half-day in-person training exploring history and culture, and the Kinship half-day program, which is an experience that provides greater insights and knowledge on traditional cultural structures, learning, and community.

Staff who are employed as local tutors through the Indigenous Tutorial Assistance Scheme, a federal government grant fund, are required to undertake the cultural competency program. Feedback from both the tutors and the students has revealed a stepwise increase in students' comfort in the tutorial sessions, increased willingness to engage with the tutoring program, and higher ratings of the efficacy of the tutoring.

At a whole-of-institution learning and leadership level, the NCCC has developed a three-day in-person immersive cultural competence leadership course, designed for staff and led by the NCCC Director. This course is coupled with online cultural competence modules and in-person half-day history and cultural awareness group activities. Key personnel from student services have been selected to participate with other professional and academic staff from across the University to form a network of leaders. Staff were chosen by their division leaders to participate due to their willingness to undertake the

INTERNATIONALIZED PROFESSIONAL DEVELOPMENT

cultural journey, as well as their commitment to bringing knowledge back to their faculty or service home and to act as a champion in driving change and pursuing the cultural competence journey with their peers.

Goals and Outcomes:

- Increased discussion of cultural competency as a core attribute in student services staff at the University.
- Development of communities of practice within student services to review policies and procedures, development of innovative and culturally inclusive programming.
- Increased opportunity of and reported comfort in accessing all services by Aboriginal and Torres Strait Islander students.
- Reflection opportunities for staff to consider their own practices, and to take ownership for promoting change.

To date, innovative proposals for new ways of working have come forward from the Student Accommodation team, the Financial Assistance Service, the Student Safer Communities Project officer, and the Mana Yura (Aboriginal and Torres Strait Islander Student Support) team. All proposals have been endorsed and put into action. For example, we have recently approved the development of an Aboriginal and Torres Strait Islander student rural placement and mobility bursary, to assist in defraying expenses incurred in taking up rural fieldwork or clinical placement opportunities.

Assessment:

While this journey has been underway in various forms at the University for the last five years, the creation of the modules and cultural competence leadership course has enabled greater uptake and visibility of the programs. This strengthens the on-the-ground resources and capability to enact the University strategy.

Assessment undertaken to monitor the efficacy of the strategy for student affairs includes tangible impact for our First Nations students in:

- Increased usage of all services.
- Increased student satisfaction ratings of the services.
- Higher rates of student retention for the undergraduate cohort.
- Higher rates of course completions and end-of-semester grades.

Lessons Learned:

We have a long way to go. While the early indications on student engagement and success are promising, and staff are mobilized to participate and generate novel approaches to supporting students, we are aware that this is an ongoing process that will require continual renewal. We are committed to pursuing knowledge in partnership with our students and staff to ensure we create a welcoming, inclusive, and empowering environment in which to learn, research, and thrive.

Recommendations for action for others embarking on this journey that have contributed to our success so far:

138

INTERNATIONALIZED PROFESSIONAL DEVELOPMENT

1. Ensuring that all staff are aware of the resources, programs, and training available, and that they are given time at work, endorsed, and supported at the local level, to undertake these opportunities.
2. Establishing a network of leaders within the local area to foster and continue the conversations, proposing improvements, and driving innovation.
3. Demonstrating leadership at all levels, with senior staff as well as new arrivals undertaking the cultural competency journey together.

Media Links:

National Centre for Cultural Competence: http://sydney.edu.au/nccc/

NCCC Online teaching and learning tools: http://sydney.edu.au/nccc/resources/teaching-tools.shtml

NCCC Publications: http://sydney.edu.au/nccc/research/publications.php

REEVALUATING THE APPLICATION OF STUDENT AFFAIRS THEORIES

Since "an important indicator of professional competence is knowledge of the field's theoretical foundation" (Jones & Abes, 2011, p. 161), to internationalize student affairs professional development means to reevaluate the application of common student development theories used. The Council for the Advancement of Standards (CAS) (2015) master's level student affairs graduate preparation program standards include student learning and development theory as one of the five main areas incorporating social identity, cognitive or learning, and psychosocial theories. Yet, many of the suggested theories were developed on and for elite, White males within the US, not minoritized and international students or women and gender non-conforming individuals. They reinforce the status quo of power differentials and US-centric perspectives that disadvantage minoritized and international students (Jones & Abes, 2011; Patton, Renn, Guido, & Quaye, 2016; Renn, Brazelton, & Holmes, 2014). Various student development and adult learning theories are based primarily on American values, communication, and learning styles (Bennett & Bennett, 2004; Fried, 2011). While student affairs student development texts do not include intercultural development, they do, more recently, reference international students as one of the populations on US college campuses but acknowledge the limited scholarship in the US on non-US student populations (Patton et al., 2016).

Scholars have critiqued theories, such as Tinto's (1975) attrition/retention theory, often used to guide organizational efforts to integrate students' social and academic experiences for positive outcomes and Astin's (1984) related theory of student involvement, for promoting an assimilation and ethnocentric understanding of student development (Tanaka, 2002; Tierney, 1992). Research on college

INTERNATIONALIZED PROFESSIONAL DEVELOPMENT

student spirituality and faith development models, such as Fowler's (1981) Stages of Faith Development, may have limited application outside of the cultural context of Western Christianity. Baxter Magolda's (2001) self-authorship theory has been applied to international and multicultural populations, such as in the edited book, *Development and Assessment of Self-Authorship: Exploring the Concept Across Cultures* (2012). The application of self-authorship can lead to incorrect analysis or incorrect cultural applications without having more knowledge of cultural contexts and non-US majority populations. Education City students in Doha, Qatar, who were a part of an international service learning trip, would ask questions about their family being able to travel with them or being able to contact their family daily while they are away (Kruse, Al-Kaldhi, & Witt, 2017). Practitioners using self-authorship without an intercultural framework may try to help students become independent and move away from their family connection without realizing that these behaviors are less about development and more about the cultural expectation and norm of centering family support and involvement (Kruse et al., 2017). With more in-depth cultural awareness, self-authorship and other theories may still be useful but would need contextualization and redefinition for what they mean and their application from multiple cultural angles.

In addition to those discussed in Chapter 3, international education literature offers guidance for student affairs with intercultural development theories that connect to various student development and learning theories (Deardorff, 2016). For example, the general nature of Sanford's (1962) challenge and support theory about how learners require an incremental amount of challenge balanced with the right amount of support and, when tipped too much in either direction, learning ceases. While not developed for the intercultural sphere, Sanford's theory is general enough to adapt to a wide variety of diverse situations. Another theory often cited is Schlossberg's transitions theory that considers individuals coping through situations, self, support, and strategies (Goodman, Schlossberg, & Anderson, 2006). Schlossberg connects to a wide application as well because it explains general adjustment and adaptation. These examples are not exhaustive, rather they offer points for consideration to prompt further critical analysis of the use of commonly applied theories to practitioners' work with students. An interculturally informed analysis of theories taught as a component of professional development would complement increasing knowledge about global practices and cultural sensitivity.

THE ADVANCEMENT OF STUDENT AFFAIRS AND SERVICES GLOBALLY

The global community of practitioners doing student affairs work is both emergent and significant as countries and regions around the world network with one another and create partnerships to advance professionally. This offers opportunity for

140

INTERNATIONALIZED PROFESSIONAL DEVELOPMENT

practitioners to learn about issues, trends, and strategies around the world. Regional cooperation has been evident in the European Higher Education Area (EHEA) for decades through the European Council on Student Affairs (ECStA), the umbrella group for the EHEA. ECStA (2010) has individual associations as members, and a philosophy of social support for student services by promoting the social infrastructure of European HEIs as stated in their Padova Declaration. The organization encompasses well-resourced student affairs and services associations such as Deutsches Studentenwerk in Germany, UK's AMOSSHE—the Student Services Organisation, the Centre National des œuvres Universitaires et Scolaires in France, and the European University College Association that has offices in Belgium and Italy. These EHEA associations have made significant contributions to student affairs and services by role-modeling collaboration and sustaining meaningful partnerships to advance knowledge and experience of their members, through myriad professional development initiatives and outreach programs.

Located within the US, both NASPA—Student Affairs Administrators in Higher Education and ACPA—College Student Educators International have been developing international partnerships and supporting internationalization of student affairs work. NASPA has been working on relationships with international partner institutions, associations, and individual HEIs for more than 25 years. NASPA has brought together colleagues from across the globe to engage in critical dialogue and discourse with the NASPA International Symposium, launched in 1996, and the Global Summit on Student Affairs and Services, established in 2012 (Callahan, 2015; Ludeman, 2014; Perozzi, Giovannucci, & Shea, 2016). To help network and connect practitioners around the world, NASPAs International Education Knowledge Community (IEKC) offers live briefings and publishes newsletters and blogs to share knowledge and resources. NASPA works with non-US countries to offer webinars in multiple languages, and offers special membership and conference pricing for greater accessibility. ACPAs Globalization Strategic Plan (n.d.) reflects their commitments to: the development of all students as global citizens; diversification through the support of international student development; and collaboration with colleagues around the world. ACPAs global initiatives include partnering with the Global Student Summit on Student Affairs. ACPA accomplishes much of its global work through the Commission for the Global Dimensions of Student Development (CGDSD), which is one of the oldest ACPA entity groups dating back to 1961. The CGDSD offers a one-day pre-conference on various themes at each year's annual convention as well as a research grant to advance knowledge.

Many countries outside of Europe and the US actively advance professional development through the creation of student affairs-oriented professional associations. The Canadian Association of College and University Student Services/ *L'Association des services aux étudiants des universités et colleges du Canada* (CACUSS/ ASEUCC) has been providing bilingual professional development and programs

141

since 1971, and approved its Student Affairs and Services Competency Model in 2016 (Fernandez, Fitzgerald, Hambler, & Mason-Innes, 2016). The Asia Pacific Student Services Association (APSSA), established in 1988, collaborates among members in the region and sponsors the Institute of Student Affairs for practitioners to develop and network. Established in 2012, the Southern African Federation for Student Affairs and Services (SAFSAS) formed as an umbrella group for Southern Africa. The Australian and New Zealand Student Services Association, Inc. (ANZSSA) is more than 40 years old and provides professional development and conferences as well as publishes the *Journal of Australian and New Zealand Student Services Association*. Additionally, *the Journal of Student Affairs in Africa* began publishing in 2013. These journals increase the availability of publications in English to incorporate into graduate curriculum and staff training. In addition to student affairs and services-oriented associations, there are also many professional associations specifically for international educators that offer related trainings and knowledge. A few of them are NAFSA—Association for International Educators, European Association of International Education (EAIE), the Canadian Bureau for International Education (CBIE), the International Education Association of Australia (IEAA), the Japan Network for International Education (JAFSA), and the Mexican Association for International Education (AMPEI).

In countries and regions without professional associations, many practitioners continue their professional development through certifications, workshops, and campus training. For example, practitioners in the Gulf Cooperation Council states of Bahrain, Kuwait, Oman, Qatar, Saudi Arabia, and the United Arab Emirates regularly engage in training to improve advising and counseling competencies and skills (Kruse et al., 2017). Through the NASPA Latin America and Caribbean (LAC) area, practitioners collaborate to create local events, such as Il Primer Congreso Internacional de Asuntos Estudiantiles, the first student affairs conference, in Bogotá, Colombia, convened in 2017 and held at the Universidad de los Andes in Colombia, in conjunction with the Pontificia Universidad Católica de Chile and the Universidad de Monterrey in México. In addition, NASPA helped create a second pilot area in the Middle East, North Africa, South Asia (MENASA) region, to support HEIs and practitioners with representatives from each of the sub-regions serving on a board. A MENASA NASPA conference has been taking place in various locations in the Middle East for more than a decade. While practitioners in the MENASA area are interested in student affairs in the US, they are much more interested in adapting promising practices to their unique cultural profiles in this broad and diverse area as described in the Promising Practice below from Qatar University.

A critical advancement in bringing practitioners together globally was with the creation of the International Association of Student Affairs and Services (IASAS), chartered in Brussels in 2013. IASAS provides free and low-cost support, resources, and networking to practitioners around the world. IASAS has led discussions about international student affairs and services, and seeks to understand common denominators that cut across various cultural contexts. Their knowledge-producing activities involve disseminating research to practitioners, supporting research in less well-represented regions, and even conducting benchmarking research such as collaborating with UNESCO on *Student Affairs and Services in Higher Education: Global Foundations, Issues and Best Practices* (Ludeman, 2014; Zereik & Seeto, 2014). IASAS also launched a Global eMentoring programme to partner established senior administrators with early career practitioners around the world to support global sharing and learning via technology (Seeto, 2016).

Global growth of student affairs work is visible by the expansion of certifications and graduate programs. In China, the Ministry of Education created the "University Advisor Development Regulations" in 2006 to mandate professional development and education to support advisors of students. Since then, 21 training and research centers to grant Ph.D. degrees in student affairs have been established (Li & Fang, 2017). The University of Botswana has been working to professionalize student affairs by creating standards and personnel development (Pansiri & Sinkamba, 2017). Some HEIs sponsor certification programs for student affairs and services practitioners to gain additional skills and knowledge to conduct their jobs within their specific cultural contexts, as shown in the MENASA area, Promising Practice from Qatar University, which developed the Student Life and Services—Professional Development Certificate Program (SLS-PDCP). Key to this program, and all others mentioned here, is the inclusion of local practitioners to serve as primary facilitators, to be sure that content is both developed and delivered using culturally appropriate methodologies. This allows for the direct learning and acquisition of knowledge and skills within local cultural context.

PROMISING PRACTICE: QU Student Life and Services—Professional Development Certificate Program (SLS-PDCP)

Institution: Qatar University

Location: Doha, Qatar

Author: Dr. Courtney Stryker, Advisor/Consultant, Student Affairs Sector; Director MENASA NASPA Area

Background and Context:

Many universities in the Middle East, North Africa, South Asia (MENASA) region have staff who are not trained specifically in student affairs. Due to cultural and familial expectations within this region, many of the student affairs employees are place-bound, and are unable to attend professional development outside of the country or workplace. More recently, political strife in the region also has contributed to this lack of mobility as several countries in the Gulf Cooperation Council (GCC) have blockaded Qatar.

INTERNATIONALIZED PROFESSIONAL DEVELOPMENT

Based on these factors, there is a great need to provide basic professional development in the region to improve staff understanding, student success, and overall staff and student engagement.

Qatar University is the national university for the country and has approximately 18,000 undergraduate students and 2,000 graduate students. Structured similarly to a US land-grant university, there are eight colleges including the medical school. The student affairs sector has approximately 320 employees and includes a full range of programs and services. The Student Life and Services—Professional Development Certificate Program (SLS-PDCP) introduces student affairs as a professional area of study to Qatar University student affairs staff. The SLS-PDCP, offered through a series of 10 two-hour classes, provides the foundation for work and professional development in the field of student affairs and is based on the ACPA and NASPA ten professional competency areas. The course focuses on the role and function of professionals in the field; the populations served; the college and university settings where the profession is practiced; the skills and competencies necessary for professional practice; and current issues in the profession. Designing, developing, and implementing the course has raised the basic understanding, performance, and engagement of the student affairs staff. The bilingual, Arabic and English, approach and the use of regional experts fills a major professional development gap.

Further Description:

Facilitator(s)

The facilitators for the SLS-PDCP are a Qatari course coordinator, who is a member of the student affairs staff, and a wide range of facilitators specific to the topics being covered, such as student development theory, assessment and evaluation, advising and supporting, leadership, etc. For example, the Dean of the College of Law facilitated the class on law, policy, and governance. In addition to the course coordinator, a student affairs-credentialed advisor/consultant helps to plan and facilitate the course as needed.

Learners

At present, the course only is open to QU student affairs staff. During the next cycle, the course will be open to student affairs employees at the Community College of Qatar. Eventually, the course will be open to all student affairs employees in the country.

When

The first pilot in Fall 2015 offered the course over 2 semesters and met 10 times. We piloted a second course in Fall 2016, and plan to offer three progressively detailed classes (Level 1-Foundation, Level 2-Intermediate, Level 3-Advanced) in the next academic year. The course is offered during the workday from 12:00–14:30 to ensure access for all staff. For example, most women would not be able to attend after work hours.

Where

The course is at Qatar University but we will pilot a similar initiative via MENASA (titled—Multaqa NASPA). We will use the materials from the SLS-PDCP and some

INTERNATIONALIZED PROFESSIONAL DEVELOPMENT

of the same facilitators. While the bulk of the professional development will come out of QU, we will coordinate with experts from around NASPA to deliver this online professional development opportunity, in English and Arabic, to a wider audience in the MENASA area. Given the current political situation, this allows for people from all countries in the GCC to participate without issue.

Language

One of the keys to delivering successful student affairs professional development programming to staff in the region is to make it accessible. Approximately 98–99% of the student affairs employees at QU use Arabic as their first language, and the language they use the most to communicate with students. The SLS-PDCP is delivered bilingually with an emphasis on creating, using, and promoting Arabic language materials and resources. The course uses an Arabic translated version of the ACPA and NASPA Professional Competencies and all other materials including presentations, articles, and other resources are translated. This helps to bring not only the concepts of student affairs practice to a wider audience, it also helps to provide participants with the vocabulary they need to use in their day-to-day practice.

Learning Outcomes:

After participating in the SLS-PDCP, staff members will be able to

- Apply basic student development and student affairs theories to their day-to-day practice.
- Create programming and services based upon best practices that are globally informed and culturally relevant.
- Utilize a common set of terms to describe, understand, and communicate within a professional context.
- Demonstrate a more informed understanding of higher education administration and structure.

Assessment:

The course is assessed using the following:

- Pre- and post-course participant feedback (6 Likert scale questions and a brief open-ended reflection piece).
- Facilitator evaluation and feedback.
- Participant feedback (4 quick questions) after each topic.
- End-of-course focus group with participants.
- Participant persistence rates.

Lessons Learned:

1. Cultural Relevance: The ACPA and NASPA Professional Competencies were very good for providing some structure and framework. However, it is important to note that while providing a global perspective of student affairs to QU staff, we needed

145

to customize topics to fit the unique culture of the GCC. We did this by using local experts, regional case studies, and examples of best practices from the MENASA area. The intercultural development comes from our program participants gaining insight and understanding from the US competencies, and discussing what works (and does not work) in a GCC context. For example, laws and policies that govern student affairs practice in the US are not necessarily applicable or relevant in this region—there is no Americans with Disabilities Act (ADA), FERPA, or Title IX. Prior to running each course, we meet with student affairs leaders at the director, AVP, and VPSA levels to gather their input and suggestions. This creates customized content to better reflect the culture of the region while discussing issues that transcend cultural boundaries. We have learned that this is a vital as well as an evolutionary process. We had to change some of our case studies based on feedback from participants and the dynamic political situation in the region. We have learned that we need to revisit the content before we run each course to ensure cultural relevance.

2. Quality Translation: When we started the SLS-PDCP course, we translated the earlier edition of the ACPA and NASPA Professional Competencies. Apparently, our translator did not do the best job and many in the class spent their time critiquing the translation rather than focusing on content. Dialect also has an impact on the quality of the translation. Be sure to consult with multiple professionals who are fluent in the language before you "trust" the work of the translator. They can give valuable insight and feedback because they work in the field.

3. Build a Professional Vocabulary Base: Building on the above point, it is very important to create a bilingual vocabulary list for the course. For example, terms like "student development" or "social justice" do not translate well into Arabic. Student affairs literature (American English) also is loaded with jargon that is difficult to explain (words like "intentional," "framing," etc.). We continue to add to the accompanying vocabulary list for the course. This has been a valuable reference tool for participants and has helped to develop a common language for professional practice at the institution. Participants also enjoy making meaningful contributions to the list.

KEY ASPECTS OF PROFESSIONAL DEVELOPMENT

Student affairs professional competencies, CAS or CAHEP Standards, and graduate preparation programs are all guiding components of professional development at early career phases for many US practitioners. It is often during graduate school where US practitioners learn a wide range of theories, practices, and assessment and research tools. After graduate school and for those without student affairs degrees or coursework, continuing professional development is critical to maintaining preparation for the complex work and challenges faced. To advance student affairs requires data-driven, intentional practice, which demands that practitioners engage in career-long learning (Komives & Carpenter, 2016). Fudan University (Chapter 4 Promising Practice) approaches professional development broadly by providing opportunities for staff across multiple levels of the organization. They follow a collaborative model using local conferences, internships, and limited exchange programs to expose practitioners to various student affairs and services paradigms and practices, while making resources and literature readily available to staff through translations.

In keeping with the importance of blending research, theory, and practice, the PREPARE model for professional development offers a framework for designing any type of training or development. In the PREPARE model activities should be:

- Purposeful, intentional, and goal related.
- Research, theory, and data based.
- Experience-based.
- Peer reviewed.
- Assessed.
- Reflected upon and reflected in practice.
- Evaluated.

(Komives & Carpenter, 2016, pp. 421–422)

Following this model, a chosen professional development or training program aligns with organizational goals so that staff see a need and purpose to the training. If the current division or department does not include internationalization, then this can be an opportunity to develop global learning objectives for professional development. To ensure the chosen program or training will be valuable and beneficial, it is best to select ideas that have some foundation or backing in research or data, such as internal assessment data.

That international education practitioners are asked to "craft decisions and account for their impact in ways that go beyond matters of intuition, self-satisfaction or anecdote" and use research and data (Hunter & Rumbley, 2016, p. 300), is a good reminder for the work of student affairs. Experience-based activities incorporate the strengths and experiences of current practitioners, within the department or across campus, to tailor trainings that leverage staff knowledge. Peer review asks others for advice, feedback, and recommendations on the training, such as with the Promising Practice from Qatar University where staff met with various key administrators to determine topics and cultural nuances that would shape the content for their SLS-PDCP. In the US, these two stages are great opportunities to collaborate with colleagues in cultural and affinity centers or international education and with faculty in related academic programs. Next, assessment determines in advance the feasibility, cost and benefits, time, and energy, and if the training will achieve the desired outcome. High quality programs include time

INTERNATIONALIZED PROFESSIONAL DEVELOPMENT

and activities for staff to reflect on the training and how they can implement them into their work. Programs, offices/departments, or institutions can implement professional development following this model for short- or long-term training to ensure that it is meaningful to those who give their time to participate.

Student affairs divisions can develop their training programs using components of the PREPARE model with an IaH framework to cater to local needs and resources. The Promising Practice from Universitat Rovira i Virgili (URV), in Spain, showcases a training program for administrative staff who had limited exposure to internationalization (Casals, 2015). Administrative staff participated in the Systemic University Change Toward Internationalization program in their native language and at their home institution. This took away barriers to professional development that involve pressure to know English at a high level and the ability to travel for conferences, and allowed greater comfort for participants at a low cost. A week-long training includes pre- and post-assessment via surveys to assess participants' changes in perspective based on the learning outcomes. At the end of the program, time built in for reflection allows participants to present ideas about how they can implement internationalization into their work after attending the training. After the program ends, facilitators evaluate if the training achieves the desired goals set through assessments to measure the impact on: 1) attitudes, 2) stereotypes, 3) communication, and 4) internationalization culture with assessment comparisons showing improvements in all four areas (Casals, 2017). Important components to developing successful professional development programs include shared communication spaces that lead to shared space of values to build community and responsibility with the hope that new solutions emerge (Casals, & Grinkevich, 2017).

PROMISING PRACTICE: Systemic University Change Toward Internationalization: Courses for Administrative Staff

Institution: Universitat Rovira i Virgili (URV)

Location: Tarragona, Spain

Author: Marina Casals-Sala, Director of International Relations

Background and Context:

Universitat Rovira i Virgili (URV) is a public research and teaching university in the Catalan region of Spain with approximately 14,000 students and just over 700 non-academic staff. In 2014, the URV drafted its second Strategic Internationalisation Plan to:

- Identify the key factors and objectives that will allow the URV to successfully adapt to the changes and challenges brought by internationalization.
- Improve the external projection of the institution.

148

INTERNATIONALIZED PROFESSIONAL DEVELOPMENT

- Plan with methodological rigor the implementation of the URV's internationalization activities and the associated resources.
- Improve the structure and internal perception of the URV's international activities.

Academic staff, mainly researchers, are supposed to already have an international outlook and work on research, which, by definition, is international. But what about non-academic staff? Part of URV's international plan was to address this question: how can we internationalize non-academic staff? What do they know regarding internationalization? The Systemic University Change Toward Internationalization (SUCTI) project, now funded by the European Commission Erasmus+ Strategic Partnership call, started in a more modest way in 2011 when the Universitat Rovira i Virgili (URV), within the context of International Days, was looking for something to offer our administrative staff. We came up with a ten-hour course with the objective to transmit the importance of internationalization in today's global context, what the university was doing in this respect, and how this important sector of the university community could participate in the internationalization process.

Further Description:

In Europe, thanks to the Erasmus program, which is already 30 years old, students have been able to study abroad and thus acquire a set of global competencies that help them afterwards in the global labor market. This same program, more recently, has included staff mobility as an option and a growing number of staff are taking this opportunity to spend five days at another institution in Europe to learn how things are done elsewhere. Nevertheless, as we know, mobility or the possibility to study abroad can only target a few of our students or staff and institutions are working toward offering ways to internationalize at home or internationalize comprehensively.

How can we then internationalize our staff at home? SUCTI is a possible answer to this and its message is clear: a higher education institution cannot call itself international if all of its components are not thinking internationally. Through a simple training, SUCTI offers information on global trends in higher education, on internationalization facts and figures relevant to the institution, region, and country, on intercultural communication and tries in a very interactive way to engage participants in a constructive debate around the internationalization of their own institution. The course is not only informative but aims at empowering participants to become true agents of change toward internationalization — ambassadors of the internationalization message — who present at the end of the course their own internationalizing project: a simple project that they can apply from their own job position to contribute to the internationalization of the institution.

Does your institution offer professional development courses to its staff? Is internationalization one of the topics? Is it offered to academic and non-academic staff alike? Is there enough widespread awareness of the importance of internationalization within your institution? Internationalization is understood not as something external, rather as something that affects deeply the institution's own development, and therefore, one's job both in the present and in the future.

INTERNATIONALIZED PROFESSIONAL DEVELOPMENT

A systemic approach to internationalize our higher education institutions is a must in today's world and the best way to succeed is by leading this process from within, transforming mindsets.

Outcomes:

After completing the SUCTI course, participants are able to:

- Understand what internationalization is and why their institution is working toward it.
- Feel part of the internationalization effort and be able and willing to contribute actively to it.
- Have a better understanding of intercultural communication and be better prepared.
- Have learnt from fellow administrative staff members.
- Be internationalization ambassadors for their institution within their own functions.

Assessment:

From a trainer's point of view, changes in the participants' mindsets are obvious, but there was the need to assess with data the impact of the course. This is why the Department of Psychology of the URV helped to develop a survey that was distributed before the course and right after the course, which assesses the progression of participants' attitudes toward internationalization, their stereotypes or prejudices, their perceived capacity to communicate with other cultures, and their take on the internationalization culture of the institution. This survey has been tested on a small number of respondents so far (27) but the first results are encouraging as they show a clear trend of slight improvement on all four areas tested. This assessment tool will be improved with the present project, including a third survey six months after the course in order to measure impact. Moreover, additional data will be collected and analyzed, which should show the effect of such training on participants and, by extension, on their institutions.

This first experience was a success in terms of attendance but also results, and it clearly showed the need for such a training within our institution, where contrary to our beliefs, stereotypes and prejudices were still very much alive regarding international students or internationalization as a whole. Since then, the course has evolved and been implemented at other higher education institutions in Spain and abroad with similar results.

Lessons Learned:

Some of the lessons learnt during this process are that we cannot take for granted the level of internationalization of our own staff, their openness to other cultures, readiness to communicate with international students or willingness to contribute to the internationalization process at our institutions. These aspects can seem basic to those working in international offices or toward internationalization of higher education, but they are not so in many other services throughout our institutions. This is why a course devoted to explaining why internationalization is important, what it entails, how can everybody

INTERNATIONALIZED PROFESSIONAL DEVELOPMENT

contribute, and what is in it for them is key to having everyone on board in this strategic process at our institutions.

If you plan on implementing your own course on internationalization to non-academic staff, these are some tips that can help you:

- Target everyone: at all levels, from all services, even those who do not deal directly with international students. Changing mindsets is not easy and you need as many on board as possible in order to reach those who are more reticent to the idea.
- Mixing non-academic staff and academic staff can be an enriching experience and it can help bridge the gap that generally exists between these two groups. But see if this can apply in your context.
- Use the course to reach the leadership as well. Not as participants maybe, but as important stakeholders. Hold a meeting and explain what you are trying to do, ask for their contribution in identifying those who should attend the course, and show them the benefits of the course and of having everyone on board the internationalization process.
- Recognize those giving the course and those attending it! A simple certificate of completion with the words "You are now an international ambassador, we are proud of you!" can be a very powerful and empowering tool.
- Bring in an international student (or video) to show what their experience at our institution is, what can be improved. Bring in a member of staff who has had an experience abroad and what that has meant.
- Make it interesting, fun, and interactive. Listen to what participants have to say, their concerns, and issues. And ask them to contribute with a personal project to the internationalization process, even a small one. Show them that they are valued.
- Enjoy the process and stay positive. Results may not show in the short term but by persevering your institution will eventually become more and more international.

Media Links:

Systemic University Change Towards Internationalization: www.suctiproject.com

PROFESSIONAL DEVELOPMENT THROUGH LOCAL WORKSHOPS, TRAININGS, AND MEETINGS

In a study of 517 student affairs and services practitioners from around the world, most respondents preferred attending organized learning events such as workshops, conferences, and training to gain professional development with many of the professional associations mentioned earlier as sources for learning, networking, and collaboration (Seifert, Perozzi, Bodine Al-Shaif, Li, & Wildman, 2014). For this group of global respondents, formal education through academic degrees and specific areas of study played a much smaller role (8%) compared to formal professional development opportunities and training (69%). More than half (52%)

151

INTERNATIONALIZED PROFESSIONAL DEVELOPMENT

of the respondents, though, cited continuous learning through reading literature related to practice and theory. These findings are consistent with a study of US and UK SSAOs' perceptions that professional conferences and association memberships are highly effective professional development methods compared to other tools (Rybalkina, 2008). For the US SSAOs in our study, the top experiences for intercultural professional development, as shown in Table 6.1, were: (1) training on working with international students or on cross-cultural understanding (86%); (2) direct experience planning culturally relevant and internationally diverse programs, services, and policies (77%); and (3) attending conference sessions about international issues, students, or internationalization (63%).

Table 6.1 Experiences Needed to be Considered Interculturally Competent

Selection of Experiences	#	%
Completed training on working with international students or on cross-cultural understanding	74	86
Experience planning culturally relevant and internationally diverse programs, services, policies	67	78
Attended conference sessions about international issues, students, or internationalization	55	64
Took a course(s) on international higher education or student affairs during graduate work	31	36
Non-US living or working experience	28	33
Non-US travel for vacation	22	26

Attending conferences for practitioners is common and clearly a valuable source of educational content; however, not everyone has access or ability to attend conferences when they require travel and/or financial resources. As such, it is important to develop opportunities where experience and knowledge can be developed at, or close to, the home campus. For those practitioners who attend conferences, they can reflect on what they learned, and how to implement ideas by sharing with other staff members at their home institution. Additionally, sharing back can be an important tool for accountability of finances, learning, and professional development but also to develop role-modeling and mentorship of staff. For example, one program from the international office at Bunker Hill Community College, Boston, was to have faculty and staff who traveled to other countries or who were from other countries create evening seminars that concluded with dinner for added benefit to the campus community in sharing of experiences and knowledge (Korbel, 2002).

The US SSAOs in our study wished to provide staff with more in-house or campus-based trainings related to internationalization and intercultural development. They offered these specific training topics and program suggestions:

- Improving communication skills and ways to disseminate information to international students.
- Developing cultural competence in the workplace.
- Supporting and providing multicultural competency education/training that is inclusive of an international perspective.
- Hearing from international students about their student experience to identify gaps in service/supports or opportunities for enhancement.
- Expanding international student orientation.
- Increasing interdepartmental collaboration and training with international services office.
- Local commitments with global connections as a framework.
- Having more culturally appropriate skills in terms of advising, supporting, and interacting with international students.
- Using an intercultural competency assessment or instrument, such as those mentioned in the previous chapter.

Many student affairs divisions may already have professional development committees or dedicated human resource staff who can assist in organizing training, sub-committees, lunchtime talks, or gatherings. Most of these suggestions fit well within an IaH framework and would offer structure to the programs and explanation of the importance behind these efforts.

While only 26% of the SSAOs in our study stated the need for intercultural competency to include knowing more than one language (see Table 3.1). International education literature and intercultural student programs reflect that individuals develop interculturally through the process of interacting and practicing language with others. Awareness of languages can assist practitioners in better understanding intercultural concepts and increasing empathy and willingness to communicate with others. Or, if staff are not interested in lunch-time language conversational programs, for example, all staff should be aware of how they communicate. Thus, working with practitioners to analyze their English communication patterns and assumptions to become better intercultural communicators can be an activity incorporated into regular staff functions or meetings. A few characteristics of effective intercultural communication in English are:

- Using fewer idiomatic, metaphoric, and jargonistic expressions.
- Being more accepting of silence as others process what has been said or construct their own utterances.
- Citing fewer own-culture reference points.

INTERNATIONALIZED PROFESSIONAL DEVELOPMENT

- Being more mindful of others' English abilities and making effort to adjust own language to meet their needs.
- Being more mindful of signs of miscomprehension or confusion in others' behaviour, facial expressions, etc.
- Using shorter and less complex syntax.

(Killick, 2015, Figure 5.1, p. 136)

Other professional development activities "at home" are to develop research teams like the example from The Hague University of Applied Sciences (see Chapter 4). Time during established staff meetings can include discussion of shared readings, such as the Promising Practices in this book, or podcasts, videos, and the like around international themes and content. Or to better understand a specific population of international students, practitioners can read journals from outside their home country to increase knowledge about the systems and cultures from which those students come (Shea, Gormley, Clarke, & Leary, 2016). While reading books and journals alone is not a substitute for direct experiential learning, it is an activity that can expand knowledge and is accessible to most student affairs staff. Additionally, any of the intercultural assessment tools mentioned in the previous chapters can offer significant value to self-discovery and professional development.

CONCLUSION

As student affairs practitioners engage in their professional development journey, whether through coursework or myriad other ways to gain competencies, there will always be more to know and understand. The incorporation of international-ization and the focus on intercultural professional development is a very specific opportunity to invoke "a process of learning and sharing across difference where no one culture dominates" (Tanaka, 2002, p. 282). Understanding that most US student development theories do not include diverse and international students suggests that practitioners look to other theories to employ in concert with appropriate models used previously, or discovered anew. Grounding learning about the work of student affairs in existing student developmental theories must be practiced carefully while new research and theories are being ethically developed. Leaders at all levels within student affairs can create contexts that support inter-cultural development for staff and students through local programs and resources. Environments that reinforce and reflect international perspectives send a signal and set the stage for knowledge acquisition and skill development. Inclusive, inquisitive, and entrepreneurial environments will motivate staff to inform their practice and guide their learning around intercultural concepts. International and intercultural development takes time and energy over a lifetime, and the many ways to gain these skills vary widely.

154

While there is not yet a global profession of student affairs, there are practitioners doing student affairs-related work on a daily basis worldwide. Providing appropriate, lifelong developmental opportunities for these individuals is varied, nuanced, and culturally relevant. Recognizing that many types and providers of training and resources are available, and some may be better suited than others due to learning styles, cultural norms, and language barriers, is a key element in intercultural student affairs work. Meanings and interpretations of concepts such as social justice and intercultural learning vary in a global context, so maintaining flexibility in professional development delivery and consumption is critical for success. This is particularly important in the professional development of US practitioners to be able to shed Western paradigms to more fully understand and embrace multiple approaches to student affairs.

REFERENCES

Arminio, J., & Ortiz, A. M. (2017). Professionalism. In J. H. Schuh, S. R. Jones, and V. Torres (Eds.), *Student services: A handbook for the profession*, 6th ed. (pp. 377–391). San Francisco, CA: Jossey-Bass.

ACPA—College Student Educators. (n.d.). ACPA's globalization strategic plan. Retrieved from www.myacpa.org/files/globalization-strategic-plan-handout-finalpdf

Astin, A. W. (1984). Student involvement: A developmental theory for higher education. *Journal of College Student Personnel, 25*(4), 297–308.

Baxter Magolda, M. G. (2001). *Making their own way: Narratives for transforming higher education to promote self-development.* Sterling, VA: Stylus.

Baxter Magolda, M. G., Creamer, E. G., & Meszaros, P. S. (2012). *Development and assessment of self-authorship: Exploring the concept across cultures.* Sterling, VA: Stylus.

Bennett, J. M., & Bennett, M. J. (2004). Developing intercultural sensitivity: An integrative approach to global and domestic diversity. In D. Landis, J. M. Bennett, & M. J. Bennett, (Eds.), *Handbook of intercultural training,* 3rd ed. (pp. 147–165). Thousand Oaks, CA: Sage.

Council for the Advancement of Standards in Higher Education (2015). *CAS professional standards for higher education* (9th ed.). Washington, D.C.: Author.

Callahan, K. (2015). *The internationalization in student affairs in the United States from 1951 to 1996* (Doctoral dissertation). Florida State University, Tallahassee, FL.

Casals, M. (2015). Targeting administrative staff. *EAIE Forum,* Winter, 36. Retrieved from https://suctiproject.files.wordpress.com/2015/11/article-forum-eaie-sucti.pdf

Casals, M., & Grinkevich, Y. (2017). Unity on campus: Professional development for administrative staff. EAIE Blog. Retrieved from www.eaie.org/blog/unity-campus-professional-development-administrative-staff/

Casals, M. (2017). The internationalisation of non-academic staff. In A. Perez-Encinas, L. Howard, L. E. Rumbley, & H. de Wit (Eds.), *The internationalisation of higher*

155

education in Spain: Reflections and perspectives (pp. 52–57). Madrid, Spain: SEPIE. Retrieved from http://sepie.es/doc/comunicacion/publicaciones/SEPIE-ENG_internacionalizacion.pdf

Deardorff, D. K. (2016). Key theoretical frameworks guiding the scholar-practitioner in international education. In B. Streitweiser & A. C. Ogden (Eds.), *International education's scholar-practitioners: Bridging research and practice* (pp. 247–264). Oxford: Symposium.

European Organisations in Student Affairs and Social Services (2010). Padova Declaration. Padova, Italy: Author.

Fernandez, D., Fitzgerald, C., Hambler, P., & Mason-Innes, T. (2016). The Canadian Association of College and University Student Services/*L'Association des services aux étudiants des universities et colleges du Canada* (CACUSS/ASEUCC) student affairs and services competency model. Toronto, Canada: CACCUS/ASEUCC.

Fowler, J. W. (1981). *Stages of faith: The psychology of human development and the quest for meaning*. New York: Harper Collins.

Fried, J. (2011). Multicultural identities and shifting selves among college students. In M. J. Cuyjet, M. F. Howard-Hamilton, & D. L. Cooper (Eds.), *Multiculturalism on campus: Theory, models, and practices for understanding diversity and creating inclusion* (pp. 65–83). Sterling, VA: Stylus.

Goodman, J., Schlossberg, N., & Anderson, M. (2006). *Counseling adults in transition*. New York: Springer.

Hunter, F., & Rumbley, L. E. (2016). Exploring a possible future for the scholar-practitioner. In B. Streitwieser, & A. C. Ogden (Eds.), *International higher education's scholar-practitioners: Bridging research and practice* (pp. 297–308). Oxford: Symposium.

Jones, S. R., & Abes, E. S. (2011). The nature and uses of theory. In J. H. Schuh, S. R. Jones, & Associates (Eds.), *Student services: A handbook for the profession*, 5th ed. (pp. 149–167). San Francisco, CA: Jossey-Bass.

Killick, D. (2015). *Developing the global student: Higher education in an era of globalization*. New York: Routledge.

Killick, D. (2017). *Internationalization and diversity in higher education: Implications for teaching, learning and assessment*. London: Palgrave.

Komives, S. R., & Carpenter, S. (2016). Professional development as lifelong learning. In G. S. McClellan, J. Stringer, & Associates (Eds.), *The handbook of student affairs administration* (pp. 411–430). San Francisco, CA: Jossey-Bass.

Korbel, L. A. (2002). Small projects that promote an international campus culture. In R. M. Romano (Ed.), *Internationalizing the community college* (pp. 125–134). Washington, D.C.: Rowman & Littlefield Publishers.

Kruse, T., Al-Khaldi, A., & Witt, E. (2017). Student affairs practices in the Arabian Gulf: The good, the bad and the foreign. *ACPA Developments, 15*, 1–2.

Ludeman, R. B. (2014). Joining hands across the seas: The genesis of IASAS. *Journal of Student Affairs in Africa, 2*(1), 67–74.

Li, Y., & Fang, Y. (2017). Professionalisation of student affairs educators in China: History, challenges, and solutions. *Journal of Student Affairs in Africa, 5*(1), 41–50.

Pansiri, B. M., & Sinkamba, R. P. (2017). Advocating for standards in student affairs departments in African institutions: University of Botswana experience. *Journal of Student Affairs in Africa, 5*(1), 51–62.

Patton, L., Renn, K. A., Guido, F. M., & Quaye, S. J. (2016). *Student development in college: Theory, research, and practice,* 3rd ed. San Francisco, CA: Jossey-Bass.

Perozzi, B., Seifert, T. & Bodine Al-Sharif, M. A. (2016). Staffing for Success. In D. Roberts & S. Komives (Eds.), *Enhancing student learning and development in cross-border higher education* (pp. 93–103). San Francisco, CA: Jossey-Bass.

Perozzi, B., Giovannucci, G. L., & Shea, R. (2016). *The global dialogue.* In L. Osfield, B. Perozzi, L. Bardill Moscaritolo, & R. Shea (Eds.), *Supporting students globally in higher education* (pp. 21–42). Washington, D.C.: NASPA.

Pope, L. R., Mueller, J. A., & Reynolds, A. L. (2009). Looking back and moving forward: Future directions for diversity research in student affairs. *Journal of College Student Development, 50*(6), 640–658.

Renn, K. A., Brazelton, G. B., & Holmes, J. M. (2014). At the margins of internationalization: Trends in publishing on international issues related to college student experiences, development, and learning, 1998–2008. *Journal of College Student Development, 55*(3), 278–294.

Rybalkina, O. (2008). Competence in student affairs administration: Perspectives from the United Kingdom and United States. In K. J. Osfield & Associates (Eds.), *Internationalization of student affairs and services: An emerging global perspective* (pp. 37–48). Washington, D.C.: NASPA.

Sanford, N. (1962). *The American college.* New York: Wiley.

Seeto, E. M. (2016). Professional mentoring in student affairs: Evaluation of a global programme. *Journal of Student Affairs in Africa, 4*(2), 47–51.

Shea, R., Gormley, B., Clarke, A., & Leary, T. (2016). Professional development for student affairs and services staff: The role of professional associations. In K. Osfield, B. Perozzi, L. Bardill Moscaritolo, & R. Shea (Eds.), *Supporting students globally in higher education* (pp. 87–105). Washington, D.C.: NASPA.

Seifert, T., Perozzi, B., Bodine Al-Shaif, M., Li, W., & Wildman, K. (2014). *Student affairs & services in global perspective: A preliminary exploration of practitioners' background, roles, and professional development.* Toronto, Canada: IASAS.

Streitwieser, B., & Ogden, A. C. (2016). Heralding the scholar-practitioner in international education. In B. Streitwieser, & A. C. Ogden (Eds.), *International higher education's scholar-practitioners: Bridging research and practice* (pp. 19–38). Oxford: Symposium.

Tanaka, G. (2002). Higher education's self-reflexive turn: Toward an intercultural theory of student development. *The Journal of Higher Education, 73*(2), 263–296.

Tierney, W. G. (1992). An anthropological analysis of student participation in college. *Journal of Higher Education, 63,* 603–618.

Tinto, V. (1975). Dropout from higher education: A theoretical synthesis of recent research. *Review of Educational Research, 45*, 89–125.

Ward, H. H. (2016). *Internationalizing the co-curriculum: Part three: Internationalization and student affairs*. Washington, D.C.: ACE. Retrieved from www.acenet.edu/newsroom/Documents/Intlz-In-Action-Intlz-Co-Curriculum-Part-3.pdf.

Universitat Rovira i Virgili. (n.d.). Strategic Internationalisation Plan. Retrieved from www.urv.cat/en/about/get-to-know/internationalisation/.

University of Sydney. (n.d.). National Centre for Cultural Competence (NCCC): Our commitment. Retrieved from http://sydney.edu.au/nccc/about/index.shtml

Zereik, R., & Seeto, E-M. (2014). IASAS: A borderless global movement. *Journal of the Australia and New Zealand Student Services Association, 43*, 25–30.

Chapter 7

Recommendations and Implications for Practice

In today's society, more than ever before, higher education plays an essential role in developing and supporting graduates who are ethically, engaged global citizens. While violence and fear permeate communities around the world, student affairs practitioners uniquely are poised to respond directly to the calls to help break detrimental cycles of oppression, hate, and ignorance that fuel divisions among individuals. Gone should be the days of isolationism and exceptionalism. Acceptance and support of differences among cultures, regions, and nations must be embraced and understood, followed by decisive action. Student affairs is a critical component of this inclusive approach, by embracing ideologies that are local/global in nature and by developing a deep understanding of worldviews while demonstrating skills and abilities to affect change "at home." Now is not the time to continue focusing primarily on travel-required programs that, while beneficial and even life-altering, remain biased towards the few and leave out approximately 90% of the student body in the US and UK alike (Killick, 2015). Instead, Internationalization at Home (IaH) shifts the emphasis to the abundant opportunity in the "home" cocurriculum to increase intentional intercultural learning opportunities that raise everyone's competencies.

Internationalization is not just connected to diversity and social justice and inclusion (SJI) work, but is the work as:

> Education in and for globalization should engage students in critical reflection on normative questions about power and equity. In the process of becoming more self-aware, students need to develop the capacity to discern their social locations in every relation, transaction, and encounter.
>
> (Cornwell & Stoddard, 1999, p. 24)

Individuals often fail to engage with culturally diverse peers even if they intellectually understand the value of intercultural interactions. Addressing equity and self-awareness at the individual, cocurricular, and organizational levels through

RECOMMENDATIONS AND IMPLICATIONS

inclusive internationalization strategies is critical for change to occur. Using international students to increase the numerical or structural diversity of US higher education institutions (HEIs) may reinforce biases, discrimination, and stereotypes. Increasing internationalization efforts through diversity and SJI frameworks can ensure ethical, international student recruitment as well as domestic and international student intercultural engagement. Therefore, the aim of this book has been to explore how SSAOs, divisions, and practitioners can internationalize their work, and incorporate intercultural competencies to advance holistic student and professional development.

There are countless ways to support internationalization in US student affairs practice as discussed in the previous chapters. Outlined in this final chapter are suggestions, implications, and recommendations based on the prior discussions and conceptualized through the original goals of this book, which were to:

- Provide Internationalization at Home (IaH) as a framework for strategic development of internationalization of US student affairs.
- Incorporate inclusive internationalization that stimulates intercultural development for all without prioritizing outbound international travel.
- Promote expanding paradigms and perspectives by incorporating practices and intercultural work from outside the US to advance the profession's knowledge base and ways of knowing and practicing.

Throughout the chapters, we offered arguments supported by international and interdisciplinary research, theories, and practice and reflected on exploratory survey data from US SSAOs' perspectives on internationalization. There is good work happening in higher education around the world, and internationalizing student affairs is an opportunity to build upon that work to improve connections, collaborations, and partnerships that can make campus climates more inclusive and educational for all students while supporting the professional competency development of practitioners. In what follows, we revisit the main goals of the book and offer some key recommendations to create a foundation for the internationalization of US student affairs. Incorporating diversity and internationalization into the cocurriculum is most effective with leadership commitment as demonstrated through strategic development; incorporation of global learning outcomes for all; international and intercultural integration into graduate preparation programs and professional development; and inclusive assessment, evaluation, and research, all done with increased knowledge on global practices.

IAH FRAMEWORK FOR STRATEGIC DEVELOPMENT OF INTERNATIONALIZATION OF US STUDENT AFFAIRS

As more and more HEIs' mission or vision statements reference being a "world class institution" or an "international university," student affairs can ensure they

160

RECOMMENDATIONS AND IMPLICATIONS

incorporate or reflect these values. SSAOs and practitioners can position student affairs as a leader and ally in advancing internationalization through an IaH framework so that global perspectives and intercultural learning is accessible and available for all, thus ensuring an inclusive cocurriculum. SSAOs can support an IaH framework through education, collaborative partnerships, and supporting documents, like strategic plans and policies. Analyzing strategic frameworks and other policy decisions for equity and ethical treatment of those involved connects to the imperative call that internationalization links to diversity and SJI as a social justice framework addresses any "discriminatory practices that involve unequal power distributions (e.g., age, language, immigrant status and disabilities)" (Chizhik & Chizhik, 2002, p. 792). Who better equipped to address this than student affairs practitioners? Educating student affairs practitioners about the value and benefits of internationalization can influence strategic development so they can, then, identity current and potential partners for collaboration, and develop creative IaH strategies and practices.

Educate Staff on the Value and Benefits of Internationalization

A paradigm shift often requires systemic and cultural changes where all stakeholders have bought into the mission and goals of internationalization efforts and see it as integral to their work (Hudzik, 2015; Leask, 2015). Promising Practices for campus-based training programs, such as with the Promising Practice from Universitat Rovira i Virgili in Chapter 6, can ensure all staff know the benefits of internationalization and develop opportunities for how they can contribute. An important part of this is internal marketing to promote the vision of internationalization within the institution and student affairs division that can increase knowledge and commitment from staff. Another way to advance education is for practitioners to seek out seats on institution-wide committees designed to internationalize and educate others on how student affairs areas are key elements in internationalizing the campus due to their connections with students. This process often begins with understanding how IaH combines local/global needs and issues and how it is not only about mobility and travel, but that it is necessary for all students, practitioners, and faculty to advance.

Creation of environments and organizational cultures that reflect and support internationalization and diversity efforts can be an essential foundation. The importance of internationalization can be further reinforced through thoughtful attention to organizational cultural elements through icons and visual manifestations of core elements (Shein, 2004). These can take the form of celebrations around successful internationalization efforts, or honors or awards for members of the campus community that recognize good intercultural and inclusive work. Infusing culturally diverse artwork, hiring international faculty, staff, and students, as well as performances and displays relating to intercultural art and topics all

161

reinforce an organizational culture that signal the value and importance of internationalization to the institution and student affairs specifically.

Identify and Collaborate with Current and Potential Partners

Educating about the value and benefits of internationalizing student affairs and the need for student affairs to be integral partners in institutional internationalization includes involving a variety of stakeholders from senior leadership, faculty, academic affairs, other colleagues across the institution, and especially students themselves (Olson, Evans, & Shoenberg, 2007; Roberts & Komives, 2016). While IaH does not require a top-down strategy, the more stakeholders involved at all levels increases commitment and sustainability of efforts.

Offices that already promote internationalization activities or support international and intercultural work, including global academic programs, international education, residential education, and multicultural education, such as cultural and affinity centers, are great first steps in establishing partnerships. A few areas to partner and collaborate on to advance internationalization include:

- Conducting an assessment inventory of all cocurriculum programming where collaboration exists or could have shared global student learning outcomes.
- Collaborating with more experienced researchers (practitioners or faculty) to promote advancing knowledge on internationalized student affairs practice and intercultural development.
- Working with faculty to infuse international frameworks, literature, and practice or experiential opportunities into curriculum.
- Using graduate students' internships or assistantships to develop internationalization plans or implement new IaH strategies within various functional areas.
- Exploring local opportunities with the globally diverse populations within local communities to help connect back to various student affairs cocurricular programs.

Empowering student affairs practitioners to work across departments and divisions and connect ideas and concepts can foster globally focused environments for students and the HEI community. It may require this outreach, and then stewardship of relationships, to move internationalization forward within student affairs, especially if there is not an institutional plan.

Develop an IaH Vision and Strategic Plan for Student Affairs

The mission and ethos of HEIs will guide organizational strategy and goal development at various levels of these organizations. In our study of US SSAOs, the more

162

RECOMMENDATIONS AND IMPLICATIONS

overt the support for internationalization was at the institutional level, the more infused the concept was in the division and with student affairs practitioners. However, even at HEIs without an explicit internationalization plan or strategy, student affairs divisions and departments can advance IaH by infusing their own missions, values, and strategic documents with internationalization goals and intercultural learning outcomes. A student affairs division can create an overall vision of internationalization that allows individual departments or programs to develop how they will support that vision. Student affairs guiding documents can support student learning and holistic development by connecting to internationalization's focus on global learning and citizenship like The Hague University of Applied Sciences' vision for THUAS students to be global citizens who are competent in culturally diverse and international settings. Or, as with Fudan University's Promising Practice Opening-Up of Student Affairs Initiative, which was a broad yet targeted strategic approach to creating a positive organizational cultural shift.

Capitalizing on the overlap of organizational goals to support internationalization and diversity and SJI within the local community and student populations can mitigate possible downfalls and potentially enhance organizational effectiveness. In the Promising Practice from the University of Sydney, their National Centre for Cultural Competence begins their intercultural work grounded in "Developing understanding and social cohesion with Australia's First Peoples [as] the appropriate starting point for the work of a Centre focused on valuing diversity, both in country and outwards across the globe" (para. 3). As vision and strategic plans inclusive of diversity are likely already in place for most US HEIs, this can be an opening conversation about how internationalization can, and should, complement broader diversity goals because this would benefit all students (Otten, 2003). Integrating global awareness and intercultural principles throughout helps all members of the HEI community remain aware and engaged in dialogue that prepares students for global citizenship and creates positive changes in climate for the inclusion of non-dominant identity students. To honor the commonalities discussed in Chapter 2, student affairs divisions and departments can incorporate more intercultural inclusivity into the system by considering the following:

- Revising, if needed, divisional and departmental missions and visions to reflect and include internationalization prioritization and intercultural values.
- Creating international and intercultural learning outcomes for students and staff within strategic documents and reflect them in assessment plans.
- Incorporating internationalization and intercultural competency into practitioner and student employee job descriptions, trainings, and performance evaluations.

163

RECOMMENDATIONS AND IMPLICATIONS

- Reviewing and revising divisional and department documents that reinforce majority cultural dominance, including customs and values, or privilege only Western, US ways of knowing and acting.
- Reflecting respect for cultural differences of US and international individuals, inclusive of race, ethnicity, nationality, religion, etc., throughout guiding documents and informal policies.

Changing organizational culture requires the implementation of new cultural icons, in the form of visible guiding documents, policy updates, and practices that reflect the importance of culturally inclusive internationalization.

INTERCULTURAL LEARNING FOR ALL STUDENTS THAT PROMOTES MORE INCLUSIVE PRACTICE

The continuous "shrinking" of the world necessitates that internationalization is a central component of helping all students succeed and not viewed as extra work or an add-on. Students require optimal learning environments, so providing access to inclusive programs and services is essential. Faculty and student affairs practitioners can use the intersection between internationalization and multicultural education to develop intercultural skills, broaden attitudes, develop local/global citizenship, and explore power and privilege in the local/global context (Killick, 2015; Olson et al., 2007). Overlaps and opportunities for intentionally connecting internationalization with current diversity, multicultural, and SJI work are meant to strengthen the focus on local intercultural and internationalization efforts while highlighting the global nature of inequalities and social justice. As such, student affairs can promote inclusive internationalization by creating global learning outcomes, conducting culturally sensitive assessment, evaluation, and research, ensuring intercultural interactions that are locally connected, and incorporating international students throughout the organization.

Develop Global Learning Outcomes that Promote Intercultural Development

An internationalized cocurriculum needs to have mutually beneficial learning and engagement because "intercultural learning is *both* continuous effort *and* educational outcome of internationalisation at home" (Otten, 2000, p. 19, italics in original). Shared student learning outcomes found across internationalization, international education, multiculturalism, and diversity work can further enhance learning outcomes for all cocurricular programs and connect back to an institution's core curriculum or general education outcomes. Three shared learning outcomes from the American Council on Education's (2014) At Home in the World toolkit directly target intercultural competency and the integration with diversity that includes:

164

RECOMMENDATIONS AND IMPLICATIONS

- Understanding culture within a global and comparative context.
- Having the ability to use knowledge, diverse cultural frames of reference, and alternate perspectives to think critically and solve problems.
- Accepting cultural differences and having tolerance for cultural ambiguity.

("Student learning at the intersection," para. 2)

The learning outcomes and goals for the critical service learning projects that comprise Global Citizenship and Equity Learning Experiences Promising Practice from Centennial College, Canada, reflect this complementary infusion of an SJI framework within local/global communities that helps students' awareness of historical inequities, their role as global citizens, and the responsibility to advocate for social change.

Ensuring that these outcomes are sustainable, achievable, and in alignment with institutional goals is essential for longevity and learning. Designating which outcomes are most appropriate for specific areas, programs, and services is part of the strategy for success, yet most programs should be able to incorporate intercultural learning. A seamless approach among academic and student affairs practitioners is a preferred way to reach critical learning outcomes. For example, while faculty can provide extra credit for students to attend programs and activities, it would be even more impactful to partner with faculty in the planning process. This could increase the likelihood that course components, content, or assignments capitalize on and complement the cocurricular programs, events, and activities. This approach demonstrates to students the benefits of blending curricular and cocurricular learning related to intercultural outcomes.

Student affairs practitioners are integrally involved with the creation, implementation, and oversight of leadership programs and activities, intercultural programming and events, and student organizations. Student employment is a similarly well-suited opportunity for practitioners and students to work collaboratively to identify, teach, and measure global learning based on overt outcomes infused and supported throughout work experiences and training activities. The essential work and collaborative efforts with students should be guided by clear learning outcomes for the students, programs, and services, within intercultural environments created because of a concerted effort to understand global issues and perspectives. Duke Kunshan University's Promising Practice is a great example of overt outcomes that infuse intercultural learning into them, and the Intercultural Communication and Learning Program joint venture between the University of Macau and Fudan University uses intercultural development theories as the genesis of their learning outcomes. There are common skill sets such as communication, problem-solving, lifelong learning, teamwork and interpersonal skills, self-awareness, and reflection, to name a few, that can all be internationalized.

RECOMMENDATIONS AND IMPLICATIONS

An internationalized student learning outcome example is where students may be able to "work effectively in teams consisting of members from a range of different linguistic and cultural backgrounds" (Leask, 2015, p. 74).

Support or Conduct Ethical and Culturally Sensitive Assessment, Evaluation, and Research

Practitioners are accustomed to the need for data-driven practice and decision-making. Thus, being able to demonstrate if domestic and international students' interactions and participation in cocurricular programs produce desired learning can be powerful in guiding decision-making, strategies, and future planning. Conducting and publishing assessment, evaluation, and research are significant professional development activities for practitioners so that successes can be celebrated, promising practices shared with other colleagues, and knowledge on internationalization and intercultural learning advanced. Culturally appropriate assessment and measurement of global student learning is a central aspect of student affairs work requiring individuals to engage in these activities with continuous self-reflection, attention to ethics, and intercultural understanding, so that they avoid harm or reinforcement of stereotypes and biases. Assessment and research can advocate for change in system, services, policies, or culture of HEIs. For example, in a study cited in previous chapters (Yakaboski, Perez-Velez, & Almutairi, 2017), the researchers partnered with international education practitioners to explore the experiences of graduate students from the Kingdom of Saudi Arabia. They developed a plan for how the data collection would be ethical and respectful to this community, including that the data would be shared with key stakeholders and senior administrators to improve services and climate. By gathering qualitative data, the stories and narratives offer rich, deep explanations and can give policy makers or administrators a fuller understanding of the trends or patterns found.

As found in the University of South Australia's assessment, intercultural interventions and programs are best when structured in a two-directional effort, meaning often there is a built-in assumption that it is the responsibility of international students to engage, adjust, and interact, but domestic students require support and skill development to perform these actions as well (Leask, 2009). Assessments and research tools can be more inclusive by employing "an intercultural [theory of student development] framework, the interactions between student, college, student major, family and close friends, and society are all considered important. Questions will avoid culturally loaded terms that might imply assimilation into a dominant culture" (Tanaka, 2002, p. 284). The Promising Practice Cultural Encounters from the Chinese University of Hong Kong's assessments of their i-Ambassadors scheme showed that students' participation through

166

RECOMMENDATIONS AND IMPLICATIONS

the program met the program's objectives of increasing intercultural interaction. The fact that international students are typically a distinct and easy to identify population makes it possible to gather basic data, such as how many international students are in attendance, from which countries, which majors, etc. Assessments on international students can be compared to larger datasets of experiences such as the International Student Barometer developed by i-graduate, which is a survey conducted twice a year of more than 3 million students, in 1,400 institutions across 33 countries. However, it is important to ensure that international students are not treated as a monolithic group but rather should allow for some disaggregation in analysis and implications (Glass, Wongtrirat, & Buus, 2015).

The complexity of assessing and evaluating dramatically increases when attempting to measure learning outcomes related to intercultural competencies. Some guidance can be found in AAC&U's VALUE rubrics (2009) that include global learning and intercultural knowledge and competence, based on Bennett's Development Model of Intercultural Sensitivity and Deardorff's intercultural framework. AAC&U's intercultural knowledge rubric addresses cultural self-awareness, cultural frameworks knowledge, empathy, communication, curiosity, and openness. As diversity experiences are one of ten "high-impact practices," AAC&U asserts these will deepen learning and have the potential to lead to students developing intercultural skills upon graduation. With more intentionality, student affairs professionals can adapt AAC&U's global learning outcomes to internationalize their programs and support student learning. On a broader institutional assessment level, the National Survey of Student Engagement offers HEIs two related optional modules—global learning and inclusiveness and engagement with cultural diversity—to assess as part of the student experience. Additionally, there are many external assessment tools that can help measure global knowledge and intercultural and competency development at the student or individual level, such as the Intercultural Development Inventory (IDI) or the Beliefs, Events, and Values Inventory (BEVI).

Ensure Meaningful Inclusive Interactions that Promote Local Connections

A primary aim of internationalization is to facilitate interactions between students of diverse cultural backgrounds because majority students largely resist diversity curriculum and engagement outside of their homogeneous groups. The creation of intentional, structured, intergroup, or cross-cultural exchanges offer all students the opportunity to "acknowledge the presence of racism, sexism, heterosexism and other forms of oppression in these interactions, and to provide opportunities to make meaning of those exchanges and experiences" (Pope, Mueller, & Reynolds, 2009, p. 648). Just as it is important to help domestic students understand and

RECOMMENDATIONS AND IMPLICATIONS

learn about international students' cultures and experiences, international students benefit from learning about the value in diversity and multiculturalism in the US (Peterson, Briggs, Dreasher, Horner, & Nelson, 1999). To do this, authentic programs incorporate learning elements that are intentional and collaborative as to avoid presenting culture as exotic or a cultural caricature. High quality global and intercultural events answer these questions:

- Is the event inclusive? Would all members of the campus community feel welcome, regardless of nationality, religion, race, or other aspects of their identities?
- Does the event **facilitate interaction** between different groups?
- Does the event align with a **global or intercultural learning outcome** defined by the institution?

(Ward, 2015, bold in original, p. 11)

While the first question may present difficulty in truly achieving inclusivity for all identities, role-modeling the importance of inclusive interactions along with the skills for intercultural communication and learning is critical.

Involving domestic students and local community members in designing IaH strategies can create awareness of the benefits of internationalization for those who may have a more local perspective, while also increasing opportunities for international students to connect to the local community. Student affairs likely already works with many community engagement programs such as Alternative Spring Break programs and local volunteer and service opportunities. These are great places to ensure that learning outcomes include intercultural competency development and the ability to think about issues locally, and how they may mirror global issues or connect to international patterns. In working with diverse local community groups and members, it is important to ensure that partnerships derive mutual benefit and reciprocal learning for those involved in the engagement opportunities. As mentioned in earlier chapters, leveraging diverse environments for domestic and international students can be a key element of IaH but only when ethical. If the local community offers areas such as rural settings and densely populated urban environments, all students can learn and grow by focusing on outcomes that are like those that have been traditionally employed in education abroad programs. For example, the Promising Practice Community-Based Experiential Learning at the University of British Columbia connects international students with local community organizations to design projects to support global citizenship volunteerism on the part of the student but also helps community members develop understanding of non-local student cultures. Ultimately, unfamiliar elements and dramatically different paradigms can exist right at home, fostering similar learning outcomes as experienced overseas.

Incorporate International Students Throughout the Institution

Supporting international students on individual campuses is a primary way that student affairs practitioners support internationalization and international students are increasingly a key component to higher education globally. As such, programs for international students are found at almost all HEIs worldwide. The Promising Practice of Nottingham Trent University's Global Lounges program is a good example of an initiative that fully embeds international students into the fabric of the institution, by helping them feel at home and providing opportunities for interaction and learning across cultures. Offering these well-planned and programmed spaces can make significant impacts on international student transition, retention, and sense of belonging at the institution. For more practices, the Center for Global Education keeps a list of international student support programs around the US and across many functional areas of traditional student affairs divisions, including career services, athletics, peer programs, mental wellness, orientation, and more.

International students themselves are important partners and student affairs practitioners can empower them by "partner[ing] to advocate, not just cooperate" (Glass et al., 2015, p. 109). Inviting and ensuring international student placements on advisory boards, student senate, graduate student council, and the like, can develop leadership skills while offering HEIs important insight into student experiences and perspectives that will benefit culture change if their ideas are implemented. To partner with international students, practitioners and programs need to first have a foundation of contact early and regularly to assist these students with transition into the institution and help sustain them throughout their academic careers. It is possible to connect with students even before enrollment by collaborating with the international student services office, and reaching out to students at strategic points in time can be beneficial for international students, domestic students, and the institution overall. Social media effectively reaches many students, and targeted use of specific media and applications with cultural considerations, for example, WeChat with Chinese students and WhatsApp for Mexican students, can be simple and impactful. The use of social media can keep domestic and international students engaged across the institution over time. Partnering directly with individual international students as well as international student services staff can be synergistic, and student affairs practitioners should feel empowered to seek out these relationships and sustain them over time for the benefit of all students.

In addition to intentional, inclusive programming, well-considered environments for both international and domestic students are essential for transmitting and supporting local/global cultures, and encouraging interaction. Campus ecology is an important element of institutional culture, and areas such as college unions, multicultural or cultural centers, residence halls, recreation centers, and career centers are among those spaces that can incorporate intentional physical design elements that embrace and reinforce internationalization and demonstrate broad support for all students and cultures. For example, residence halls are often designed with smaller room or suite configurations and more ample common spaces, lounges, dining areas, etc. to encourage students to come out of their rooms and interact with others. Such is the case in Stellenbosch University's Listen, Live and Learn Promising Practice where students in themed houses are required to have weekly group meals together in their residences.

PROMOTE NON-US KNOWLEDGE AND INTERCULTURAL WORK TO ADVANCE THE US PROFESSION

Holding global or international perspectives as practitioners means recognizing the complexity of the world and the subsequent impact on HEIs and individuals. It is about preparing self and others to truly be holistic in the approach to the work of student affairs. In expanding beyond structural diversity, "student affairs professionals should not shy away from but indeed, seek ways to create learning environments that encourage different and conflicting points of view" (Pope, Mueller, & Reynolds, 2009, p. 648). This is a good guideline when conceptualizing professional development opportunities for staff to create cognitive dissonance combined with new skills acquisition. Paradigms vary so dramatically cross-culturally that it is essential for practitioners to recognize various methodologies and conceptualizations of student affairs and services in cross-border education. Cultural appropriateness is everything, as reinforced throughout this book. It is incumbent upon US practitioners to understand that this work takes place globally and in various contexts, and that what is a "best" practice in one area or region may have little applicability in another. Moreover, professional development alone will not create a paradigm shift toward inclusive internationalization, but rather, graduate preparation programs and professional standards must reinforce the importance of internationalized knowledge and other ways of knowing in addition to providing pathways to achieve this.

Foster Professional Development Opportunities

Internationalization of professional development can begin with incorporating intercultural development into job descriptions or annual evaluations at the systems level and, then, follow through to where staff create personal learning plans that incorporate how they will advance these skills. There are numerous tools to encourage reflection and offer guiding thoughts and questions. For example, one reflection tool for intercultural competence guides the individual through questions in attitudes, knowledge, skills, internal outcomes, and external outcomes (see Berardo & Deardorff, 2012). Sample questions under internal and external

RECOMMENDATIONS AND IMPLICATIONS

outcomes are: "do I know how others want to be treated, or do I assume they want to be treated by my cultural standards" and "what could I do differently in the future to be more appropriate and effective in my communication and behavior and in interpersonal interactions?" (pp. 51–52). Training and staff meetings are ripe for incorporating a variety of tools, ideas, and concepts to advance IaH efforts and intercultural development, such as in intercultural training (e.g., Berardo & Deardorff, 2012) and diversity and social justice training (e.g., Adams & Bell, 2016).

Creating and reinforcing organizational cultures that value internationalization and interculturalism can be achieved through incorporating topics, discussions, readings, and reflections regularly into staff and students' training, retreats, and programs to capture most staffs' intercultural and international learning. Some ideas for how practitioners can develop their own intercultural competency adapted from within an IaH mindset include:

- Becoming familiar with institutional international programs by shadowing or conducting informational interviews with staff in these direct line support positions.
- Encouraging the development of skills in another language, through lunch-time language groups for staff and students for example, which may help reduce bias against non-native English speakers detailed previously.
- Encouraging the translation of key student affairs documents for wider sharing and discussion about cultural context application.
- Working on identifying and improving effective intercultural communication skills.

Ultimately an intercultural lens can frame Komives and Carpenter's (2016) PREPARE model described in the previous chapter to best align professional development activities with the needs of the participants, and the directions of the institution, division, and areas.

Learn About Practices and Professional Development Outside of the US

Increasingly, there are many ways and opportunities for learning about practices outside of the US, whereas just a decade ago this would have been a challenge. Some ideas to gain this more global perspective on student affairs are:

- Incorporating discussions into staff meetings that may include the Promising Practices showcased in this book to advance understanding of current practices from colleagues outside of the US. Many of the

171

RECOMMENDATIONS AND IMPLICATIONS

Promising Practices offer additional reading weblinks or resources about their programs. Read chapters for staff meeting discussions developed around the Promising Practices included. Numerous points could be discussed such as:

- What can you learn about internationalization or intercultural development from the context of this promising practice? How is their practice of student affairs similar and different from your own?
- How are they advancing internationalization or intercultural development in the practice showcased?
- How would you redesign this program to fit your context?

■ Exploring opportunities for international education and professional development provided by professional associations around the world via technology (e.g., online publications, webinars, asynchronous programs) and social media platforms. There are many online options to learn about other professional associations and organizations around the world.

■ Engaging students, practitioners, and faculty who have participated in education abroad, exchange travel programs, or international conference by presenting professional development or workshops.

■ Inviting international students and scholars to share and engage with staff and students.

■ Using technology and social media to read and learn about non-US perspectives of global issues, to connect and collaborate with professionals and faculty from around the world, and to explore non-US-based professional associations.

■ Reading and staying current in the more recently expanding research and journals published outside of the US related to student affairs and services, such as the *Journal of Student Affairs in Africa* and the *Journal of the Australia and New Zealand Student Services Association.*

Organizational structures and cultures can support and reward learning broadly, yet individual student affairs practitioners are primarily responsible for their own learning and development and must find ways to advance without need for funding and international travel. HEIs, in collaboration with student affairs divisions, can assist by providing a global context and support for internationalization broadly. In the case of Fudan University's Opening-Up Strategy, they developed a rich range of opportunities for student affairs practitioners to avail themselves of and to create momentum. Their cooperative work and outreach efforts with other countries and global associations have helped facilitate a new synergy for the Fudan and Shanghai area student affairs practitioners, and, ultimately, students. As in other countries, this increased knowledge and resource base leads to more questions about home students, and their success.

Shift US Graduate Preparation Program Curriculum

To be successful in internationalizing any curriculum, global learning outcomes can be woven into and throughout rather than separated out in stand-alone modules, units, or classes (Jones, 2011). If students see internationalization, just like diversity and SJI work, as integrated and reflected in the curriculum and student affairs broadly, rather than one week out of the semester or quarter or some other separated piece, then optimal socialization and learning occurs to support or encourage intercultural development and the internationalization of student affairs. All of this assumes that US graduate preparation programs include international or comparative coursework and seminars or incorporate international students into multicultural and diversity courses. While waiting for more direct recommendations from professional competencies or curriculum standards, graduate faculty can review existing course offerings and work to ensure multiple courses or most of the curriculum incorporates international and intercultural perspectives and learning outcomes. For programs engaged in a social justice perspective, they must view this as imperative to the work. A social justice perspective presumes that "students have the right to appropriate and effective education that respects their identities and backgrounds; that is culturally, nationally, and internationally relevant; and that equips students to recognize and challenge structural and societal barriers to equitable opportunities for all" (Broido & Schreiber, 2016, p. 65).

For practitioners to better support and work with all diverse students, they require the knowledge, attitudes, and skills of intercultural competency. Practitioners often help domestic students process new cultural elements when they transition to higher education and how these experiences influence personal change or questioning of values and worldviews through various student development theories. It would be socially unjust to apply these same theories to all students because they lack cultural appropriateness and context as they prioritize Western cultural values (Broido & Schreiber, 2016). As practitioners commonly select student development theories that resonate most with them, they must know themselves, including their own intercultural development, and understand their cultural, national, and international assumptions and biases.

US graduate preparation curriculum can use some of the best practices for teaching diversity and culturally responsive pedagogies to incorporate internationalization into both the curriculum and pedagogical practice. Part of working with culturally diverse students is remaining open to new knowledge and ways of knowing, in addition to developing reflection on one's own ethnocentric tendencies that arise from individual cultural values, attitudes, and behaviors as failure to do so limits moral reasoning and empathy development, which are critical elements in effectively developing intercultural competency (Killick, 2015, 2017). Some related ideas include:

RECOMMENDATIONS AND IMPLICATIONS

- Doing self-work. Exploring biases and stereotypes and how they manifest themselves in class interactions with diverse students.
- Exploring gaps in personal and program knowledge and how these gaps of international and intercultural perspectives limit and shape curriculum design.
- Developing strategies for teaching intercultural skills including in group work and reflection or assessment of other's work that do not further isolate diverse students.
- Ensuring assignments and class activities use and value all students' cultural, social, and personal knowledge without placing the burden of teaching on diverse students.
- Teaching appreciation for linguistically diverse speakers, including how to be an effective intercultural communicator as reviewed previously.

These are just a few ideas from the many other tools that already exist for teaching, promoting, and advancing classroom pedagogy and curriculum revision. There are many general resources available, such as internationalizing curriculum, see Leask (2015) and Hudzik (2015) or teaching diversity and social justice, see Goodman (2011) and Davis and Harrison (2013) to start.

CONCLUSION

This book has addressed the importance of the internationalization of student affairs in the US and the need to focus on the "at home" cocurriculum and professional development. Chapters showcase examples and Promising Practices from other countries; however, these are just a few of the outstanding illustrations of global practices. Driven by the globalization trend, and supported by higher education's concomitant move toward internationalization, student affairs and services has become more globally connected and networked, stimulating increased partnerships, sharing of information, and learning from one another. Despite nationalistic trends, the interconnectedness among HEIs with their joint enterprise efforts, along with the notable collaborations among student affairs associations, will continue to drive knowledge production, and the likely proliferation of student affairs as an emerging profession in many countries and regions.

Intercultural competency development through increased knowledge, skills, and attitudes will remain a key element of the ongoing learning and development for student affairs practitioners. A global view and fostering of collaborative environments that support and engage global concepts are necessary for student affairs to appropriately work with and assist students in becoming competitive and engaged citizens of the world. It remains essential for practitioners to understand connections between intercultural, diversity, and SJI work. Further, making connections across departments and divisions is central for the intentional development of both domestic and international students. This can happen across

RECOMMENDATIONS AND IMPLICATIONS

numerous programs, services, activities, and creative initiatives that welcome students, help them transition, and foster dynamic environments within which they feel a sense of belonging, can excel and practice skills, and assume leadership and other roles of significance at their institutions. The IaH framework promoted here provides practitioners with tools and options to offer students rich experiences that provide similar learning and outcomes as education abroad programs and others that require travel, right on students' own campuses.

Student affairs practitioners have the responsibility to understand global perspectives on issues, and to exercise their skills in acting locally and impacting their HEI communities in positive ways. This book has addressed concepts related to internationalizing US student affairs hoping to provide a foundation upon which others can build. We have raised awareness, presented some initial ideas and thoughts, and have suggested potential solutions and courses of action. It is now up to all of us to leverage this foundational information by infusing global and international perspectives into the daily work we do on our own individual campuses.

REFERENCES

AAC&U (2009). Inquiry and analysis VALUE rubric. Retrieved from www.aacu.org/value/rubrics/inquiry-analysis

American Council on Education. (2014). Student learning at the intersection: At home in the world toolkit. Washington, D.C.: Author. Retrieved from www.acenet.edu/news-room/Pages/AHITW-Student-Learning-at-the-Intersection.aspx

Adams, M., & Bell, L. (Eds.). (2016). *Teaching for diversity and social justice*, 3rd ed. New York: Routledge.

Berardo, K., & Deardorff, D. K. (2012). *Building cultural competence: Innovative intercultural training activities and models*. Sterling, VA: Stylus.

Broido, E. M., & Schreiber, B. (2016). Promoting student learning and development. In D. Roberts & S. Komives (Eds.), *Enhancing student learning and development in cross-border higher education: New directions for higher education* (pp. 75–84). San Francisco, CA: Jossey-Bass.

Center for Global Education (n.d.) Retrieved from http://globaled.us/internationalization/index.asp#introduction

Chizhik, E. W., & Chizhik, A. W. (2002). Decoding the language of social justice: What do privilege and oppression really mean? *Journal of College Student Development, 43*(6), 792–808.

Cornwell, G. H., & Stoddard, E. W. (1999). *Globalizing knowledge: Connecting international & intercultural studies*. Washington, D.C.: AAC&U.

Davis, T., & Harrison, L. M. (2013). *Advancing social justice: Tools, pedagogies, and strategies to transform your campus*. San Francisco, CA: Jossey-Bass.

Glass, C. R., Wongtrirat, R., & Buus, S. (2015). *International student engagement: Strategies for creating inclusive, connected, and purposeful campus environments*. Sterling, VA: Stylus.

RECOMMENDATIONS AND IMPLICATIONS

Goodman, D. (2011). *Promoting social justice and diversity: Educating people from privileged groups*, 2nd ed. New York: Routledge.

Hudzik, J. (2015). *Comprehensive internationalization: Institutional pathways to success*. New York: Routledge.

Killick, D. (2015). *Developing the global student: Higher education in an era of globalization*. London: Routledge.

Killick, D. (2017). *Internationalization and diversity in higher education: Implications for teaching, learning and assessment*. London: Palgrave Teaching & Learning.

Komives, S. R., & Carpenter, S. (2016). Professional development as lifelong learning. In G. S. McClellan, J. Stringer, & Associates (Eds.), *The handbook of student affairs administration* (pp. 411–430). San Francisco, CA: Jossey-Bass.

Jones, E. (2011). Internationalisation, multiculturalism, a global outlook and employability. *ALT Journal*, *11*, 21–49.

Leask, B. (2009). Using formal and informal curricula to improve interactions between home and international students. *Journal of Studies in International Education*, *13*(2), 205–221.

Leask, B. (2015). *Internationalizing the curriculum*. New York: Routledge.

Olson, C., Evans, R., & Shoenberg, R. E. (2007). *At home in the world: Bridging the gap between internationalization and multicultural education*. Washington, D.C.: ACE.

Otten, M. (2000). Impacts of cultural diversity at home. In Crowther et al., *Internationalisation at Home Position Paper* (pp. 15–20). Amsterdam, The Netherlands: EAIE.

Peterson, D. M., Briggs, P., Dreasher, L., Horner, D. D., & Nelson, T. (1999). Contributions of international students and programs to campus diversity. *New Directions for Student Services*, *86*, 67–77.

Pope, R. L., Mueller, J. A., & Reynolds, A. L. (2009) Looking back and moving forward: Future directions for diversity research in student affairs. *Journal of College student development*, *50*(6), 640–658.

Roberts, D. & Komives, S. (2016). *Enhancing student learning and development in cross-border higher education: New directions for higher education.* San Francisco, CA: Jossey-Bass.

Shein, E. (2004). *Organizational culture and leadership*, 3rd ed. San Francisco: Jossey-Bass.

University of Sydney. (n.d.). National Centre for Cultural Competence (NCCC): Our commitment. Retrieved from http://sydney.edu.au/nccc/about/index.shtml

Ward, H. H. (2015). *Internationalizing the co-curriculum: Part one: Integrating international students*. Washington, D.C.: ACE. Retrieved from www.acenet.edu/news-room/Documents/Intlz-In-Action-Intlz-Co-Curriculum-Part-1.pdf

Yakaboski, T., Perez-Velez, K., & Almutairi, Y. (2017). Breaking the silence: Saudi graduate student experiences on a U.S. campus. *Journal of Diversity in Higher Education*. Advance online publication. http://dx.doi.org/10.1037/dhe0000059

Biographies of the Authors and Promising Practices Contributors

Tamara Yakaboski, Ph.D., is Full Professor of Higher Education and Student Affairs Leadership at the University of Northern Colorado. She has been a graduate faculty member for over a decade and, prior to that, served as a student affairs administrator at the University of Arizona in the Arizona Student Unions. She earned her master's and Ph.D. from the University of Arizona's Center for the Study of Higher Education, with a minor in sociology. Dr. Yakaboski is active in numerous professional associations including ACPA, ASHE, and NASPA, where most recently she served as the Faculty Liaison for the International Education Knowledge Community (IEKC). Also, she has been involved with the Consortium of Higher Education Researchers (CHER) and European Association of International Education (EAIE) in Europe.

Dr. Yakaboski has teaching and research specialties in higher education organization and administration; international higher education and student affairs; and women and gender issues. She has experience in curriculum redesign and new course creation that infuse technology, internationalization, social justice and inclusion into and throughout undergraduate, graduate, and education abroad opportunities. Dr. Yakaboski has published over 20 juried articles in both US and international higher education and student affairs venues including *Journal of Studies in International Education*, *Journal of Student Affairs in Africa*, *Review of Higher Education*, and *Journal of Student Affairs Research and Practice*. She has given over 50 presentations and invited keynotes to academic and practitioner audiences worldwide.

For Dr. Yakaboski's sabbatical in 2017, she received a grant as a visiting researcher at the Finnish Institute for Education Research/Koulutuksen tutkimuslaitos at the University of Jyväskylä, Finland, to research multi-institutional implementation of tuition fees for international students. Dr. Yakaboski was lead PI on a summer 2015 grant to The Netherlands to investigate Dutch international education staff and faculty efforts to internationalize 9 higher education institutions, which developed her interest in IaH. Other experiences that have helped shape her worldview and

BIOGRAPHIES OF THE AUTHORS AND CONTRIBUTORS

fueled her passion for interculturalism include English language teacher training in Kraków, Poland; teaching English as a Second Language in South Korea; writing her dissertation in Bangalore, India; and developing education abroad trips to Kenya and Mexico. Recent campus-based research projects include assessing Saudi and Chinese students' college choice and decision-making to improve institutional services and student experiences.

Brett Perozzi, Ph.D., is Vice President for Student Affairs at Weber State University, a public university of 28,000 students located 30 miles North of Salt Lake City, Utah, USA. Over his 30-year career he has served as faculty in higher education/student affairs administration graduate programs at Colorado State, Arizona State, and Indiana Universities. Brett earned his undergraduate degree from the State University of New York, a master's degree in higher education administration from the University of Arizona, and a Ph.D. in higher education administration from Indiana University.

Dr. Perozzi has been an active volunteer with NASPA for more than a decade, supporting their international efforts and agenda. He established the Global Advisory Board and served as Chair, Past-Chair, and North American representative. Brett continues to work closely with NASPA on initiatives in China, the Middle East, and Latin America. He is also a founding member of the International Association of Student Affairs and Services (IASAS). Dr. Perozzi has delivered educational content and interfaced with global colleagues in more than a dozen countries.

Brett has been a faculty member on study abroad programs for graduate students and has helped plan the NASPA International Symposium for ten years. He has coordinated international administrative exchanges and has helped execute numerous international education programs, such as NASPA's International Student Services Institute and the biennial NASPA-IASAS collaboration: the Global Summit on Student Affairs and Services. Brett has published three books and dozens of monographs, articles, and book chapters on student employment during college, and international student affairs and services.

PROMISING PRACTICE CONTRIBUTORS

Bader Al-Sayed Ahmed has more than five years of professional experience and served as the Coordinator for Student Organizations & Student Employment at the American University of Kuwait (AUK). Bader supervised programs and activities directly related to Student Clubs and Organizations, and the Student Employment Program at AUK. Before joining AUK, Bader worked for two years as a sales support and business development supervisor at Ooredoo Telecommunications Company in which he used to audit and train sales representatives on customer service techniques.

178

BIOGRAPHIES OF THE AUTHORS AND CONTRIBUTORS

Jordi Austin is the Director of Student Support Services and elected Fellow of Senate at The University of Sydney, Australia. She has worked in the community mental health sector, as well as nearly two decades in the University industry. She has been at the University of Sydney since 2006. She is responsible for a broad portfolio that includes nine significant teams of support on campus. Jordi is also President of the Australian and New Zealand Student Services Association, Inc. (ANZSSA) since 2013. Jordi is currently participating as Assistant Editor (Asia and Oceania) for the UNESCO/IASAS Student Affairs and Services in Higher Education (third edition) due to be released in 2018.

Neil Buddel, Ph.D., has more than 17 years of experience in the post-secondary education system through various roles (including residential and career education, academic student success, and overall student affairs) at multiple institutions, including the Universities of Alberta, Guelph, Toronto; McMaster University; and Centennial College. Neil completed his Ph.D. at the University of Alberta, exploring the storied experiences of first-generation students through a social class lens. Currently, as the Dean of Students at Centennial College, Neil has responsibility for wide range of student affairs programs and services. Neil is also a Lecturer with the Ontario Institute for Studies in Education (OISE) at the University of Toronto where he teaches in the Student Development and Services program.

Marina Casals-Sala is the Director of International Relations at Universitat Rovira i Virgili in Tarragona, Spain. She has worked in international education since 1999, also in Finland and Morocco. She is a member of the General Council of the European Association of International Education (EAIE) and an EAIE Trainer, member of the Management Board of the Centre for Higher Education Internationalisation at Università Cattolica del Sacro Cuore, and coordinator of the Systemic University Change Towards Internationalisation (SUCTI) Project.

Tadd Kruse is the Assistant to the President for Institutional Planning and Effectiveness at the American University of Kuwait (AUK). He has more than 18 years of professional experience at higher education institutions in the US, the UK, and with more than a decade in Kuwait. Tadd has served as a senior student affairs officer, founded the Department of Student Life at AUK, and has worked in a variety of professional areas within student affairs. He has developed and facilitated professional staff development programs and experiential learning and culture at both national and regional conferences. Further, he has served as a mentor to graduate students and young professionals, and serves as the Professional Development Coordinator for the MENASA NASPA Area and on the leadership team for the International Association of Student Affairs & Services (IASAS).

María Soledad Cruz has a psychologist degree from Universidad de Chile, and a Masters in Educational Psychology from Universidad de Barcelona, Spain. She

BIOGRAPHIES OF THE AUTHORS AND CONTRIBUTORS

started her career working in student counseling in high school institutions. She has been working for 8 years in Pontificia Universidad Católica de Chile, with the last 6 years as Student Life Director in Student Affairs Division of Pontificia Universidad Católica de Chile.

Priscila Gallardo has a Social Work degree from Pontificia Universidad Católica de Chile. Since 2014, she has been responsible for Student Representation in Student Affairs Division of Pontificia Universidad Católica de Chile.

Raymond Leung has been serving in the higher education sector for 25 years. With postgraduate training in business administration and counseling, he is now the Director of Student Affairs at the Chinese University of Hong Kong. He coordinates activities and services in student development, internationalization, career development, and mental wellness.

Dun Mao is a senior student affairs officer of Fudan University's College of Foreign Language and Literature, in China. Dun Mao graduated from Cambridge University, UK in 2011. He started his career in student affairs at Fudan University, China. He was the chief student affairs officer of Zhide College (one of five residential colleges at Fudan) from 2013–2015. He works as the liaison of Fudan University with NASPA's cooperation.

Ivonne Moraga has a Social Work degree from Pontificia Universidad Católica de Chile. She has specialized in design and projects evaluation, social rights and public policy, and youth issues. She has experience in coordination and implementation of social and entrepreneurship projects. Since 2014, she has been responsible for Student Organizations in Student Affairs Division of Pontificia Universidad Católica de Chile.

Orla Quinlan is the Director of the International Office at Rhodes University and elected Deputy President of the International Education Association of South Africa. She leads IEASA's Internationalization of the Curriculum and Internationalization at Home efforts. Formerly a teacher, teacher trainer, and education project manager, Orla has worked in Ireland, France, Bangladesh, Cambodia, Burundi, Haiti, South Africa, and the UK. As part of Oxfam GB's Senior Management for 13 years, Orla provided strategic leadership to a team located across 70 developing countries.

Yasmin Razack has worked for and led teams in diverse divisions across multiple higher educational institutions for 17 years. In her current role as Director of the Centre of Global Citizenship Education and Inclusion at Centennial College, Yasmin works with a team to strategically lead the integration of the principles and practices of an engaged citizenry that reflects the valuing of global citizenship, human rights, and equity and inclusion. This role includes the integration of

BIOGRAPHIES OF THE AUTHORS AND CONTRIBUTORS

appropriate curricular/cocurricular programming and policy development. Her past professional career roles include positions across many institutions in Toronto, Canada, including the University of Toronto, Seneca College, York University, Harmony Movement and the Wellesley Institute. Yasmin also is a certified coach with her own coaching practice, and has worked with clients from various sectors on personal and professional goals.

Cheryl Rounsaville, Ph.D., is originally from Maryland, USA. Working as an English teacher in Japan on the JET Programme from 1996–1999 sparked her interest in promoting internationalization and working with students from different cultures. In 2012, she completed her Ph.D. in International Education at the University of Nottingham. Dr. Rounsaville has worked for Nottingham Trent University since April 2013, first as their Internationalisation Coordinator, and in early 2016 was made Global Student Experience Manager responsible for supporting international students as well as developing and overseeing projects that help all students internationalize their learning experience.

Birgit Schreiber, Ph.D., is the senior director of Student Affairs at University of Stellenbosch, South Africa. She has worked in higher education for 20 years and has gathered extensive experience in South Africa, Africa, and abroad. She has published widely and has presented research papers and keynotes. She was a visiting faculty at various universities, including the University of California, Berkeley, and has been a member on the National Executive of various national and international professional organizations including SAFSAS and is the Africa Chair for IASAS. She is on the Global Advisory Board of NASPA. She is on the editorial board of a number of journals and on the executive of the *Journal for Student Affairs in Africa*. She is the course co-convener for the Postgraduate Diploma in Higher Education Management at the US Business School.

Juanita Sherwood, Ph.D., is the Academic Director at the National Centre for Cultural Competence at the University of Sydney, with a mandate to engage, innovate and lead in cultural competence. A proud Wiradjuri woman, Professor Sherwood is a registered nurse, teacher, lecturer, researcher, and manager with a depth of working experiences of some 30 years in Aboriginal and Torres Strait Islander health and education. Professor Sherwood has pushed boundaries from a grass roots, community-based position that seeks to engage with and build capability within communities, deliver culturally safe models and research methodologies in partnership with communities and recognize in policy and practice the straight line between world views and social justice. She has a Ph.D. from the University of New South Wales, and has previously worked in lecturing, research, management and consultative roles in health, education, and Indigenous studies, with her most recent role being Professor of Australian Indigenous Education at the University of Technology (UTS).

181

BIOGRAPHIES OF THE AUTHORS AND CONTRIBUTORS

Courtney Stryker currently serves as a consultant for Student Affairs at Qatar University, in Doha, Qatar. Courtney earned her bachelors and master of arts degree from Columbia University in the City of New York, and her doctorate at Montana State University where she served as Dean of Students. She accepted a position at the United Arab Emirates University in Al Ain, UAE as Assistant Provost and Dean of Students, and served in a similar capacity at Zayed University in Abu Dhabi. Courtney has consulted with universities in the US, Canada, Mexico, Fiji, and the Middle East. She is the founding director of the MENASA NASPA Board, and serves on the NASPA Global Advisory Board and International Symposium Committee.

Sisi Sun is currently a Resident Fellow at Cheong Kun Lun College, University of Macau. She is also a doctoral candidate in international investment law at University of Montreal and a barrister and solicitor admitted to the Ministry of Justice of the People's Republic of China. Her educational experiences in China and Canada have enabled her to develop a remarkable understanding of diversity issues among students both in the West and the East.

William Young has been working in university administration for 18 years. He began his career in the Physical Sciences and Mathematics Department at the Universidad de Chile and has been at the Pontificia Universidad Católica de Chile for the past 11 years. Having held positions in academic administration and student affairs, he is now the Director of Student Affairs at the University, and serves as Director of the Latin American and Caribbean Area of NASPA—Student Affairs Administrators in Higher Education.

William also works as an Associate Adjunct Professor in the School of Engineering, teaching a Marketing course. William holds an Industrial Civil Engineer bachelor's degree and a master's in Management and Business Administration from the Universidad de Chile.

Xiaoming "Peter" Yu, Ph.D., is an experienced practitioner in student affairs, working with students in the United States and Asia. His education in China, the UK, and the US has equipped him with an insight into diverse student populations. He joined the University of Macau in July 2012 as its founding Dean of Students and became the founding College Master of Cheong Kun Lun College in July 2016.

Howard Wang, Ph.D., began serving as the Associate Dean for Student Affairs in 2014 at the Duke Kunshan University in China. He is also an adjunct professor in Education at Beijing Normal University, Faculty of Education, as well as at Duke Kunshan University. Howard has served in senior administrative posts for more than 30 years, at the University of California Los Angles and two California State University campuses. Previously, he served as the Executive Officer to the Assistant Vice Chancellor and later as both Assistant and Associate Vice President for Student Affairs with the California state university system. He received a bachelor's

182

BIOGRAPHIES OF THE AUTHORS AND CONTRIBUTORS

degree in Biology from the University of Oregon, and a master's in Clinical Microbiology from Wisconsin. He earned his master's and Ph.D. degrees in Higher Education Administration from UCLA.

Peter Wanyenya is currently pursuing a Ph.D. at the University of British Colombia's Social Justice Institute, and has supported and championed resiliency among vulnerable young people in inner-city and Indigenous communities for many years. While at UBC, he has worked as a student affairs professional with hundreds of international, undergraduate merit and need-based award students, student refugees, and other student leaders to help them meet their full potential. For many years, Peter has engaged with various community-based organizations serving vulnerable youth through the media arts, including the Access to Media Education Society and Kick Start Arts.

Jin Xu, Ph.D., is the Director of the Student Affairs Office at Fudan University, China since 2014. Dr. Xu graduated from the School of International Relations and Public Affairs of Fudan University, China. She started her career as a student counselor at Fudan's Foreign Language and Literature College, then she was promoted as deputy dean (student affairs) in 2008. During this period, she finished her Ph.D. degree in moral education. In 2012, Dr. Xu was transferred to Fudan's Human Resources office as deputy director for two years.

Jia Zheng joined Duke Kunshan University in 2014 working as the Residence Life Officer. Jia oversees significant housing responsibilities and coordinates the Student Leadership Development Program to promote living-learning community on campus. Jia is a member of NASPA and is passionate about supporting student growth and development through Student Affairs. She graduated with a Master's degree in Education Policy from the University of Washington and received her bachelor's degree in Education (Honors) and in English Language (Secondary) from the Hong Kong Institute of Education.

Index

Page numbers in *italics* refer to Promising Practice case studies.

academic affairs 1; collaborations with 82, 91, 97, 104, 119, 126, 162; separation from student affairs 89, 96

ACPA audience xvii; graduate programs xvi; internationalization efforts 17, 141; Strategic Imperative on Racial Justice and Decolonization 31; Student Learning Imperative 69; *see also* ACPA and NASPA Professional Competencies

ACPA and NASPA Professional Competencies: Arabic translation 145–146; globalism thread x, 59; history of 56–58; in relation to graduate preparation curriculum 61; limited guidance from 62, 75, 133, 173; part of professional development 146; *see also* intercultural competency; multicultural competency

Africa, practices in: African diaspora 35; internationalization trends 5; the *Journal of Student Affairs in Africa* 142; Kenya 23, 113; Nigeria *15*, 114; politics 2; programs *14–15*, 119; *see also* South Africa, practices in

American Council on Education 4–5; *At Home in the World* 36, 164–165

American University of Kuwait xv, 122, *123,* 178

Asia, practices in: internationalization 5; students from 12, *46,* 48; *see also* Asia Pacific Student Services Association; Chinese University of Hong Kong, The; Duke Kunshan University; Fudan University; MENASA

Asia Pacific Student Services Association 142

assessment collaboration 91, 92, 162; ethical and culturally sensitive 166–167; graduate curriculum 146; in IaH 7–8, 160, 164; in IoC 6; of intercultural learning outcomes 36, 65, 83, 126–127, 163, 174; National Survey of Student Engagement 167; Oakton Community College *19;* part of professional development 147–148, 153, 154; of promising practices *15, 22, 46, 68, 74, 94, 100–101, 112, 117, 125, 138, 145, 150*

Association of College Unions International xvii

Australia and New Zealand, practices in: IaH 6; internationalization 37, 90; IoC 5; global citizenship 55, 69, 96–97, 120; multiculturalism 35; University of South Australia 163,

185

INDEX

166; University of Sydney 135, *136–139; see also* Australian and New Zealand Student Services Association

Australian and New Zealand Student Services Association 142, 172; *see also* Australia and New Zealand, practices in

Baxter Magolda's self-authorship theory 140

Beelen, J. 6, 7, 47, 120

Canada, practices in: Canadian Association of College and University Student Services 141; Canadian Bureau for International Education 32, 142; Centennial College 70, *71–74*, 165; internationalization *20*; The University of British Columbia 19–22

Centennial College xiv, 70, 71, *71–74, 165; see also* Canada, practices in

Chile, practices in *see* Pontificia Universidad Católica de Chile

Chinese University of Hong Kong, The xiv, 43, *44,* 119, 166; *see also* Asia, practices in

citizenship: as privilege 48, 64; being inclusive of 2; defined as nationality 35

cocurricular; cocurriculum x, 1, 6, 107–108 cocurricular transcript 38, 117; Intercultural Semester program 19; Leadership and Student Activism Development program *116–117;* not inclusive 88; related to global citizenship 69; role in internationalization 5, 7, 9, 108; strategies 7–9, 17, 18, 87, 108, 120, 162, 164–165, 166; *see also* multiculturalism: student learning; student leadership

college unions: as a place of belonging ix, 169–170; support of student engagement 97, 113–114, 120

colonization 34, 35, 41, 55, 65, 135; decolonization 71; neo-colonization 17, 34, 70; *see also* discrimination

Comprehensive Internationalization 4–5, 34, 70

contact hypothesis 34, 48

Council for Advancement of Standards (CAS): in professional development 133, 146, 170; in relation to graduate preparation curriculum 17, 61–62, 139, 173; *see also* curriculum, graduate preparation: combined with professional development

Council for the Advancement of Higher Education Programs 61–62; in relation to graduate preparation curriculum 146; *see also* Council for Advancement of Standards; curriculum, graduate preparation

cultural and affinity centers: centralization of inclusivity work 2, 7; collaboration with 9, 12, 24, 50, 82, 97, 103, 134, 135, 147, 162; as facilitators of intercultural learning 31, 119; history of 2, 34; as a place of belonging ix, 170; *see also* international education; multicultural competency

curriculum, graduate preparation: combined with professional development 146; culturally responsive pedagogy 173–174; goals for xiii; the need for inclusive internationalization 8, 16–18, 34, 47–49, 75, 102; role of competencies in 56, 60–62; *see also* graduate preparation programs

curriculum, undergraduate: Centennial College 71; connection to global social justice 41; culturally responsive curriculum 48, 136, 173; difference from cocurriculum x; in Europe 83; internationalized and intercultural learning outcomes in 1, 9, 107, 162, 164; language requirements 57, 65; Leeds Metropolitan University 37;

186

INDEX

Nottingham Trent University *100;* stages of internationalization 81–82; student activism curriculum 114; student resistance to 42–43, 167; The Hague University of Applied Sciences 83, 86; within Comprehensive Internationalization 4–5; within IaH x, xvi, 7, 8; within IoC 5–6; *see also* inclusivity: student resistance; Internationalization of the Curriculum; Internationalization at Home

Deardorff, D. xi, 3, 56, 58, 64, 167, 171
Deardorff's Intercultural Competence Model xi, 58, 64–65, *68*, 126, 167
Development Model of Intercultural Sensitivity (DMIS) 42, 62–64, 167
Dewey, J. 69–70
discrimination 2, 10, 11, 31, 42, 61, 71, 160; ethnocentrism 17, 41, 42, 63; White privilege 6; White Supremacy 32, 41, 64; xenophobia 15, 22, 47; *see also* racism; neo-racism
diversity: Centennial College's Statement of Diversity 70–71; cocurriculum programs 1, 10, 99, 117, 119, 120–121, 168; connection to internationalization 3, 9, 34–37, 47, 49, 82, 83, 88, 104, 135, 159; domestic diversity xi, 6, 13, 31, 32, 43, *45*, 47, 86; IaH 8, 9, 55; inclusive of intercultural ix, xi, xvii, 3, 11, 32, 56, 58, *111*; inclusive internationalization 2, 3, 9–10, 32, 50, 135, 171; institutional strategic documents 33, 126, 160–161, 163; learning outcomes 108, 122, 164–165, 167; local–global xiii, 41, 113, 163, 164; professional development 56, 133, 134–135, 171, 173; 32, 35, 36, 42, 43, 56, 86 self-work 55–56, 63, 174; Stellenbosch University *38–40*; student employment 121; THUAS model 86; *see also* cultural and affinity centers;

global citizenship; inclusivity: student resistance; indigenous; international students; international student recruitment; linguistically diverse; social justice and inclusion competency; structural diversity
documents, internationalization: includes international activities 87; institutional policies 88, 103; mission and vision statements 86–88; strategic development *44*, 82–83, 161, 163–164; THUAS Institutional Strategic Plan 83–86; *see also* policy, internationalization
domestic students: Chinese University of Hong Kong 43; defined x; engagement with international students 7, 9, 12–13, 120, 122, 160, 166; IaH for xvi, 168; intercultural learning 10, 18, 24, 34, 96, 104, 167–168; Nottingham Trent University 98; resistance to intercultural learning 43, 97, 121; services and programs for 1, 32, 109, 113, 169, 173, 174; University of Cape Town in South Africa 19; University of South Australia 120, 166; *see also* student interaction, domestic and international
Duke Kunshan University xv, 109, *109, 110,* 165; *see also* Asia, practices in

education abroad: in graduate preparation programs xiii, 4, 17; as internationalization strategy 3, 8, 9, 81; Johnson County Community College 19; learning from those who have participated in 172; limitations with *15*, 18, 70, 86, 159; local community as alternative to 168; as not required in IaH xvi, 6, 175; Nottingham Trent University 101; participation in 7; part of international education x; supervised

187

INDEX

by student affairs 95, 96; Universitat Rovira i Virgili *149*

employability 1, *21*, 71, *73*, 108, 113, 122, *125*, 126, 128; definition 16; *see also* student employment

ERASMUS 83, *100*, 134, *149*

Europe, practices in 5–6, 10, 32, 43, 49, 57, 83, 90, 96, 108, 127, 134, *149*; Deutsches Studentenwerk 141; European Higher Education Area (EHEA) 83, 89, 141; Finland 12, 23–24, 89, 114; Germany 114; *Kaunas Declaration* 32; The Netherlands 83–86, 89; Sweden 6; *see also* ERASMUS; *individual promising practices*

European Association of International Educators (EAIE) 6, 142

European Council on Student Affairs 141

extra-curricular *see* cocurricular

Fowler's Stages of Faith Development 140

Freire, P. 69

Fudan University xiv, xv, *66*, 92, *92–94*, 147, 163, 165, 172; *see also* Asia, practices in

global citizenship: about and history 69–71; assessment 126; Centennial College *71–75*, 165; as cocurricular activity 8, 108; connection to inclusivity and interculturalism 56, 69, 164; ethics and responsible global citizenship 70; graduate attribute 55, 60; outcome of internationalization 1; as part of IaH 164; The Hague University of Applied Sciences 83, 86, 163; The University of British Columbia *21–22*, 168; *see also* multiculturalism: student learning

global competencies ix, xvi; in graduate preparation curriculum 60; importance for professional development xvi; National Education Association's definition 57; for students 2, 149; Weber State University 122; *see also* intercultural competency

globalism: defined x, 57; in graduate preparation curriculum 17; new staff hiring 102; in professional development 59, 75; as student learning outcome 88; *see also* global competencies; intercultural competency

globalization 23, 24, *39*, 41, 69, *95*, 120, 159, 174; ACPA's Globalization Strategic Plan 141; defined x, 2–3

Goodman, D. 33, 42, 49, 174

graduate preparation programs xvi, 2, 4; connection between internationalization and diversity 134; cross-pollination research 49; dominant privileges in 6, 34; internationalization strategies 173–174; need to internationalize 16–18, 102, 170; as professional development 133, 146; *see also* curriculum, graduate preparation

Hague University of Applied Sciences, The (THUAS) 83–86, 91–92, 154, 163

Hofstede, G. 47

home students *see* domestic students

Hudzik, J. 3, 4, 5, 81, 161, 174

human resources: hiring international students and staff 96, 122, 161; new staff hiring 102–103; on-boarding 103, *137*; *see also* student employment

immigrant x, 6, 11, 12, *14*, 18, 34, 61, 161; *see also* domestic students; international students

inclusivity: cocurriculum 42; global inclusivity 20; IaH connection 9; institutional strategies 163; in programming 168; social conflict 2;

INDEX

student resistance 42–43; understanding of 56; *see also* diversity; international students; social justice

indigenous: in Canada *22,* 32, 70–71; Centennial College *72;* part of racial justice movement 2; University of Sydney *136*

interaction, international and domestic student: assessment of 166; avoidance of 11, 159; Chinese University of Hong Kong 43–46; cocurriculum 107–109, 120; employment, student 121; IaH strategies 7–9, 12–13, 164; inclusive interactions 167–169; JAMK University of Applied Sciences 12; peer programs *101*, 120; reliance on structural diversity 33–34; role of student affairs 24; student resistance 42–43; teaching privilege 48; University of Leeds 13; *see also* contact hypothesis; curriculum, graduate preparation; international students; structural diversity

intercultural communication 57–58; Cheong Kun Lun College and Zhide College 65, 66–68, 165; effective intercultural communication 58, 153–154, 171; Johnson County Community College 19; as learning outcome 12, 113, 135, 149, 150, 168; *see also* intercultural learning; intercultural competency

intercultural competency xi, 3, 58; additional language requirement 57, 60, 153; assessment of 126–127, 153, 167; campus culture change 32, 104; Chinese context 65, *66–68;* cocurriculum 108, *110–112,* 119–121; component to internationalization 3–4; connection to inclusivity 55–56, 58, 134–135, 173; curriculum, graduate preparation 47, 173–175; curriculum, undergraduate 43, 60; global citizen requirement xvi, 10 *45,* 55, 69; hiring

new staff 102–103, 163; history of 56, 57; local–global connection 168; NAFSA competencies 57–58; misapplication/assumption from structural diversity 34; as a personal process 36, 58, 174; professional development 23, 59–60, 75, *93–95,* 153, 160, 170–171; related to social identity development 55–56; student activism 114; theories to support 64–65; travel, international 134; used in international education 49, 133; within IaH xiii, xvii, 7, *15–16,* 24, 50, 55, 164–165; *see also* Deardorff's Intercultural Competence Model

intercultural learning xi; for all students 10, 164; assessment 65, 122, 126–127; Cheong Kun Lun College and Zhide College 65; cocurriculum 119–122, 164–166, 168; contact hypothesis 34, 47–48; IaH 159, 161, 163; internationalization x, 50; limitations of mobility programs 7; local connections 17, 18, 97; professional development 155, 166; role of educators 55, 60; strategic documents 163–164; student resistance 42–43; THUAS 92; University of Leeds 13; *see also* cocurricular; curriculum, undergraduate; intercultural competency: assessment of

International Association of Student Affairs and Services (IASAS) xvii, 142–143

International Association of Universities (IAU) 5, 50

international education x, 7, 58; collaborations with 82, 97, 119, 120, 126, 134, 162, 166; connection to intercultural xi, 133; data driven decisions 147; infuse into graduate preparation 17, 61; intercultural centralized in 24, 49, 50, 89; limitations 41; literature and theories

189

INDEX

from xii, xvii, 57, 63–64, 140–142; NASPA's International Education Knowledge Community 141; as a part of all positions 102–103; professional associations for 142, 172; reporting to academic affairs 95–96; shared learning outcomes 164; student resistance 42; *see also* intercultural competency

internationalization x, 1, 3, 24, 50, 107; argument for the internationalization of student affairs xvi, 1–4, 23, 43, 55, 81, 104, 127, 160–161, 164; barriers 87, 90, 91; CAS 61–62; cocurriculum 107–108; connection to diversity and SJI 32–33, 34–36, *38–40*, 58, 134–135, 159, 167–168; culture of internationalization 96, 148, 161, 164, 171; curriculum, graduate preparation 16–17, 18, 47–49, 62, 173; global social justice 41–42, 47; inclusive internationalization 9–10, 24, 50, 70, 133, 159–160, 164, 170; partnerships 162; research group 91–92, 93, 166; student affairs supervision of services 95–96; taskforces 89, 91, 96; US SSAOs understanding of 9, 12, 18, 33, 86–88, 103, 152–153; *see also* Comprehensive Internationalization; international student recruitment; Internationalization at Home; Internationalization of the Curriculum, organizational structure; policy, internationalization; prioritization of internationalization; senior internationalization officers; structural diversity

Internationalization at Home (IaH) x, xvi, 3, 6–7; community colleges 37; connection between inclusivity and intercultural 9, 24, 55, 70, 82, 159; history of 6; local–global connections 18, 31, 37, 168; strategic development 160–163; strategies 7–9, 83, 119, 120, 148, 153, 171

Internationalization of the Curriculum (IoC) 5–6, 43, 81, 107

international student recruitment 1; as financial gain 32, 41; focused internationalization activity in US 5, 9, 24, 31–32, 33, 89; inclusivity in 10–11; Sweden 6; *see also* structural diversity

international students: assimilation 32; Chinese University of Hong Kong 43; curriculum, graduate preparation 18, 23, 34, 48, 61, 173; defined x–xi; employment 122, 128; engagement 8, 9, 10, 12, 17, 18, 113, 119–120, 164, 169–170, 172; experiences of 10–12, 34; as a focus of assessment and research 91–92, *93–94,* 166–167; inclusivity of 10, 35–36, 37, 88, 121, 135, 160; international student committees 91, 113, 169; Leeds Metropolitan University 37; local connections 18, 168; Nottingham Trent University *98–101;* Organisation for Economic Cooperation and Development's Programme for International Student Assessment 127; orientation 10; professional development 152–153, 154; related to internationalization 2, 24, 33–34, 37; Rhodes University 13, 15; Saudi students 43, 88, 166; services and programs for 1, 7, 95–97, 169–170; Stellenbosch University 40; theoretical limitations 139, 154; University of British Columbia *19–22;* University of Leeds 13; Universitat Rovira i Virgili *150–151; see also* discrimination; interaction, international and domestic student; international student recruitment; linguistically diverse; mobility

Jones, E. x, xi, 6, 35–36, 37, 42, 43, 55, 56, 57, 62, 69; centering students in internationalization 83, 86

190

INDEX

Killick, D. xi, 11, 18, 31, 36, 41, 43, 70, 88, 97, 133, 153–154, 159, 173
Komives and Carpenter's PREPARE model 147–148, 171
Kuwait, practices in 122, *123–125*, 142; *see also* American University of Kuwait; MENASA

language: barriers and discrimination 11, 43, 48, 57, 88, 155; benefits of additional languages 19, 57; English language 11, 65, 88; English language programs 95; knowledge of more than one language 59, 60, 120, 153, 171; Oakton Community College 19; as a part of internationalization programs x, 4, 8, *15*, 18, 57, *99*, 120; as a part of social identities 2, 161; programs in languages other than English 141, 145, 148; *see also* linguistically diverse
Leask, B. 5–6, 43, 55, 58, 70, 120, 165–166, 174
linguistically diverse 10, 19, 174; bi- and multilingual 141, *144–146*, 171; resistance to and stereotypes 43, 48, 60, 88; *see also* language
local: connection to social justice 41; key element to IaH 31, 37, 55; local curriculum 7, 19, *40*, 43, 67; local communities and needs 7, 9, 17, 18–19, *21–22*, 24, 31, 37; local diversity xiii, 6, 8, 33, 36, 56; *see also* diversity; Internationalization at Home

MENASA 142, 143, *144*, *146*
Mexico, practices in 48, 120
mobility: component of internationalization 3, 4, 9, 96; in Comprehensive Internationalization 4; faculty and staff 1, 134, 138; IaH 6–7, 24, 134, 161; movement from a reliance on ix, 2, 5, 6, 7, 36; Nottingham Trent University 100, 101; outbound mobility xii, 5;

privilege in mobility programs 31, 134; stage in Parsons and Söderqvist's model of institutional internationalization 81–82; Universitat Rovira i Virgili *149; see also* international student recruitment; education abroad
model of institutional internationalization 81
multicultural centers *see* cultural and affinity centers
multicultural competency *40*, 49, 56–57, 58
multiculturalism xi, *15*, 33, *38–40*, 82; connection to interculturalism and internationalization 3, 34–36, 49; 81, 164; multicultural education xii, 34–35, 36, 43, 56; student learning 168; *see also* diversity; inclusivity; cultural and affinity centers
multilingual/bilingual *see* language; linguistically diverse

NAFSA xvi, xvii, 4, 142; NAFSA professional competencies 57–58
NASPA xvi, xvii, 17, *94*, 141, 142, *143; see also* ACPA and NASPA Professional Competencies
neo-nationalism 11, *16*, 34, 64; exceptionalism 41
neo-racism *see* discrimination; racism
Nottingham Trent University xiv, 97, *98,* 169; *see also* United Kingdom, practices in

organizational structure for internationalization: CI 4; related to activities' supervision 95–96; separated international education 7; as a stage in Parsons and Söderqvist's model of institutional internationalization 81; structure to promote internationalization 89–92, 121, 172; structure of student affairs 89, 104, *124; see also* documents,

191

INDEX

internationalization; prioritization of internationalization

People's Republic of China, practices in *44*, 62, 65, *66*, 89, *92, 109*, 143; *see also* Asia, practices in

policy, internationalization: Australia's colonialism 136; Canadian International Education Strategy *20;* China's Ministry of Education 65, *93*; European Union 83; IAU's call for 50; inclusive of social justice framework 161; *see also* documents, internationalization

Pontificia Universidad Católica de Chile xv, *115,* 142

prioritization of internationalization: for higher education institutions globally 5; impact on student engagement and interaction 12; reflect in documents 163; US SSAOs 87–88, 90, 91, 103, 134; *see also* documents, internationalization; organizational structure for internationalization

Qatar, practices in 142, *143–146*, 147; Education City 140; *see also* Qatar University

Qatar University xv, 142, 143, *143, 144,* 147

racial justice *see* social justice

racism *16*, 31, 33, *39*, 48, 64, 120, 167, neo-racism 11, 34; *see also* discrimination; neo-nationalism

refugee students x, 12, *14*, 18, *20*, 34; refugee crisis 2; *see also* domestic students; international students

Rhodes University xiv, 13, *13,* 119

Sanford's challenge and support theory 140

Schlossberg's transitions theory 140

senior internationalization officers 81–82; use outside of the US 90–91; US SSAO interactions with 91

senior student affairs officers (SSAOs): capacity building 82; collaboration 18, 119, 120, 135; cultural competency 9–10, 59, 60, 62, 160; international goals/goal setting 37, 75, 86–89, 103, 162; internationalization at home 161; mobility/travel 9, 134; organizational structure 33, 90, 91, 95–96, 113; professional development 152–153; student employment 122; as study respondents xii, xvi, xvii, 12, 23; *see also* senior internationalization officers

service learning: assessment 126–127; Centennial College *71–74*, 165; Education City 140; IaH strategy 8; Johnson County Community College 19; in the local community 18, 119; Rhodes University community engagement 14; supervised by student affairs 96; University of British Columbia 19; *see also* local

social identity development: Chinese students 110, 112; combined with intercultural *38,* 47–48, 58, 120, 163; combined with an understanding of culture 35, 36, 56, 61; curriculum, graduate preparation 139; DMIS 63–64; *see also individual theories and models*

social justice xi, 10, 41, 155; Centennial College *72–74*; curriculum, graduate preparation 48, 61, 173; global SJ 32, *38,* 41–42, 47, 50, 69, 71; inclusive of intercultural and international 36, 75, 108, 159–160, 164; organizational and culture change 33, 43; reflective sense of self 58; social issues *14*, 50, *66*, 71, *73–74, 111,* 114, 127; SJ framework 12, 17, 47, 48–49, 55, 161, 174; student affairs educators 6, 58, 171; *see also* indigenous; global citizenship; inclusivity: student resistance; social justice and inclusion competency

INDEX

social justice and inclusion (SJI)
competency 31, 56, 58; connection to
intercultural and internationalization
xvii, 2, 3, 24, 32, 33, 34, 43, 58;
curriculum, graduate preparation 56;
learning outcomes 36; local–global
connection 41; need for global
framework 59–60; as a personal
process 56; professional development
133–134; *see also* diversity;
intercultural competency;
multiculturalism; multicultural
competency; social justice
Sorrells, K. 41, 42, 55, 69, 70; definition
of intercultural competency 58
South Africa, practices in 6, *13–16*, 19,
37, *38–40*, 109, 114, 119, 142
see also Africa, practice in; Rhodes
University; Stellenbosch University
Southern African Federation for Student
Affairs and Services 142
Spain, practices in 148, *148–151*, 161;
see also Europe, practices in
Stellenbosch University xiv, 37, *38, 40,*
120, 169, 170
structural diversity 10, 33–34, 47, 86,
160, 170
student activism: assistance with
intercultural competency 58, 109,
114–115; Chilean higher education
115–118; IaH strategy 8; *see also*
student leadership
student affairs globally 23–24, 140–143;
*see also individual promising practices and
countries*
student development theories *124,*
134, 139–140, *144–145,* 154, 173;
see also individual theories
student employment: American
University of Kuwait 123–125; on
campus programs for 121–123;
through cocurriculum 107, 127, 128,
165; *see also* employability

student government 109, 113–114, *118;*
National Union of University Students
in Finland 114
student interaction, domestic and
international: buddy or ambassador
programs 120, 166–167; Chinese
University of Hong Kong *43–45;*
IaH in student affairs 24, 107;
needs intentionality of design 12,
33, 47, 48, 109, 164; residence
halls 13, *38–40*, 120, 170;
programming 7, 120–121, 167–169;
student employment 121; student
resistance 11, 42–43, 159; *see also*
contact hypothesis; structural
diversity
student leadership *93,* 109, *109–112,*
114, *115–119; see also* cocurricular;
student activism
student union *see* college unions; student
government
study abroad *see* education abroad

Tinto's attrition and retention theory
139–140

undocumented students x, 34, 48;
see also domestic students;
international students
United Kingdom, practices in 2, 6, 9–10,
13, 23, 36–37, 43, 55, *98–101,*
113–114, 121, 141, 159 *see also*
Europe, practices in
Universitat Rovira I Virgili xv, 148, *148,
149,* 161
University of British Columbia xiv, 19,
19, 20, 168
University of Macau xiv, *66, 67,* 165
University of Sydney xv, 135, *136,* 163

Weber State University 122
White Racial Identity Development
Model 64

Taylor & Francis eBooks

www.taylorfrancis.com

A single destination for eBooks from Taylor & Francis with increased functionality and an improved user experience to meet the needs of our customers.

90,000+ eBooks of award-winning academic content in Humanities, Social Science, Science, Technology, Engineering, and Medical written by a global network of editors and authors.

TAYLOR & FRANCIS EBOOKS OFFERS:

- A streamlined experience for our library customers
- A single point of discovery for all of our eBook content
- Improved search and discovery of content at both book and chapter level

REQUEST A FREE TRIAL
support@taylorfrancis.com